SCIENCE AND
TECHNOLOGY ETHICS

The world has undergone a radical transformation during the past 200 years. The Industrial Revolution, the development of mass-production techniques and recently the plethora of technological advancements in medicine, engineering, computation, communication and entertainment products have drastically changed the ways in which we live, our expectations of the future, and our moral landscapes.

Science and Technology Ethics re-examines the ethics by which we live and asks whether we have in place the ethical guidelines through which we can incorporate scientific and technological developments with the minimum of disruption and disaffection. Bringing together a range of expertise, this book assesses the ethical systems already in existence and proposes new approaches to our scientific and engineering processes. It considers the social contracts in practice, the developments in biology and informatics and how these can influence our ethics, the role that the military industry can play, and our environmental responsibilities.

Science and Technology Ethics is a much-needed discussion of the scientific developments that have major effects on the way we live. It will be of interest to all students of science and technology and all professionals involved with administrating laws in these fields.

Raymond E. Spier is Professor of Science and Engineering Ethics at the University of Surrey.

PROFESSIONAL ETHICS
General Editor: Ruth Chadwick
Centre for Professional Ethics, University of Central Lancashire

Professionalism is a subject of interest to academics, the general public and would-be professional groups. Traditional ideas of professions and professional conduct have been challenged by recent social, political and technological changes. One result has been the development for almost every profession of an ethical code of conduct which attempts to formalize its values and standards. These codes of conduct raise a number of questions about the status of a 'profession' and the consequent moral implications for behaviour.

This series seeks to examine these questions both critically and constructively. Individual volumes will consider issues relevant to particular professions, including nursing, genetic counselling, journalism, business, the food industry and law. Other volumes will address issues relevant to all professional groups such as the function and value of a code of ethics and the demand of confidentiality.

Also available in this series:

SCIENCE AND TECHNOLOGY ETHICS

Edited by Raymond E. Spier

London and New York

First published 2002
by Routledge
11 New Fetter Lane, London EC4P 4EE

Simultaneously published in the USA and Canada
by Routledge
29 West 35th Street, New York, NY 10001

Routledge is an imprint of the Taylor & Francis Group

Typeset in Times by
The Running Head Limited, Cambridge
Printed and bound in Great Britain by
TJ International, Padstow, Cornwall

British Library Cataloguing in Publication Data
A catalogue record for this book is available
from the British Library

Library of Congress Cataloging in Publication Data
Science and technology ethics/edited by Raymond E. Spier.
p. cm. — (Professional ethics)
Includes bibliographical references and index.
1. Science–Moral and ethical aspects. 2. Technology–Moral
and ethical aspects. I. Spier, R. (Raymond) II. Series.

Q180.55.M67 S32 2001
174′.95—dc21   2001041857

ISBN 0–415–14812–X (hbk)
ISBN 0–415–14813–8 (pbk)

CONTENTS

CONTRIBUTORS

Michael Atiyah was a Professor of Mathematics at Oxford and Princeton, and subsequently President of the Royal Society and Master of Trinity College, Cambridge. He is currently President of the Pugwash Conferences on Science and World Affairs, and an Honorary Professor at Edinburgh University.

Stephanie J. Bird is a neuroscientist and Special Assistant to the Provost at Massachusetts Institute of Technology where she works on the development of educational programs that address the responsible conduct of research, and ethical issues in science and more generally. Her research interests now focus on the ethical, legal and social policy implications of scientific research, especially in the area of neuroscience. She is co-editor of the journal *Science and Engineering Ethics.*

Rufus Black, who holds degrees in politics and law from the University of Melbourne, has just completed a doctorate in ethics at the University of Oxford where he was a Rhodes Scholar and taught ethics. He is currently a Tutor in Philosophy at Ormond College in Melbourne.

Susan B. Hodgson is a Sustainability Training Manager at the Centre for Environmental Strategy, University of Surrey, having worked in the environmental field for fifteen years. Her wide interests cover the interrelationships of the private and the public sectors in taking responsibility for sustainable development.

Brad Hooker is Senior Lecturer in Philosophy at the University of Reading. He is author of *Ideal Code, Real World: A Rule-Consequentialist Theory of Morality* (2000). He is also co-editor of *Morality, Rules, and Consequences: A Critical Reader*, *Well-Being and Morality* and *Moral Particularism*, all published in 2000.

Slobodan Perdan is a research fellow at the Centre for Environmental Strategy, University of Surrey. His research interests are primarily concerned with environmental philosophy and discourse ethics.

Andrew Reeve is Professor of Politics and International Studies at the University of Warwick. He is author of *Property* and co-author of *Electoral Systems in Britain*. He is also editor of *Exploitation* and co-editor of *Liberal Neutrality* and *Modern Political Theory from Hobbes to Locke*. His main interests are in the history of political thought and contemporary political theory.

Simon Rogerson is Director of the Centre for Computing and Social Responsibility and Professor in Computer Ethics at De Montfort University, UK. He is author of *Ethical Aspects of Information Technology: Issues for Senior Executives*. He was the winner of the 1999 IFIP Namur Award for outstanding contribution to the creation of awareness of the social implications of information technology.

Raymond E. Spier is Professor of Science and Engineering Ethics at the University of Surrey. He currently edits/co-edits the journals *Vaccine, Enzyme and Microbial Technology* and *Science and Engineering Ethics*.

Vivian Weil is Director of the Center for Study of Ethics in the Professions at the Illinois Institute of Technology. She is co-author of *Owning Scientific and Technical Information* and editor of *Whistleblowing – Defining Engineer's Responsibilities*.

1

SCIENCE AND ENGINEERING ETHICS

Overview

Raymond E. Spier

Introduction

New knowledge about our world and the way it works is accumulating at an ever-increasing pace. Along with this is a burgeoning of engineering activities leading to new, improved and life-changing products. These two activities feed off one another so that we may expect the rate of change in both these areas to either maintain present levels or increase.

For example, our increasing knowledge of the way we work as human beings has spawned a profusion of guidelines as to what we should eat, how we should exercise and how we should refrain from exposing ourselves to toxic materials which could lead to heart disease, cancer or liver failure. In another area the insinuation of massively increasing computer power into the domestic environment has connected people to an abundance of information whose magnitude is almost beyond comprehension. This, and the advent of satellite and cable television, has provided individuals with an exposure to world-wide events and cultures. A consequence is that we are beginning to change the way we think about our own upbringing, traditions and way of life. Global attitudes and considerations are now on most agendas.

The ubiquity of the private car has led to enormous changes in how we behave and how we build and use our towns and cities, just as the prevalence of relatively inexpensive air travel has led to an apparent shrinking of our globe by many orders of magnitude. And the new technologies that are in the realm of our 'defence' sectors have radically changed the way we think about defending our territorial possessions. This has led to international collaborations which would have been unthinkable some fifty years ago.

But to cap all the above, our modern answers to questions about origins (energy/matter, universe, Earth, life, humans) mean that we are beginning to see ourselves in a different light. We do not need to invoke an involvement of supernatural elements in these areas. This in turn may have a profound influence on our ethics and the way we relate to one another.

For these reasons it is timely to review our position with regard to the nature of our science and engineering activities and to re-examine and consider in greater depth the way these powerful influences are actually affecting our lives. We might also ask whether the present ethical systems are sufficiently well honed to allow such behavioural changes. Indeed, while we may learn from our past and immediate present, we have also to consider the near, medium and long-term future positions. Here we must again ask the question, have we the most appropriate ethics for the careering progress evidenced by the continuing advances in science and engineering?

The range and scope of science and engineering

Science

For various reasons, culminating in C.P. Snow's declaration of the 'two cultures' in 1959,[1] science seems to have been relegated to those activities effected by the white-coated personnel frequenting forbidding fortresses called laboratories. This dichotomous treatment of how we acquire and process knowledge has created unnecessary boundaries between areas of investigative activities effected in all subject areas by people trained in a variety of disciplines. If we are to resolve this issue, it would be appropriate to revert to the original meaning of the word 'science' (Latin *scientia*) which, in translation, is simply 'knowledge'. This latter word leads us to consider the thoughts, impressions, ideas, beliefs, concepts, abstractions, images and models we hold in our conscious and unconscious brains as representations of the world (which would include ourselves and the seat of such thinking and ideation). We acquire this knowledge via a process known as the 'scientific method'. This involves observing one or several states of nature (or the same state a number of times) and then making a hypothesis (or guess) as to what it is that is being observed, or any relationship which may pertain between the different things observed. Such a hypothesis is then tested by experiments or examinations to determine the level of confidence we may place in the original guess or hypothesis. At one time it was thought that it was possible to 'prove' the 'veracity' or 'truth' of a hypothesis by virtue of a sophisticated series of unequivocally determinative experiments. However, K. Popper[2] cast serious doubt on this: 'Theories are not verifiable, but they can be corroborated . . . we should try to assess how far it has been able to prove its fitness to survive by standing up to tests. In brief, we should try to assess how far it has been "corroborated".'[3] Notwithstanding this, it is clear that the same arguments, which eliminated the possibility of proving the truth of a hypothesis, may be applied to showing that it is impossible to disprove a hypothesis. So the 'product' of the application of the scientific method is not the proof of a hypothesis nor yet its disproof, but rather a change in the level of confidence with which we may hold and use that hypothesis. It follows that if the hypothesis passes stringent and difficult tests then we may have more confidence in the hypothesis than if a weak or uncritical test was effected with a similar pass result. A consequence of such an increase in confidence is that we may use the hypothesis with greater assurance and reliability to generate new hypotheses or guesses to explain different phenomena. When our hypotheses have been so well tested that we hold them with virtually complete assurance, we refer to them as knowledge.

Some people write about 'knowledge' which is 'unscientific' or 'non-scientific'. Although at first examination this implies a contradiction of terms (science is a word which translates directly to knowledge) it actually denotes a kind of knowledge which has not been tested by methods of sufficient stringency to ascertain with any significant reliability the degree of confidence which can be placed in that 'non-scientific' knowledge.

But this testing-of-guesses procedure is not an activity unique to people who wear white coats. People who work in libraries and test their hypotheses by using the published literature are no less scientific than those who have to make convoluted tubes of glass act as condensers and connectors. The former might be called 'library scientists' as opposed to the latter who might be termed 'laboratory scientists'. (It should be noted that the laboratory scientists do not have to work in closed buildings for such a designation. Rather such individuals might be characterized as doing experiments with appropriate controls in the wider context of the social, biological and geophysical worlds to name but three such extramural environments.) Moreover, science can also be effected 'on the street corner'. When we question other people about our thoughts and ideas we are using the scientific method by testing our version or concept of the world against the version which may be held by a respected colleague or neighbour. I would designate such science 'street science'. We may also test ideas within the confines of our own minds, in which case we may consider applying to such an activity the denotation 'conscious science'. It is even possible to 'do science' subconsciously, hence 'subconscious science'.

A simple introspection of the way we work will reveal that we have done many things without thinking consciously about them. In typing or playing an instrument we do not consciously tell each finger what to do, yet our bodies must sense where each finger is and by activating the appropriate muscles achieve an effect which has a broader intention than the mere moving of a particular digit. That the intended effect is achieved is a test of the hypothesis that the finger in question is doing the correct thing at the correct time. Additional examples of having effected subconscious science may be realized by considering what we were thinking about when driving a car between an origin and a destination, or hitting a ball with a squash racquet or just walking along a road. In each case our thoughts may be elsewhere than with the activity in hand. The need to use knowledge of our position in relation to external physical objects has been taken care of by our subconscious acquiring 'knowledge' of the external world, testing that knowledge and using the result to control the workings of our muscles to achieve our predetermined ends.

Thus science is not just for the physicists, chemists and biologists among us. We have to recognize the work of the sociologists, historians, psychologists, theologians, economists, musicologists and a myriad of other -ologists, not excluding those who research literature and politics, and include them in the realms of scientific investigation. We may, therefore, choose to describe those who call themselves 'scientists' as people who, for material or immaterial reward, research those areas of nature which are difficult to penetrate without the use of refined and generally unavailable instruments or difficult and elaborate techniques. (This differs from the original definition of Whewell who, in 1840,[4] considered scientists as those who use the scientific method and tested guesses; as we all test guesses to obtain a new purchase on our knowledge, this definition becomes less than adequate.)

As the product of science is an emotive sensation of confidence or assurance rather than a 'truth' or 'proof', science may be said to lack 'objectivity'. This does not automatically mean that because science is subjective it lacks reliability. As expressed above, the more stringent the experiments we use to determine the confidence we may have in our hypotheses, the more assurance we can have in the closeness of the relationship of such hypotheses to something in the world outside ourselves. So as our knowledge is not absolute it has to be relative. Indeed it relates to how we 'feel' about the observations and tests we effect. This in turn is informed by our previous experiences and the way in which we hold ideas and concepts in our minds. It has therefore been influenced by our exposure to whatever social conditioning has prevailed during our mental development. While such preconditioning may be held to pervert the appropriate level of confidence we attribute to a tested guess, this process cannot get too far out of line with the state of the world outside the individual. Because, were the distorting effects of preconditioning too severe, a model of the external world would be conveyed which would put the individual at a disadvantage in activities relative to his or her survival. It is therefore pragmatism (learning about the world outside ourselves by our actions and the consequences of those actions) which prevents us from straying too far from concepts of the actual world outside; nevertheless we cannot discount the occasional perversion of our concepts by such preconditioning. However, having recognized this possibility our students and citizens need to be prepared so that they may avoid those influences which prevent them from arriving at a perception of reality which will serve them with the greatest reliability.

While the examination of hypotheses leads to a level of confidence which is also influenced by previous conditioning, the areas of interest which are examined by scientists and others are determined in part by the prevailing state of society and the social 'agenda'. For example, at this state of our being we are obsessed with issues which relate to our health. But we can easily imagine that we will soon conquer infectious disease and learn to implement ways of eating and exercising that considerably decrease the risk of heart disease and cancer. So the focus for our questioning may shift to environmental issues or even to ways we might colonize other planets in our solar system or other planetary systems. That society can prioritize the questions for which it requires answers is not a reprehensible state; after all, most scientific (laboratory and library) investigation is supported by money provided through the tax system and, thereby, provided by the citizens. In a system which is solely dependent on the state of energy and matter in the universe, scientific questions do not arise *de novo*. Likewise curiosity is not *sui generis*. Rather, those who accept public funding to pursue investigations or test hypotheses need to recognize that there is an implicit (covert) or explicit (overt) social contract to which they commit themselves.

Engineering

The word 'science' is often inappropriately applied to engineering. Scientists are held to be fully responsible for nuclear reactors, aeroplanes and communication systems. Such notions must be challenged. As has been described above, scientists are responsible for developing and testing the knowledge base. Some of such knowledge is incorporated into engineering activity and indeed many engineers contribute to the extension of the knowledge base as the questions asked by scientists do not necessarily generate the knowledge required to build bridges, design a printer or enhance the energy of a laser.

In addition to using and extending the knowledge base, engineers are distinguished from scientists in that the product of their activities is generally a material entity. (In this context a new system, organization, work of 'art' or law may be regarded as 'material' products.) These products are characterized by having two additional features. In the first place they provide benefit to society, while in the second they express inventiveness or the 'genius' of the word engineering. To cover the issue of the generation of social benefit most engineers enter into a social contract (see Andrew Reeve, this volume, chapter 6) via their commitment to a code of conduct or practice as administered by their representative institute or body. Although this is one way of recognizing the requirement for the engineer to progress social benefit, it is not always clear as to what constitutes such benefit. To some, a healthy armaments industry is an unalloyed social benefit while to others this self-same industry is an anathema (see Michael Atiyah, this volume, chapter 10). Such disputes need to be resolved and Brad Hooker (see this volume, chapter 5) has indicated how such resolutions might be achieved.

When considering the issue of inventiveness we may augment the term by the use of an extended expression such as *the introduction of significant novelty* into a product. Again we might look to the experience generated and reported by patent examiners who make a first assessment as to whether a proposed patent has within it something which is inventive, or something which would surprise a worker who is already 'gifted in the art'. If the latter conditions are fulfilled a patent may be issued. Engineers may not always be engaged in writing patents. But I would suggest that the thrust of their day-to-day activities is to arrive at something that is patentable; they work with the *intent* of eventually generating something which has significant novelty. Those whose daily work does not have the commitment to arriving at this degree of novelty might be termed 'technicians'. Even though each decision they make might require them to do something different, these differences do not constitute the kind of novelty which is required for the issue of a patent. To meet the innovation provision for the award of a patent, the inventor has to produce something which would be a surprise to someone working in the same area and gifted in the existing arts.

While this definition of engineering requires a certain, and assessed, level of knowledge, skill and experience along with the commitment to social benefit and inventiveness, it is yet possible to satisfy the criteria by application to an engineering institute. In place of the assessed formal qualifications, one would be allowed to substitute an appropriate suite of experiences acquired over a significant period. Indeed many inventors may qualify for 'engineer' status as a result of the uptake and use of their inventions via the patent system.

It is not possible to examine the nature of the engineering activity without addressing the issue of the nature and role of 'design' in engineering. Some might regard this as the essential and creative process. Others view it as those activities that make a material product functional, aesthetically acceptable and efficient to fabricate. It derives from the sixteenth-century French word *'disseigne'*[5] which has clear connotations of purpose, intent or determination. There is a sense in which there is a desire to achieve an end, as in a plot or intrigue, an interface between intent and realization. So a material entity which is so formed as to achieve an objective might be seen as the product of a process that began with a 'design'. Clearly, some designs may be innovative while others are variants of an existing theme. The former would qualify as engineering designs and the latter as technical designs. What is important is that while design is necessarily part of an engineering process, all that is designed is not necessarily that which has been engineered.

The range and scope of ethics

Verbal issues

Ethics is a word which graces the front pages of our newspapers and magazines on a regular basis at this time. It is generally associated with a behavioural issue that is prominent either because there has been misconduct or because an example to others of approved behaviour has been realized. In this sense the dictionary definition of ethics as 'relating to morals; the science of morals; the department of study concerned with the principles of human duty'[6] is suitable. Nevertheless, the word is often used in association with other words such as laws, values, good, right and benefit. So it would serve us well in this introductory chapter to examine the relationship of ethics to these other concepts.

'Moral', we find, is defined as 'of or pertaining to character or disposition, considered as good or bad, virtuous or vicious; of or pertaining to the distinction between right and wrong, or good and evil, in relation to the actions, volitions or character of responsible beings; ethical'.[7] Its relationship to ethics may be determined from the etymology of the two words. In the *Oxford Dictionary of Etymology* (1966), Latin *moralis* translates to Greek ηθικος, ethics.

While some philosophers and writers seek to maintain a distinction in meaning between the two words, in a work such as this I would hold that this is not necessary, and that the two words, ethics and morals (and their derivatives), may be used interchangeably and denote identical meanings.

There is less of a problem with the word 'law'. The latter is the verbal product of a social institution that requires that certain defined actions or behaviours of the members of that society do or, more commonly, do not take place. When behaviour is in default of the law, sanctions can be expected to result. Laws may be promoted as rules, regulations, statutes, guidelines, codes, injunctions, commandments or customs. Also, laws may be subdivided into categories such as civil, ecclesiastical and criminal with further subdivisions. It is clear that there are ethical guidelines which exist in areas not covered by laws, in any of the latter's manifestations. For example, we do not have laws requiring that people should be polite to other people and respect their privacy; but it is not ethical to be rude, abusive or intrusive. However, I would also contend that all that is required by laws is also ethical. One might regard the death penalty as unethical but legal, but it is necessary to remember that a majority of some societies think otherwise and regard the death penalty as acceptable. Although acceptability *per se* is not necessarily grounds for ethicality, it is often used as such. Again, as will be discussed in other chapters in this volume (such as Brad Hooker, chapter 5), there are ethical systems whose guideline products may be in conflict so what is ethical for one system may be unethical for another.

A 'right' is that for which one can properly make a claim. In this sense it is part of ethics as it denotes a suite of ethically acceptable actions. Similarly ethically approved actions may be considered right while ethically endorsed things or objects may be described as good. While most laws proscribe actions, rights provide entitlements. Thus the United Nations Declaration of Human Rights (1948), Article 12: 'No one shall be subject to arbitrary interference with his privacy, family, home or correspondence, nor to attacks upon his honor and reputation. Everyone has the right to the protection of the law against such interference or attacks.'

We do not have laws that state that individuals shall have privacy, nor that a family is immune to interference. Such dispensations come to individuals by way of rights as defined internationally or adopted nationally. Yet these notional 'rights' may be waived by criminal investigation agencies in the pursuit of alleged criminals, so the declared rights may be outside the law and yet within ethics.

It is useful to examine the concept of value. Some individuals regard ethics as being dependent on values; I would hold that the reverse is a more sustainable position. The word 'value' comes from the Latin verb *valere*, which means to be strong, healthy, effective or worthy; to have worth. This leaves open the question of how values are assigned. When we begin to perceive the world as a child, the objects and actions we encounter have preassigned values. Those with a high positive value are encouraged, others are not. Clearly, values are assigned by adults to objects and actions on the basis of what it is that they wish to encourage and promote as a way of progressing or advancing their ethical positions. In this regard the seemingly outrageous values placed on rare works of art or jewellery do not so much signify the value of the item *per se*, rather they act as a signal to society of the wealth (status) of the possessor of such items. Hence they become instruments in establishing a dominance hierarchy which seems to be akin to the behaviour patterns of our primate forebears. This hierarchy in turn requires a suite of appropriate behaviours. In this way the values which result become ethically determined values.

An envelope for ethics

We might ask, are there limits to what behaviours may be judged for their ethicality? It would seem that our interactions with other people, animals and even the material substance of this and other planets might be adjudged to have ethical aspects. Does this also apply to our private behaviour *vis à vis* ourselves? We have (in the UK) laws forbidding suicide and have laws restricting our possession and use of specified drugs. Some ethical systems proscribe the eating of certain foods: pigs are off-limits for Jews and Muslims; the latter also may not consume alcohol or smoke. But in liberal societies there are not limits to what I might read (from what is the legally available literature), or to how I might treat my body (exercise), or which curtail my imagination or thoughts. Yet there is a way in which all these activities impinge on my well-being and hence on the prosperity of society at large and can, therefore, be the subject of socially generated direction.

As a mature and functional (which excludes the young, old and infirm) member of society there is an unwritten contract between the individual and society (see Andrew Reeve, this volume, chapter 6). Some people do not recognize the existence of such a contract, even when the possibility of its existence is drawn to their attention, but that does not invalidate or efface its being. It may be envisaged that any such contract contains provisions such that individuals may not so damage themselves that they become less capable of making their contribution to the society or demand more of society's services. In which case what an individual does in private is subject to ethical guidance.

As thinking may be considered a human activity, is it appropriate to consider the ethicality of the way we think? It is a commonly held view that an omniscient deity may have access to our thoughts and reward or punish us on the basis of that knowledge. Also, our thoughts are implicated in the control of our bodily functions: wrong thoughts may lead to wrong actions. Additionally, we are beginning to learn that the way we think changes the properties of our immune systems – an increase in mental stress may render us more susceptible to infectious disease. Nevertheless, we would contend that we would not wish our thoughts to be necessarily controlled by the ethical principles of whatever society we happen to inhabit; this evokes the fearful image of the 'thought police'. So whatever ethical constraints are applied to our bodies they are generally not applied to what and how we think. Indeed, we can argue for a hands-off approach to thinking because this is one of the most cost-effective ways of conducting experiments (thought-experiments) which enable us to think through the possible outcomes of future actions, thus enabling us to select the one which is most propitious. Such an examination may require us to think the 'unthinkable' and to consider options that are clearly the opposite of those required by the prevailing system of ethics. I would contend that such thinking is itself ethical if, and only if, the *intent* of the thinking individual is to arrive at outcomes that

are personally and socially beneficial. To think thoughts that are contrary to ethical guidelines for the purpose of perpetrating evil
(disbenefit) is an activity that may be ethically proscribable.

Ethics as a component of a human social control system

The behaviour of living organisms is controlled by a variety of mechanisms. At the microscopic level, bacteria and protozoa control the
directions in which they move and their reproductive systems through
molecular mechanisms whose nature is subject to intense and successful study. Much is known about the way a gene is switched on and off,
and often the consequences of such a switch are also understood.
With multicellular organisms additional chemical elements enter into
the control arena, and we are familiar with the way hormones modulate our emotionality and the consequences for the way we behave and
act. Another way of explaining the complex behaviour of animals is
to assert that they are responding to their instincts. These constitute
'an innate propensity in organized beings (especially in the lower
animals), varying with the species, and manifesting itself in acts which
appear to be rational, but are performed without conscious adaptation of means to ends'.[8] The building of a hive by bees or anthills by
ants, the nesting or mating activities of birds and the hunting
stratagems of wild hyenas and lions may be said to be based on
instinctive behaviours. By contrast, conscious adaptation of means to
ends may be identified in birds and mammals. But only the higher primates may be both conscious and self-conscious. Hence we now have
another source of stimuli for action which is based on the coordinated
activity of brain neurons and the messages such cells dispatch to
muscles for fulfilment. It is a unique feature of humankind that they
are able to communicate with one another with words (introduced
over an extended period some 100,000 to 200,000 years ago and represented by tangible symbols about 7,000 to 30,000 years ago). By
contrast non-human animals communicate using tweets, barks,
howls, hoots, squeaks, bellowings and shrieks. Humans, on the other
hand, using words, are able to formulate expressions with the intent of
controlling human social and individual behaviour to achieve beneficial ends. It is my view that these words constitute our ethics and
ethical systems.

The verbal formulation of an ethical guideline serves as a 'set point'
in both the feed-forward (quality assurance) and feedback (quality
control) systems which operate in contemporary societies.[9] These set
points derive from answers to questions concerning the nature and

the 'purpose' of life. Much of the material used in such answers is found in answers to more basic questions about the origin of the various components of the material world (including ourselves as humans) and the way the original entities became the components we presently experience. Thus knowledge which bears on the origins of matter, the universe, our solar system, the planet Earth, life, humans and thought contributes to our concepts of ourselves and our place in the scheme of things. From such considerations we nominate guidelines for behaviour (ethics) and having used them we review the consequences. We may then ask questions as to whether, by using such guidelines, we have achieved the purposes for which the guidelines were designed (engineered): if not, then we can change the guidelines; if so, we can reinforce them.

The foregoing clearly applies to a system of beliefs which does not involve either divine intervention or instinct as an origin of those verbal formulations which are used to guide behaviour (ethics). Were such sources to be invoked it would be difficult to prevent the inevitable conflicts that would occur as a result of either differing views as to what the divine intentions are or different interpretations of divinely inspired writings. In either case it is held that it is not possible to argue from knowledge of the present world as to what to regard as acceptable in ethical terms. Divine backing for a particular set of ethical guidelines may once have been of value to the promoters of those guidelines in that it gave them authority and power. An alternative, non-materialistic view was presented by Immanuel Kant (1724–1804), who argued that the fundamental principles of ethics have to be derived through the application of reason in such a way that all such considerations are entirely free from the taint of the influence of entities of the material world. (He recognized that such a condition may, indeed, not have a physical reality; just where this leaves the manifestations of reason free of material influence is an apt question.)

However, in a modern world we gain confidence in our rules and regulations by observing their beneficial applications in practice. Should the execution of the rules turn out to be a disbenefit then we would choose to remove or change them. In neither case would we need to obtain guidance from sources that are supernatural.

The exposition of science and engineering ethics

It is convenient to divide this volume into sections so as to cover the four main aspects of science and engineering ethics: the process of doing science, the products of science, the process of engineering and the products of engineering. The three chapters by Stephanie J. Bird, Rufus Black and Vivian Weil achieve this end. The following seven chapters show some of the areas in which science and engineering ethics can be applied and which are the objects of current attention. These are not the only areas, as the concept of engineering applies to systems such as the governmental, educational, commercial, legal and what we call cultural (the arts) facets of our society.

While there are some who hold that the ethical principles which guide our behaviour throughout life are embedded within us as a result of our early childhood experiences, others maintain that these principles are continually modified by our experiences and encounters and constitute a dynamic reservoir of concepts by which we live our lives. As we move forward into the twenty-first century we are coming to realize that our education is a process which continues throughout our lives and one may glean from this that our ethical education has similar characteristics. Our parents do not generally prepare us to integrate new knowledge into our scheme of being, nor do they prepare us for the behaviour-changing inventions that beset us on all sides. For these reasons we have to generate new ethics to encompass such developments. Those engaged in these advances are yet further obliged to become acquainted with the perils inherent in the developments they are bringing into a largely unprepared world. For these reasons scientists and engineers have to redefine the way in which they work so as to be more aware of the ethical implications of what they are seeking to achieve. They should also be appraised of various ethical systems and be able to apply them to the solution of such questions as what should we do now in relation to cloning, information, nuclear power, the motor car, CO_2 emissions and so on? In addition, and because different ethical systems may provide contradictory answers, it is necessary for scientists and engineers to be adept in the application of methods which can be used in all cases where conflicts need resolving.

Can ethics be taught?

Plato, in his work *Meno*,[10] is quite clear 'that virtue is neither natural nor acquired, but an instinct given by God to the virtuous'. His main argument is that some fathers who are virtuous have children who are not, while other, non-virtuous, fathers have children who are virtuous; therefore in spite of the most intensive and focused parent-based education it is possible that the outcome is not what is intended. From this he concludes that virtue (or ethics, as translated into right actions) cannot be taught.

There are two aspects to the teaching of ethics. The first involves the understanding and appreciation of ethical issues and what might be appropriate behaviour in any defined situation requiring a decision as to how to behave. The second is the actual implementation of a particular behavioural response to that defined situation. We may know what we ought to do but our actions may or may not follow that intellectual determination. Teachers in higher education may be able to heighten awareness of ethical issues and provide ways of thinking which can give rise to determinations of how one might most appropriately behave given a defined set of circumstances. However, it would not be judged practicable to follow such intellectual determinations through to the stage of action. Action takes place on the stage of the 'real world', for which the educational process is but a preparation.

Most educators in the field of ethics would assert that there is more than one way of imparting ethical sensitivities. Classically, a study of the history of ethics was the traditional method of teaching ethics to would-be philosophers. They would then be trained to make intellectual contributions to the subject based on a combination of the venerated texts and their own thoughts based on their unique experiences and knowledge. This method does not generally commend itself to would-be scientists and engineers. An alternative approach is to summarize the variety of ethical systems available and to indicate both compatibilities and incompatibilities. Methods for conflict resolution then become necessary (see Brad Hooker, this volume, chapter 5) when people take conflicting ethical systems as a basis for their behaviour. It is generally found that when scientists and engineers are left to make a decision (that is, they are faced with two contradictory and equally defensible ethical solutions) they are uncomfortable and dissatisfied. Ways and solutions have to be provided which avoid equivocation.

The discussion of, generally authentic, 'case studies' is a common means of inculcating ethical awareness. Such discussions are best effected with relatively small class sizes (up to twenty) and where each member of the class makes a contribution. This kind of approach has been highly formalized by the teaching techniques of leading exponents K. Pimple and M. Bebeau.[11] When this is underpinned by the identification of particular ethical issues germane to specific subject-based courses, a reinforcement of the considerations stimulated by the case-study discussions occurs. Thus academic staff in all subject areas need to be aware of the ethical issues pertinent to their specific subject expertise. This requirement also influences the more general consideration of the way ethics might be taught through example. It is obviously not productive to discuss and intellectualize about ethical issues in the abstract when examples of behaviour by those in authority are less than salubrious. This in turn calls inevitably for all the members of staff of academic institutions to be aware of the ethicality of their actions and so to set an example to students of the most appropriate behaviour in the specifics of their calling.

The message which seems to be emerging from those who teach ethics to scientists and engineers is that a variety of techniques should be deployed. Also it must be realized that education cannot be achieved in a 'once-and-for-all' fashion. Rather a multifaceted long-term approach has to be taken and the whole exercise has to be couched within an institutional ethos that promotes and positively seeks to improve the standards of behaviour of its members on a day-to-day-basis.[12]

A personal view

In the teaching of science and engineering ethics it is common to seek to improve the ability of students to perceive the ethical issues in the way they practise and in the products which result from that practice. This may be achieved through the use of case studies or seminars on current ethical issues or through a discussion of the ethical issues thrown up by the more academic subjects studied. One may then ask for the possible ways in which one might act according to the issues raised. By way of justification, such courses of action may then be attributed to a particular approach to ethics. As the teacher may seek to lead a balanced discussion which draws out as many possible courses of action as possible, each justified by reference to one or other ethical system, the students become bewildered and uncertain. What they want most of all from such teaching is clear guidance as to how they should behave, or what behaviours they should recommend, in a given set of circumstances.

While it is clearly important to realize that there may be more than one way of arriving at a number of conclusions, in a 'shop-floor' work situation only one such course of action can be carried forward. How then might one encourage the students to judge for themselves what that action might be? They could, of course, refer to individuals who might be considered 'ethical experts'. These people may have spent a major part of their lives learning to glean moral messages venerated or holy texts. Interpreters of such writings (hermeneutics) carry titles like priest, rabbi, mullah, monk, brahman, scholar or guru. Philosophers who have engaged in the examination of the nature and origin of ethical systems or who have suggested ethical systems different from those of the recognized religions may also be sources of ethical expertise. For each such case the basis or origin of the moral messages would be clear. One may also encourage the students to pick an ethical system in which they place the greatest reliance and use it to choose courses of action without reference to nominated authorities. A possible method for enabling students to take this latter course is to offer them an example of how that might be done. To engage the students' attention and supply the most meaningful learning experience it might be appropriate to offer a personal example of how a teacher of ethics has approached one or another ethical issue.

I provide such a model below; it seeks to come to a conclusion as to how to behave in the face of emerging techniques which could lead to the cloning of human beings on the one hand, or the production of headless 'humans' for the purposes of organ harvesting on the other hand. Students and readers should realize that what follows is but an example and its author does not assert that this is the only or correct way of arriving at an answer; it is intended to serve merely as a heuristic.

First, select an ethical system

By accident of birth most children find themselves immersed in the ethical system which is promulgated by their parent(s). During the early years of life it is expedient to adopt this system as it supplies the needs of a growing child. On achieving material independence it becomes possible to think again about the ethical system of one's youth and to determine whether it is the most fitting for the rest of one's life. When I made such a review, I was not impressed by concepts that derived from phenomena which were outside the system of cause and effect. I resolved to derive my ethics from the messages that emanated from the four-billion-year history of life on planet Earth. This system includes all aspects of the nature and reactions of the material and energetic entities perceived by my senses. So I took the key message from biology: survive.

Biology is complex. It involves chemicals, cells, individual organisms and collectives of organisms, be they clones or mobs (kangaroos) or societies. Each such entity and collection of entities seeks to survive. There are occasions when individuals compete, as in the determination of a mating hierarchy; there are times when individuals collaborate, as when the group is threatened by predators or by other similar groups seeking an expansion of their territory. As humans we view our survival in a continually changing manner which may be influenced, for the most part, by two defining parameters: age and wealth. As babies we behave as selfish autonomous systems seeking food and comfort in a manner which does not take into account the well-being of the other biological entities in our surroundings. We act in a manner that seeks to promote our own unique and selfish survival. As we mature we begin to realize that our well-being is in some measure dependent on the well-being of our family so we may devote some effort to the survival of our parents and siblings. Again, on further ageing, our tribe, township, society and beyond become the objects with which we see our own survival connected. So we devote some of our efforts to the survival of these more extended entities. Clearly, when the society is threatened by external aggression, individuals commit their lives to its protection. In the absence of such pressures, individuals get on with their own survival and that of their families as well as they might.

The second parameter which determines our behaviour is wealth. Under conditions where individuals can barely obtain sufficient nutrients for their personal survival, they do not have excess resources to contribute to the survival of others. When they can acquire additional resources they turn their attention to the survival of others in their society and even lavish their attention on the survival of other parts of the biota such as whales and rare butterflies and, latterly, the environment. This illustrates that while survival is a core concept, the way it makes itself manifest is a function of time, place and circumstances. But it does constitute a guideline for behaviour and it is possible to measure the outcome of its application in terms of survival so as to modify behaviours and thus increase survivability. It follows that those actions that promote survival (of individuals and/or groups and communities) are right, good and beneficial.

Following from the principle that we act to increase our chances of survival (for self, society and so on) we should note that virtually all tools may be used for benefit or harm. For example, when the early hominids met fire they would have been burned and damaged. As they learned to use this tool to ward off predators, cook (thereby decontaminating food sources) and preserve food and eventually master the arts of metal production and manipulation, the survival or beneficial properties of what was once a harmful tool became more apparent. (We are the only animal species that uses fire deliberately;

some plant species take advantage of fire incidentally to initiate germination of heavily protected seeds following forest fires). So in principle the development of any tool that can extend our ability to do things may be used beneficially; but how do we move from having the potential for benefit to the achievement of benefit without incurring irreparable harm in the process? This question is particularly germane when we acquire new tools whose use and application is unknown.[13] For this we have to consider how to apply the guideline we have decided to follow.

Second, determine the method by which the teachings of the ethical system may be applied

The same principle that was used to determine the guideline may be used to delineate the method by which it is implemented. We wish to increase and enhance survival or benefit as we apply the new tools that become available. The problem we face is that, as the tools are new, we do not know from experience the directions that will lead only to benefit and not to harm. (We regulate the use of hammers through laws and customs which restrict their use to knocking in nails or moving inanimate objects rather than making holes in living human crania except in times of war or self-defence.)

We could look to theories about the potential use of the new tools. One such theory might be that to use a tool for the deliberate fabrication of a new life form will create a biological competitor or toxin (of the mind?) which will be detrimental to the survival of present-day humans. Using the example of the use of fire, we might adduce that although the use of the fire-tool might have been most harmful with the techniques available some 200,000 years ago, perseverance and experiment resulted in methods and applications that drew out its beneficial properties. It is therefore unwise to use blanket restrictions on the use of new tools for all times and circumstances. How then might we proceed?

Most of our new tools have been tested through a trial-and-error process. This empirical approach to the exploration of the possible uses of a tool has, on balance, stood us in good stead. We have made mistakes, generated harm and, unfortunately, caused human suffering in this process. Yet we have learned a great deal about how to control the implementation of a new technology so as to minimize harm and maximize benefit. In this we proceed with our experimentation in controlled environments, where we try to think ahead about possible harmful outcomes ('HAZOP procedures') either to prevent their happening or to render them harmless by making sure that humans do not get in the way of the new tool. Such developments have to be effected with care and at a scale that is manageable. (Victor Frankenstein's first experimental creature was 8 feet tall and so powerful that it could not be controlled.)[14] The work should also be done in a manner which is not secretive; the public should be informed about the intent to effect the experiment and the manner in which it is to be performed and even asked to comment and make suggestions as to improvements in its design. The outcomes likewise should be open for public scrutiny and the evaluation of the experience should also involve a contribution from the interested citizenry. So might we proceed with caution, openness and in concert with the social will. Where other humans become involved or damaged in the testing of the tools then immediate compensation should be available for them and their families. In learning from our actions, as opposed to our theoretical notions, we adopt a realistic approach to the adoption of a new tool, a pragmatic approach.

Test the application in practice; if necessary revise the guideline to obtain more beneficial results

When a new drug (read tool for drug) is tested prior to licensing for introduction into the market place, it undergoes extensive evaluation of its safety and efficacy and of the ability of the manufacturer to produce it consistently. The introduction of a new tool might be similarly assayed. It, too, could be introduced under licence. Abreactions or misuses of the tool would be reported back to the licensing authorities. Laws might be written which define the areas of appropriate tool use and the manner in which it should be applied. This might be followed up with education, in specialist institutions, of how the tool should be used for maximum benefit. Society then licenses individuals who have received the appropriate training in the approved uses of the new tool. They have the obligation to continually update their understandings and proficiencies. All these procedures will be kept under review and modified to enhance the applicability of the new tool.

With regard to the cloning of humans, it is clear that I have taken a standpoint that asserts that we may look for an appropriate set of times, places and circumstances for the necessary trial-and-error experimentation. For this new tool we have to take account of the possible future scenarios as depicted in such books of fiction as *Brave New World* (Aldous Huxley 1931), *The Boys from Brazil* (I. Levin

1976) or *The Cloning of Joanna May* (Fay Weldon 1989). So we have some idea of how things might work out and of some of the pitfalls we should avoid (through thought experiments effected by the authors). Nevertheless the cloning of childless individuals or people whose unique abilities have resulted in outstanding contributions to our social well-being might well become the paradigms through which we could introduce the use of the new tool for cloning humans in an acceptable manner.

The potential uses of human foetuses which have been genetically modified so that the head (and presumably the brain, the seat of the soul?) does not develop have been thought of as being useful as a source of organs for transplantation purposes. Such beings, thought to be incapable of feeling pain, nurtured initially in the womb of a human female, cannot have an independent existence after gestation unless they are successfully attached to the equivalent of a heart and lung machine. I cannot rule out *a priori* the possibility that such entities might not be of use in promoting the survival of humans at some time in the future. However, in view of the psychological distress to the carrier of such a foetus as well as the negative reaction of many objectors, it is unlikely that, in the foreseeable future, there will be a call for their production.

Conclusion

One of the universally agreed defining events of the year 1997 was the cloning of Dolly the sheep by the team of Ian Wilmut at the Roslin Institute in Scotland.[15] Other such events like the discovery of planetary systems around stars, the richness of the mineral deposits in the vicinity of vents in the floor of the oceans, a vaccine protective against the AIDS disease, a doubling of the speed of computer chips and a halving of their cost and other such developments can be expected with a reasonable degree of confidence to happen in the short-term future. What are the ethical implications of such developments? How may we be expected to modify our behaviours in the light of such events?

It is an aspiration of the authors of this volume that its readers may become sufficiently fortified in their appreciation of the ethical aspects of science and engineering to answer such questions and to lead our citizenry to a deeper understanding and appreciation of the dynamically evolving world in which we live. Our political leaders and the press have a due concern with the way we are progressing. They are overcome by the rapidity of advances, by the far-reaching

implications of the new discoveries and by the absence of the necessary ethics which would have enabled them to be comfortable with the
way they and other members of society come to behave. It is hoped
that by focusing attention on the ethical aspects of these events we
may encourage the development of the ethical skills necessary to
provide such behavioural guidance. This work is intended as a small
step towards that objective.

Notes

1 C.P. Snow (1993) *The Two Cultures*, Cambridge: Cambridge University
   Press.
2 K. Popper (1983 [1934]) *The Logic of Scientific Discovery*, London:
   Hutchinson, p. 480.
3 Ibid., p. 251.
4 *The Compact Oxford English Dictionary*, second edition, 1989.
5 *Oxford Dictionary of English Etymology* (1966) (ed.) C.T. Onions.
6 *The Compact Oxford English Dictionary*, second edition, 1989.
7 Ibid.
8 Ibid.
9 R.E. Spier (1996) 'Ethics as a control system component', *Science and
   Engineering Ethics*, vol. 2, pp. 259–62.
10 *Great Books of the Western World*, Mortimer J. Adler, editor in chief, vol.
   6, *Plato*, p. 190.
11 M.J. Bebeau, K.D. Pimple, K.M.T. Muskavitch, S.L. Borden, D.H.
   Smith and E. Agnew (1995) *Moral Reasoning in Scientific Research:
   Cases for Teaching and Assessment*, Indiana University, K. Pimple, TRE
   Project Director, Indiana 47450.
12 D. Callahan and S. Bok (eds) (1980) *Ethics Teaching in Higher Education*,
   New York: Plenum Press, p. 315.
13 R.E. Spier (1999) 'An approach to the ethics of cloning humans via an
   examination of the ethical issues pertaining to the use of any tool',
   Science and Engineering Ethics, vol. 5, pp. 17–32.
14 M. Shelley (1818) *Frankenstein, or The Modern Prometheus.*
15 I. Wilmut, A.E. Schnieke, J. McWhir, A.J. Kind and K.H.S. Campbell
   (1997) 'Viable offspring derived from fetal and adult mammalian cells',
   Nature, vol. 385, pp. 810–13.

2

THE PROCESSES OF SCIENCE

Stephanie J. Bird

Introduction

Science is an intensely human activity and as such it reflects the full range of human strengths and weaknesses. It is based on our curiosity about the world around us; the desire to know and understand everything from the outer limits of the universe to the inner recesses of the mind. Scientific research also exemplifies the application of human creativity in many and varied forms to satisfy our curiosity. At the same time, the doing of science provides the opportunity to express human frailties and fallibilities: hubris, greed, avarice, insensitivity, stubbornness, ignorance, even cruelty and other examples of abuse of power.

As professionals, research scientists expect that they have a shared sense of professional values and standards of behaviour. Some professional societies in some disciplines have spelled out these standards with varying degrees of detail in a professional code of ethics (e.g. the American Chemical Society, the Association of Computing Machinery, the American Psychological Association, the Ecological Society of America, the Society for Neuroscience). However, the overarching values of scientific research are generally assumed to be understood and shared by all, and the specifics of accepted practice are only rarely explained in detail (e.g. the National Academy of Sciences' *On Being a Scientist*). It is also assumed that trainees will learn the standards and values of the profession, and how they are expressed in the details of behaviour, by observing the example set by senior science professionals. Yet observation by itself leaves much to interpretation, and the potential for confusion, misunderstanding and misinterpretation is considerable. Thus it is appropriate, even essential, to make explicit what generally has been implicit.

Ethical concerns are inherent in the various stages of conducting and reporting research (Bird and Housman 1995a, 1995b, 1997) as well as in the application of research to real-world problems (see chapters in this volume; Longino 1990; Shrader-Frechette 1994). In the limited space of this chapter it is not possible to explore in depth all of these issues – moreover, this is a growing field where professional standards and the expectations of colleagues are evolving. Rather, this article will focus on some of the recurring themes and thorniest aspects of scientific research. A brief description of key stages and components of scientific research, from an initial idea or question through to publication and subsequent research, lays the foundation for further discussion.

Stages of scientific research

Research begins with the initial question – the why, what and how of the universe: why do bees visit flowers? What are stars made of? How do I remember my own name? From the question comes speculation on what the answer(s) might be, that is, *hypothesis development*, and methods to test the hypothesis. Embedded in the design of the tests, the *research* design, are assumptions about what the relevant variables are or might be (e.g. age, sex, species, season, genetic make-up, distance, and so on), which variables need to be held constant and at what value, and what is a reasonable answer.

Once the research design is laid out, experiments or observations are carried out and data collected. Critical to this step is identifying which data are 'real' and to be included in data *analysis*, and which are artefacts of the methodology and therefore to be ignored. This process of data *selection*, of identifying the signal in the noise, is a critical process at the very heart of science. It is also a dynamic process reflecting the interaction of data interpretation with the evolving understanding of researchers of the phenomenon they are investigating. This stage is vulnerable to both overly narrow and overly broad assumptions of the nature and range of variables to be considered. Early pilot studies attempt to frame both the problem and the set of possible explanations, and they lay the foundation for describing the cause-and-effect relationship under study. Often some or all of the data collected in pilot studies are ultimately discarded because they are considered too unreliable since they are observations made in the uncertainty of development and refinement of techniques. In addition, data gathered by individuals who are very new to the particular research project, whether established researchers or new students, trainees or technicians, are usually dropped since they reflect the learning curve of the new investigators.

That data are discarded is neither surprising nor inappropriate (indeed it is just the opposite) since the purpose of research is to discover the nuggets of reality in the morass of relevant and irrelevant information, and to assist collaborators and colleagues (who will build on the work) to see the signal in the noise, too. Nonetheless, it is a process that is widely misunderstood and criticized (sometimes with good reason), at least in part because of the real possibility for bias to consciously or unconsciously influence the identification of data that should be and/or will be discarded (Segerstrale 1995). Inappropriate bias in the evaluation of data is an anathema to the core tenets of scientific research. Thus data are collected, selected, analysed and interpreted before they are ultimately described in a written document. The widely held notion that the scientific method is a straightforward process of hypothesis testing misses the subtle, dynamic and evolving nature of actual scientific research. Publication of scientific research papers is the primary means the scientific community has of disseminating the results of its work. It is the mechanism for expanding the body of knowledge, for providing additional information on which further research can be built, for adding pieces to the jigsaw puzzle of our understanding of a phenomenon. Publication also identifies those individuals who have made the contribution. In so doing, it serves as a tool to indicate those who have demonstrated skill and scientific ability, and thus those who have earned the respect of the scientific community based on their peers' evaluation of their contribution. By extension, research publications confer on authors a corresponding right to claim resources in the form of research funds, space, equipment and other potentially scarce resources. In short, authorship is in many important ways the 'coin of the realm' that is tendered for employment, promotion, research grants, scientific awards and prizes, honorary degrees and other elements and prerequisites of career advancement.

Ownership of ideas

Hypotheses, that is, possible explanations for a phenomenon under investigation, are central to many of the processes of science – and many of its problems. What we *think* might be the underlying mechanism or basis for what we observe in large measure frames how we determine whether what we think is true actually is. It affects how we look for the answer, what instruments we use, what changes we watch for and where we watch for them. Our ideas about what might be happening are grounded in our understanding of the phenomenon: what other studies about it have revealed, and what we know about other phenomena we believe, rightly or wrongly, are analogous. A new discovery, a flash of insight, a novel interpretation are valued within and beyond the research community as much as, if not more than, diligence and hard work in clarifying and expanding on the limits of a previous finding (Kuhn 1970). Often an idea, and who can lay claim to originating that idea, are the crux of controversy, debate and disagreement.

Where do ideas come from?

It seems doubtful that any idea springs into the mind fully formed. Rather it bubbles up to consciousness after some degree of unconscious rumination, even if it finally surfaces with a noticeable 'pop'. It is not surprising that two intelligent individuals with similar training and education, working independently in the same research area on a related problem, attending the same lecture or discussing related topics with each other or with the same colleagues, might eventually, and 'independently', arrive at the same novel explanation for a particular phenomenon. If both have the required facilities and equal resources to test the hypothesis, then independently each may produce a publishable manuscript. (This is an important 'if' to be discussed further since the distribution of resources may not be the same for researchers in different laboratories or even in the same laboratory.) Yet primacy, who first had the idea and adequately demonstrated its viability, is a fundamental concern for much of the research community (even when patent rights are not involved).

It is important to note that although each may have a potentially 'publishable manuscript', it rarely happens that both will be published, especially for particularly noteworthy findings. The editors of scientific publications seek to publish new findings that have not been previously published. Those who are asked by editors to review manuscripts in order to ascertain suitability for publication are expected to reject manuscripts that present work published elsewhere. Of course this may not be an entirely realistic expectation. Reviewers are selected for their knowledge of the field, and in any field there are a finite number of professional journals to which manuscripts may be submitted (particularly prestigious ones). At the same time, there are generally many more papers published, especially in active areas of research, than an active researcher can be depended upon to be familiar with. It is even less likely that, however knowledgeable a reviewer may be, he or she will necessarily know of all similar work in progress.

Being the first to have one's name widely associated with an idea *and* proof of its reliability (Merton 1968) is a complex process, dependent on a variety of factors: the order of the authors on the relevant publication(s), the notoriety and seniority of other authors on the paper, the circulation of the scientific journal in which a paper appears, that journal's reputation and whether articles published in it are peer-reviewed, participation of the authors in relevant scientific meetings at which prestigious colleagues are in attendance, citation of the paper in other relevant and important publications and so on. Because authorship and reputation are the basis for the recognition that results in jobs, career advancement and funding for further research, the quest for recognition is not purely idle ego-pampering but in many ways a necessity if one is to have the opportunity to make further contributions to science. Yet one side effect of the emphasis on primacy (which many would identify as unfortunate) is that it tends to undermine the fundamental openness of the scientific process. In particular it exacerbates the tension and conflict between openness and secrecy in science, between collaboration and competition.

The scientific community depends upon the free exchange of information between fellow researchers: the work of each is built on the foundation laid by others. Because of the research done by others, we can avoid 'reinventing the wheel', thereby conserving scarce resources whether money, chemicals, cell lines, research subjects (either animals or human volunteers), time or energy. Instead, resources are invested in finding information that is not already part of the body of knowledge.

At the same time, revealing one's idea or theory prematurely, that is, before it is in publishable form (i.e. before sufficient data demonstrate its validity) allows others working in the same research area, on the same family of research questions, to pursue the idea and perhaps produce the prized 'publishable paper' more quickly. Some researchers may have greater expertise than others, a better model system, more resources (including research assistants) or some other factor that makes it possible for them to pursue a particular idea, or a refinement of it, more effectively and, as a result, produce the definitive demonstration that makes possible the production of a publishable paper. Thus the advantage can go to those who are most prepared and indeed already advantaged, not only when they develop an idea independently and simultaneously, as indicated previously, but also when they obtain it from someone else in a more fully developed form.

It is not the case that, until it is published, a research project is known only to those investigators actually working on it. Invariably, from conception to the submission of a publishable manuscript, it is discussed to varying degrees and in some detail with colleagues in the same research group working on related but different projects, with colleagues in the same department and with colleagues in the same field at other institutions or organizations. The discussion may be informally held in the hall or over lunch, or more formally as an invited talk at a lab meeting, departmental seminar or scientific conference. It may even be written up in an abstracted form for the proceedings of a scientific symposium. These early discussions are primarily to obtain other perspectives, advice, suggestions and evaluations to assure one is exploring the problem effectively, leaving no alternative explanation unexamined. There is a tension between, on the one hand, vetting an idea sufficiently to assure its validity and acceptability and, on the other, retaining ownership of it. As the discussion becomes more formal, and presentations are given to a wider audience, the investigator stakes out and lays claim to the research problem or a particular theory. Indeed, to enhance that subtle process, sometimes researchers imply that certain experiments are under way, even if they are barely on the drawing board, in part as an attempt to discourage others from investing resources to pursue the question, especially those with the potential to take over the problem.

Negative findings

Within the scientific community there is a widespread reluctance to publish negative findings, that is, research results that do not support the hypothesis. In general, scientific journals and researchers are reluctant, even opposed, to publishing what does not work. The assumption is that only cause–effect relationships are informative. If a relationship is not demonstrated, it may be as much because the research design, methodology and/or the researcher's technique was flawed as because the relationship does not exist.

Yet resistance to publishing the demonstration of no apparent relationship can also have a detrimental effect on the progress of science because it can result in the squandering of resources and ultimately the lost careers of promising investigators. Because similar education and training are likely to lead several investigators down the same path, not knowing that others have tried the same approach to no avail results in wasted effort and resources – analogous to reinventing the wheel in reverse. Moreover, given the finite research funding available, especially to new investigators, and the interrelationship between funding and employment, researchers who pursue a dead end may, through no fault of their own, find themselves unable to pursue the research career for which they have trained.

Giving credit where it is due

In publishing a manuscript, dissemination of information within, and beyond, the scientific community is only one function that is being served. If dissemination were the only goal, research findings could be published anonymously.[1]

In fact, as we have seen, authorship serves multiple functions. It not only identifies those who have made a particular contribution to the fund of knowledge embodied in the publication but, in so doing, also identifies those who may be deserving of employment, promotion, and further allocation of resources with which to carry out additional research. These various functions of authorship reflect the assumption that relevant information is embedded in the list of authors, i.e. that both the nature and extent of contribution that fulfil criteria for inclusion in the group of authors, and the order of authorship, convey information that can be deciphered and used in making decisions about professional advancement.

Although the consensus is that all who make a significant contribution to the original, new scientific information that is the core of the paper are potential authors, there can be some considerable variability about which contributions qualify as 'new' and 'significant'. Contribution, like beauty, can be 'in the eye of the beholder'. While all would agree that anyone who developed the hypothesis, designed the experiments to test it, carried out all of the experiments, analysed the data and wrote the manuscript should be an author (if not the author), the extent and nature of a lesser contribution that nevertheless merits authorship may be, and often is, debated. Power, politics and personal and professional philosophy often enter into the process of conferring authorship. Laboratory heads, technicians and those who provide unique materials (e.g. clones or reagents) or services (e.g. statisticians and geographers) are in a grey zone so that some may be included in a list of authors and others may not. The final decision is usually made by the more senior researchers, some of whom may by nature be more inclusive than others. Moreover, it is possible that the lab or project head who determines authorship policies and makes authorship decisions may or may not have been the primary force at any particular stage of the research project. Problems and disputes often arise when expectations are not fulfilled.

Various schemes have been developed for 'giving credit where it is due'. They range from simple to complex, from practical to theoretical. In 1986 the policy of the Martin Marietta corporation (Martin Marietta 1986) was that anyone who made a 'major' contribution to one, or an 'important' contribution to two, of the fundamental components of publishable research (i.e. concept or idea, experimental design, data collection, data analysis, interpretation, writing) qualified as a potential author. (Note, however, that 'major' and 'important' have definitional problems akin to those of 'new' and 'significant' described above). In 1983 the Council of Biology Editors (CBE 1983) identified as a basic requirement for authorship that every author must be able to take public responsibility for the content of the manuscript as a whole. In other words, each author must be able to explain the rationale for the research, and how experimental observations were made and how the conclusions follow from the data. More recently the International Committee of Medical Journal Editors, also known as the Vancouver Group (International Committee of Medical Journal Editors 1997), has revised this to require that all authors participate in research design, in experimental observation and interpretation and in writing or revision for intellectual content. This pronouncement on the part of medical journal editors, regarding the criteria for authorship of articles involving medical research, coexists with several proposals in various fields that the specific contributions of each author be described as part of the manuscript itself: AC did the statistical analysis, TR carried out the biochemical experiments and wrote the first draft of the manuscript, and so on (Resnik 1997; Rennie *et al.* 1997; Tarnow 1999).

Equally as unsettled is the significance of the order of authorship. There are no definite rules and, therefore, the order of authors may reflect

1   the extent or nature of an individual's contribution (e.g. who did 'the most' work, had the central idea, carried out the central experiments, authored the first draft, and so on)
2   the senior scientist or project leader (formerly listed first, now first or last)
3   alphabetical order (this is standard practice in some disciplines, e.g. experimental physical sciences, is required by some journals and is standard policy in some research groups)

4   some other agreement among the authors. Most problematic about the order of authorship are the assumptions made by readers (and the assumptions made by authors regarding the assumptions made by readers) about the significance of order.

Discussion and debate about the criteria for authorship and the significance of the order of authorship continue, and as yet there is no consensus – except, perhaps, that, unless one has first-hand knowledge of the specific research project described in a publication, it is possible to infer from the list of authors neither the nature nor the extent of the contribution of any individual.

Because authorship serves multiple functions, because the research process itself is complex and dynamic and the role of researchers multifaceted, and because there are no clear-cut rules so that authorship policies continue to reflect the idiosyncratic experience and perspective of the decision-maker, 'giving credit where it is due' remains problematic. Moreover, because of the multiple functions authorship serves, plagiarism, the usurpation of another's work (whether ideas or writings) and its presentation as one's own, is considered a heinous crime within the scientific community. It deprives the rightful owner of appropriate recognition and attendant benefits in professional development and advancement.

A potentially problematic situation arises in the peer review process, whether in the course of publication or in efforts to obtain research funding. In either instance, reviewers are selected to evaluate the work of researchers in the same field. The more similar the work of the author or grant applicant and the reviewer, the more likely it is that the reviewer will be able to accurately assess the ideas, capabilities and quality of work represented in the manuscript or grant proposal. Yet given the increasingly competitive nature of many areas of science, it is possible that a reviewer may, on the one hand, have access to the ideas, hypotheses, preliminary data and research findings of fellow investigators (even competitors) and, on the other, be in a position both to adopt or integrate that information into his or her own work, and to undermine or block the publication or funding of the author or applicant. Thus the appropriate functioning of science through the review process depends upon the integrity of members of the community.

Integrity in science

Integrity is central to the process of science. Society depends on the honesty and incorruptible moral character of investigators as it seeks to use scientific findings as the basis for public policy in a wide range of arenas from the environment to health to national security and national defence.

Individuals, too, depend upon the integrity of the scientific process as they make personally important decisions regarding products and services from foodstuffs to health care to home insulation. Within the scientific community researchers depend on the uprightness and sincerity of their colleagues in order to justify the investment of finite resources, whether time, effort, materials or research subjects.

Definitions of scientific misconduct

Because they strike at the heart of scientific integrity, fabrication and falsification of scientific findings have always been abhorrent and unacceptable. Given the many important roles of authorship, plagiarism is the third member of the scientific misconduct triumvirate (FFP) (National Academy of Sciences 1992). Although some favour limiting the definition of scientific misconduct to these three misbehaviours, others recognize the limitations and vagueness of these concepts and that other behaviours in the context of scientific practice do not fit under the rubric of any version of FFP and yet are considered serious deviations from the range of practices accepted by members of the scientific community itself (Buzzelli 1999). Recently the Commission on Research Integrity of the US Department of Health and Human Services proposed a revision of the working definition of scientific misconduct to be used by the US Public Health Service in responding to allegations of scientific misconduct (Commission on Research Integrity 1995). This definition emphasizes misappropriation, interference in scientific research activities and misrepresentation as the principle aspects of scientific misconduct. The notion of misappropriation includes not only plagiarism but also the misuse of information obtained through the confidential review process (as discussed above). The interference component includes any behaviour that is meant to impede or disrupt the research of another, including stealing, hiding or damaging research equipment, materials or data. Misrepresentation expands on fabrication and falsification to include omission of relevant findings or information that, as an intended or foreseeable consequence, results in deception.

While proposing a revised definition, the Commission also recommended that Federal agencies work together to produce a common, shared definition of scientific misconduct. The definition of scientific misconduct will continue to evolve as discussion of the meaning of the concept continues within and beyond the scientific community (Bird and Dustira 1999; Spier and Gorski 2000). Moreover, numerous scientific societies have ethical codes or guidelines, and still other societies are developing them (or revising those they have) as the scientific community attempts to make explicit the professional standards and ethical values that have for so long been implicit yet inherent in the sometimes contradictory elements of research practice.

Conflict of interest

The integrity of members of the scientific community is generally assumed because it is universally recognized as critical to the scientific process. Nevertheless, a number of factors can influence judgements and decisions made as a part of the scientific process, either intentionally or unintentionally. Most frequently discussed, especially by observers of the scientific community, is the potential for financial gain as a result of patenting, licensing, subsequent product development and marketing of a product and/or stock in a manufacturer. However, the possibility of financial gain is only one, relatively limited, source of competing concerns and interests in the larger context of the scientific process. Widespread emphasis on competition, especially in some fields, reflects avid interest and extensive activity that may be only loosely tied to the marketability of research findings. Researchers generally agree that competition between pet theories about fundamental principles of science can be as intense as a race for patentability.

Moreover, individuals may feel pressured by professional commitments to teaching, training junior researchers, writing, peer review of the manuscripts and funding proposals of others in the field, institutional and departmental responsibilities, meeting organizational needs and expectations and the need to secure continued funding for research. Such commitments and responsibilities, combined with uninformed and unstated assumptions about the standards and significance of aspects of research practice, and the lack of clear definitions regarding acceptable practice, can undermine high standards of integrity. Researchers may be motivated to take shortcuts and 'push the envelope', sometimes stretching the concept of acceptable practice to, and even beyond, the boundaries of commonly held assumptions regarding what is acceptable.

Competing interests and concerns may have an intentional or unintentional impact on how individual researchers present research findings (both their strengths and limitations). Competition can also influence the evaluation of the work of a competitor. This can be especially problematic in the peer review process.

Training others

The complex, multifaceted character of the research process requires close interaction and one-on-one training to a greater or lesser degree at every stage. For example, subtle differences that may not be discernible to the untrained observer may embody the essential distinction between the sought-after signal, or data, in the irrelevant 'noise'. How to collect and select data reliably for analysis is one of the most important skills an experienced researcher can teach a student. This one-on-one training can be both highly productive and a potential source of problems and conflict.

Mentorship

Beyond the basics of scientific concepts and laboratory techniques, the science professional must learn a variety of additional skills including how to write and review manuscripts, obtain funding, manage a research project, give an oral presentation and so on. Equally as important is an understanding of departmental and institutional politics, the machinations of institutional committees and, most especially, the professional standards and ethical values that are expected of and by members of the scientific community. The range of conventions and accepted standards may differ from one discipline to the next. Nevertheless this is information that is critical for professional success, and it is this type of information that mentors can help to provide.

Mentors are those who share their experience and expertise, and who are interested in the professional development and success of those they mentor. While this definition often leads to the expectation that thesis advisors and research supervisors will be mentors to students and trainees, this is not necessarily the case, although it ought to be (Bird 1994; Swazey and Anderson 1996; National Academy of Sciences 1997; Bird and Sprague 2001). Rather, advisors are expected to see to it that students fulfil departmental and institutional requirements for an advanced degree. The job description of research supervisors of postdoctoral trainees and other research staff is even less well defined with regard to oversight of professional development and advancement.

Through mentors the trainee can learn about the nature of science, and especially about the community of scientists and the processes of science. Because the role of the researcher and the processes of science are many and diverse, junior researchers need multiple mentors. This contradicts the widely held perception that a trainee usually has only one mentor. (This view may be linked to the tendency to use the terms 'mentor' and 'thesis advisor' interchangeably.) Multiple mentors are essential not simply to provide numerous professional contacts, but also as a variety of sources for learning fundamental skills. After all, a single individual cannot know all techniques and skills that a trainee may need to learn, and different mentors will have different strengths and experience. Furthermore, junior scientists benefit from hearing various perspectives regarding the issues and implications associated with the full range of practices and conventions that are part of the scientific process. For example, trainees need to be aware of the spectrum of views about where best to publish; the criteria for and responsibilities of authorship; effective matching of the presentation of research findings to a given audience whether students, peers or the general public; funding strategies; project management; departmental politics and so on. At the same time, the mentoring relationship is, more than many other workplace relationship, a personal as well as a professional relationship.

Those seeking the advice of a mentor should recognize the advice for what it is: a unique perspective on a given situation based on experience the mentee does not have. It is invaluable but not infallible. It is advice based upon a different time and place and potentially different values and goals. Thus a mentor's advice should always be carefully evaluated in light of the mentee's own background, needs, values and goals.

Discrimination and harassment

The research setting, like any workplace, is a microcosm of society to which co-workers bring their values, concerns, tensions, unconscious perceptions and biases. It is a structured, hierarchical setting with a differential distribution of power. There exist the same potential for stereotypic thinking regarding roles and responsibilities and the same possibility of differing expectations, miscommunication and misunderstanding. Often these expectations are played out unconsciously, but they can serve as the basis for discrimination and even harassment in the research setting.

The mentoring relationship, too, can reflect differential power distributions. The personal as well as professional nature of the relationship, shared interests and enthusiasm for the research topic, and differing expectations, miscommunication and misunderstanding can also lead to discrimination and even sexual harassment.[2] Thus both members of the mentoring relationship need to be aware of and attentive to the potential for unstated assumptions and expectations to creep into the relationship.

Research subjects: willing and unwilling partners

In 'giving credit where it is due', an often under-recognized contribution is that of the research subject. Both human volunteers and research animals play a role in the research process. Although some areas of scientific research are independent of life processes, life and social science research are dependent on the participation of living organisms. While computer models and tissue and cell culture can replace some experiments, computers depend on information obtained from real living systems, and individual cells cannot fully inform our understanding of how a whole, complex and dynamic organism will be affected by different variables. Thus research subjects are an essential part of some areas of research if that research is to progress.

Animals in research

There is a certain arrogance in placing the thirst for knowledge, for whatever purpose, above the interest of individual organisms. The scientific community has come to recognize that the financial cost of procuring and maintaining research animals militates for using as few animals as possible, while at the same time it is necessary to use enough animals in an experiment to ensure that the data obtained from each animal are statistically meaningful. Similarly, the physical well-being (and, where appropriate, the psychological well-being) of research subjects is essential in order to make certain that the data obtained are accurate and reliable.

However, the more thorny question of the justification of research that subordinates the suffering and interests of other life forms to the goals and interests of humans has yet to be adequately addressed by either the scientific community or the society in whose name the research is carried out.

Human volunteers

The participation of human subjects in research is critical to understanding the details of human health and disease, and to developing therapies for treating human illness. The fully informed decision to choose voluntarily to participate in clinical trials without expectation of any benefit is a noteworthy act of altruism. Yet all too often what is represented as informed consent on the part of human volunteers is far less. Too often research subjects are motivated by misconceptions of the fundamental nature of the protocol itself.

While much has been achieved since the use of concentration camp inmates in Nazi experiments, much more remains to be done to improve the process of participation of human volunteers in research.

Conclusion

The processes of science are multiple, complex, interactive and dynamic. To one degree or another, those engaged in the research process believe that research and the accompanying expansion of knowledge will make the world a better place. The application of scientific research has done much to alleviate suffering of various kinds and to extend opportunity and human potential.

Yet the scientific process does not automatically provide progress or improvement. Moreover, there is often a burden embedded in the research process, in addition to the costs integral to the specific allocation of resources in one area over another. Choices are inevitable and the winners and losers often go unacknowledged and even unrecognized. Inherent in nearly every aspect of conducting, reporting and funding research are ethical issues, concerns and sometimes dilemmas.

Over the last few decades, there has been growing awareness of the ethical issues and implications associated with the practices of science as well as with the application of research findings. The scientific community, and the society of which it is a part, have much to gain from recognizing and addressing these ethical concerns.

Notes

1   However, it could be argued that authorship links the present and future reputations of the authors to the work and thereby serves the reader by providing a professional context for the paper that confers credibility on the work (or not) by making it possible to identify both underlying assumptions and bias in the authors. Note that this professional context is useful to readers only to the extent that they know the literature, including the previous work of the authors, and other potentially relevant information about the authors.
2   Even if the institution is the same, different people and policies can make a dramatic difference in organizational dynamics.

References

Bird, S.J. (1994) 'Overlooked aspects in the education of science professionals: mentoring, ethics, and professional responsibility', *Journal of Science Education and Technology*, vol. 3, pp. 49–55.

Bird, S.J. and Sprague, R.L. (2001) 'Mentoring and the responsible conduct of research', *Science and Technology Ethics*, vol. 7, no. 4, pp. 451–639.

Bird, S.J. and Dustira, A.K. (eds) (1999) 'Scientific misconduct', *Science and Engineering Ethics*, vol. 5, no. 2, pp. 129–304.

Bird, S.J. and Housman, D.E. (1995a) 'Trust and the collection, selection, analysis and interpretation of data: a scientist's view', *Science and Engineering Ethics*, vol. 1, pp. 371–82.

Bird, S.J. and Housman, D.E. (1995b) 'Conducting and reporting research', *Professional Ethics*, vol. 4, nos 3 and 4, pp. 127–54.

Bird, S.J. and Housman, D.E. (1997) 'Conducting, reporting and funding research', in D. Elliott and J.E. Stern (eds) *Research Ethics: A Reader*, Hanover, NH: University Press of New England, pp. 98–108, 120–38.

Buzzelli, Donald (1999) 'Serious deviation from accepted practices', *Science and Engineering Ethics*, vol. 5, pp. 275–82.

Commission on Research Integrity (1995) *Integrity and Misconduct in Research: Report of the Commission on Research Integrity*, US Department of Health and Human Services, Public Health Service.

CBE Style Manual Committee (1983) 'Ethical conduct in authorship and publication', in *CBE Style Manual*, fifth edition, Bethesda, MD: Council of Biological Education, pp. 1–6.

Gadlin, Howard (1994) AAAS presentation, San Francisco.

International Committee of Medical Journal Editors (1997) 'Uniform requirements for manuscripts submitted to biomedical journals', *New England Journal of Medicine*, vol. 335, pp. 309–15.

Kuhn, Thomas (1970) *The Structure of Scientific Revolution*, second edition, Chicago: The University of Chicago Press.

Longino, Helen E. (1990) *Science as Social Knowledge: Values and Objectivity in Scientific Inquiry*, Princeton, NJ: Princeton University Press.

Martin Marietta Document Preparation Guide (1986) Section 3.1.4.3: guidelines regarding criteria for authorship, May 1986.

Merton, Robert K. (1968) 'The Matthew effect in science', *Science*, vol. 159, pp. 56–63.

National Academy of Sciences (1992) *Responsible Science: Ensuring the Integrity of the Research Process*, vol. 1, Washington, DC: National Academy Press.

National Academy of Sciences (1997) *Advisor, Teacher, Role Model, Friend: On Being a Mentor to Students in Science and Engineering*, Washington, DC: National Academy Press.

Olson, Steve (1995) *On Being a Scientist*, Washington, DC: National Academy Press.

Rennie, Drummond, Yank, Veronica and Emanuel, Linda (1997) 'When authorship fails: a proposal to make contributors accountable', *Journal of the American Medical Association*, vol. 278, pp. 579–85.

Resnik, David B. (1997) 'A proposal for a new system of credit allocation in science', *Science and Engineering Ethics*, vol. 3, pp. 237–43.

Segerstrale, Ullica (1995) 'Good to the last drop? Millikan stories as "canned pedagogy"', *Science and Engineering Ethics*, vol. 1, pp. 197–214.

Shrader-Frechette, Kristin (1994) *Ethics of Scientific Research*, Lanham, MD: Rowman and Littlefield Publishing.

Spier, R.E. and Gorski, A. (eds) (2000) 'Scientific misconduct: an international perspective', *Science and Engineering Ethics*, vol. 6, no. 1, pp. 1–144.

Swazey, Judith P. and Anderson, Melissa S. (1996) *Mentors, Advisors, and Role Models in Graduate and Professional Education*, Washington, DC: Association of Academic Health Centers.

Tarnow, Eugen (1999) 'The authorship list in science: junior physicists' perceptions of who appears and why', *Science and Engineering Ethics*, vol. 5, pp. 73–88.

3

ETHICS AND THE PRODUCTS OF SCIENCE

Rufus Black[1]

> Whether we will acquire the understanding and wisdom necessary to come to grips with the scientific revelations of the 20th century will be the most profound challenge of the 21st.
>
> (Carl Sagan)

As humans unravel the biochemical foundations of their nature and as they come to a clearer understanding of both their own origins and the very origins of the universe itself, it has become possible to ask whether ethics is really a subject apart from science and, if it is, to query whether it is capable of resolving the moral dilemmas that arise as people consider the products of modern science and the uses to which they might be put. This chapter will begin by considering a significant scientific challenge to the very possibility of ethics itself. It will then turn to consider how the moral dilemmas raised by modern science might be resolved. Finally, an important approach to the resolution of moral dilemmas will be applied to some of the difficult problems relating to modern scientific products.

Modern science has produced a range of challenges to the notion that ethics is a subject with even a relative independence from science. These challenges have ranged from deterministic arguments based on the nature of physics to arguments drawing upon psychology. It is beyond the scope of this chapter to treat all of these challenges in detail. However, the particular currency and apparent resilience of one of these challenges – that arising from a certain line of contemporary evolution theory – is worthy of special attention not only in itself but also in order to advance the more general thesis that there is *not* an inherent tension between a scientific world view and a world view which affirms that there are truths beyond those knowable by science.

Ethics is not just genes

With the help of some eloquent writers on science, various fields of scientific enquiry have captured the public imagination, usually because they ask, or appear to answer, the sort of much larger questions which might once have been thought the domain of philosophy or theology. One of these fields of enquiry is genetics and a subject which it has, at times, purported to overthrow is ethics. The most famous of those attempting such an overthrow by applying neo-Darwinian theory to explain not just animal behaviour but human behaviour as well was E.O. Wilson in his (in)famous book *Sociobiology* (1975) – the book which gave the name to this field of enquiry. Every few years, the general thrust of Wilson's argument has been given new life by some – often very engaging – writers on science. Rather than revisit the storm that surrounded Wilson, clouded as it is by political recriminations, it may be helpful to focus instead on a more recent and balanced rendering of his general approach, John and Mary Gribben's *The One Per Cent Advantage: The Sociobiology of Being Human*.[2]

The Gribbens begin by distancing themselves from those accounts of sociobiology which argue that human behaviour is simply genetically determined. In this regard, they take issue with Konrad Lorenz and Robert Ardrey's widely discussed proposal that 'human beings are driven by innate aggression'.[3]

Such arguments, the Gribbens maintain, are unsound because

> culture *is* a big influence on human behaviour (thanks to our genes) and we have the intelligence (thanks to evolution) to analyse situations and *act on the basis of reasoned argument*, instead of instinct. People are rather *unusual* African apes, and our unusual attributes have to be taken into account.[4]

Having sought to distance themselves from such theories, the Gribbens articulate the central thesis of current sociobiology: a gene which contributes to the bringing about of behaviour that increases that gene's survival chances will, in the long run (all other things being equal), come to predominate over a competing gene or genes. The long-run result will be that an animal's behaviour will be determined by what is most advantageous for its genes. The Gribbens then highlight the explanatory power of this theory in relation to the behaviour of non-human animals. At this point, those familiar with popular genetics will be on clearly recognizable and fairly uncontroversial territory. The Gribbens call upon the work of eminent biologists to demonstrate how elegantly this theory of 'selfish genes' can account even for what appears to be altruistic behaviour in animals. Other than noting that anthropomorphizing animal behaviour with morally loaded terms, such as 'selfish' and 'altruism', helps to gloss the transition to the discussion of human behaviour, the ethicist has relatively little to complain about.

It is with this transition to the discussion of human behaviour in terms of evolutionary theory that the problem for ethics appears to arise. For if, ultimately, it is genes which cause people to behave the way they do – albeit by the indirect mechanism of generating 'predispositions that incline us in certain directions'[5] – then ethics will simply represent the codification of behaviours which have an evolutionary advantage. Indeed, the Gribbens conclude as much when they observe that 'ethics, moral codes, and the teachings of the great religions are powerful forces in human affairs because . . . the code of behaviour they represent has been tried and tested in the evolutionary struggle for survival'.[6]

The Gribbens do not, however, end, as some sociobiologists are wont to do, by viewing ethics as being inescapably determined by evolutionary forces. Rather, they argue that once we realize that we act in genetic self-interest *'then* we shall be able to see how best . . . to make our lives better and more secure'.[7]

This move is common in such discussions. Richard Dawkins, for example, concludes his discussion in *The Selfish Gene* even more affirmatively with the rallying call that 'we, alone on earth, can rebel against the tyranny of the selfish replicators'.[8]

Yet what the Gribbens and many other supporters of sociobiology do not make clear is how they know what making our lives 'better' – a claim which can only be a value judgement – means if all the existing ethics and moral codes which might give meaning to such value judgements are simply codifications of our genetic self-interest. The explanation appears to lie in the fact that, as the Gribbens observe, 'we have the intelligence (thanks to evolution) to analyse situations and *act on the basis of reasoned argument,* instead of instinct'.[9]

The result is that reasoned argument has, over time, given rise to moral understandings, such as that 'altruism' as a matter of value judgement is 'better' than 'selfishness' and is not simply a way of describing a subtle form of selfishness. This means that it is *not necessary*, as the Gribbens claim, to know about sociobiology *before* it is possible to make genuinely reasonable value judgements about what 'better' might mean in moral terms. This conclusion does not, however, discount the potential support which knowledge of sociobiological forces can provide to assist people to act on the basis of reasoned argument. For example, the identification of sociobiological reasons which might have shaped the behaviours defining the social role of our female ancestors, *together with* the recognition of the extent to which men, who benefit most from such behaviour, have decided what is reasonable, might add considerable weight to the argument that such behaviour is not required by reason.

Although some behaviour might, at least in part, have a valid sociobiological explanation, once the role of reason in shaping human behaviour is recognized, existing ethics and moral codes can no longer be reduced to codifications of genetic advantage *unless* it can be shown that the reasoning itself will be controlled by genes. In terms of evolutionary theory, any significant degree of such control would seem very difficult to demonstrate. For once people who possess language and a measure of self-determination are acting to some extent on the basis of reason rather than instinct, the power of evolutionary forces will be substantially reduced. In fact, there appear to be only two essential ways in which evolution can control the knowledge and reasoning which shape behaviour.

First, evolution could control a person's knowledge and reasoning if it gave rise to patterns of behaviour which significantly disadvantaged that person *vis à vis* others and those others were prepared to exploit that disadvantage so that, in the long run, sustaining a community which transmitted those reasons inter-generationally became impossible. For example, if a community reasoned that they should be pacifists and they lived next to an aggressive, acquisitive community which was prepared to take advantage of their behaviour, their particular account of pacifism might be eliminated. Or, more realistically, a community which lived and behaved according to simple technical knowledge will survive (all other things being equal) unless they encounter a more technologically advanced (e.g. industrialized) people who are prepared to exploit that advantage.

Second, evolution could eliminate reasons for behaviour if those reasons led to forms of behaviour which give the genes of the non-human world an evolutionary advantage so that those acting on the basis of such reasons do not allow their genes to replicate. A good example of such reasoning is to be found in the economic 'rationality' which threatens the world with environmental destruction.

These broad 'genetic controls' on reasoning allow people to behave on the basis of a very wide range of reasons for action. In other words, they allow for cultural diversity. What is more, they enable these culturally embodied systems of thought to be transferred across generations, while remaining little affected by evolution. As a result, far more proximate causes for the shaping of the reasoning – which is the subject of ethics and the content of moral codes – are to be found in the interaction between people, their ideas and their environment down through the ages of history, rather than in the far slower work of evolution.

The apparent irresolvability of moral problems

Restoring the possibility that ethics could – in theory – be a matter of 'reasoned argument' may seem a pyrrhic victory as a measure of scientific certainty is lost for the gain of apparently intractable exchanges on moral issues. In decades of arguing, little or no resolution has been reached between the disputants of bio-medical questions such as abortion or, more recently, the use of embryos in medical experimentation. There is often a sense that such disputants are simply speaking past one another, and are so lacking in common ground that their arguments never really engage. Voices become louder and the arguments harder to hear. The conflicts appear to be more than matters of priority. They seem to have the nature of conflicts about the whole way of thinking about ethics. To a greater or lesser extent, such observations probably reflect the reality of these exchanges because they arise from the fact that, in the modern world, it is possible to employ a range of incompatible moral systems to analyse ethical problems.

What makes resolving moral disagreements more complicated still is that much moral argument has ceased to employ systems of moral reasoning at all.[10] Instead, it involves the sewing together of insights drawn from diverse and often incompatible systems of ethical thought in response to some intuitive sense of their rightness. The result is that the real cause of the intractability of so many contemporary ethical problems, not least in scientific fields, is not the inherent irresolvability of the questions themselves but the failure to resolve the prior question of ethical methodology. This problem is difficult to overcome because the acceptance of the apparent irresolvability of these questions has become so widespread that there has been a loss of confidence that there can even be 'right' answers to moral questions. This is not to say, however, that this common presumption should be lightly or quickly accepted. Rather, the problem needs to be tackled at its core, by determining which general approach to ethical decision-making is most satisfactory.

Ethics is not just a feeling

Today the attempt to seek for one system for ethical analysis and for objective answers to moral questions is likely to be met by the casual observer with the claim that 'there are no objectively right or wrong answers to moral questions; they are just a matter of what people feel'. This observer, it should be noted, has effectively proposed a system for ethics – that one should act in accordance with one's feelings – on the basis of a strong objective claim about the nature of ethics – that there are no right or wrong answers. Unless the observer is to lapse into self-contradiction by claiming that all truth is just a matter of what people feel (i.e. by claiming that this is an accurate or true description of reality), she has also, at least, made the general nature of ethics the subject of rational argument. This becomes clear if we disagree with her claim because she would have to resort to commonly agreed canons of sound reasoning (such as that one should not propose self-contradictory arguments and that one should favour a theory which best accounts for the evidence) in order to seek to demonstrate the truthfulness of her position.

There have, however, been moral philosophers who have accepted that the nature of ethics can be the subject of a rational quest yet who have also sought to defend the essential thrust of the casual observer's claim. Pre-eminent among them is C.L. Stevenson. According to his approach, a moral statement such as 'it is right to protect privacy', is an expression which is equivalent to saying, 'I approve of protecting privacy and I want you to approve of it as well!'. However, as other moral philosophers have pointed out, the problem with this approach is that the everyday use of moral language simply cannot be reduced to expressions of feelings.[11]

Rather, 'moral' language – language which is concerned with answering the question 'what should I, or we, do?' (as distinct from the language of commands and commendations) – is concerned with communicating *reasons* why a person or group should *choose* to do one thing rather than another. This becomes particularly apparent when we think about being confronted by a moral statement about which we are uncertain – perhaps, 'you *ought* to keep an individual's genetic information confidential'. In such a case, we will ask 'why?', with the expectation that we will receive some *reason(s)* as to why we should keep this information confidential. We will then assess the quality of the reason(s) or reasoning we have been given. This means that, in seeking to determine which methodology we should adopt for making moral decisions, we must assess the reasoning offered by different approaches. In a brief chapter such as this, a comprehensive evaluation of all the available major options is impossible. This problem can be substantially reduced, however, by focusing consideration upon the widely used form of ethics in which people claim to be trying to bring about 'the greatest good' by their decisions and upon a modern restatement of an approach which integrates the central insights from a number of other highly plausible accounts of ethics.

Proportionalism and its problems

Let us turn first to the approach to ethics which centres on the notion that one should choose that option which will bring about 'the greatest good'. When Mill first proposed this in the nineteenth century, it was known as *utilitarianism* because the right option was the one which maximized utility, which was equated with pleasure or happiness. As pleasure was thought to be an inadequate goal for the moral life, other worthwhile objectives of human life (or human goods) were substituted for what should be maximized. Questions about the notion of maximizing things led to a shift to choose that which would bring the optimal consequences – thus the label *consequentialism* in the 1950s. Despite these varying labels and emphases, all these approaches share a common methodology: that the morally right choice is 'the one that will bring about a *better proportion of benefits to harms* than any other available choice'.[12]

These proportionalist approaches to moral reasoning gain an initial plausibility because in everyday speech there are uses of phrases like 'greater good' ('the greater good of the community lies in caring for the poor') and 'better option' ('it would be a better option to spend our money on our children's education') which *are* meaningful. However, these everyday uses are not usually those of proportionalists. In everyday use we commonly have some reason, such as fairness or the priority established by our commitments, which is the basis of our evaluation of the known good(s) or options. Proportionalists, however, seek to make their evaluation by *comparing* the *expected* good(s) or consequences *themselves*.

It is with this proportionalist methodology of basing a moral judgement on what can, at best, only be the *expected* utility, consequences,

harms or benefits that the real problems begin to arise. For the proportionalist, what makes a particular option the right choice is that it will
actually bring a greater proportion of benefit to harm. If we followed
this approach, we would not judge a choice good if it turned out that in
fact more harm than good resulted from it. Yet knowledge of all the
good and bad consequences which will flow from our decisions is
exactly the sort of knowledge which it is impossible for humans to
obtain. Even with decisions about the use of the products of science
where predicability is likely to be higher than in more strictly social
policy choices, the problem remains. We know this all too well when
even well-trialled drugs end up causing very undesirable and unforeseen side effects. Even if the technical barriers of imperfect knowledge
and the unpredictability of complex systems could be overcome, there
is the ultimate unpredictability of exactly how humans will regard and
use the products of science.

What makes matters more difficult is that, logically, this approach
does not allow us to place a limit on the consequences (such as those
which are foreseeable) which we should take into account, because
what makes the particular option morally good or bad is the *actual*
harms and benefits brought about. There is nothing in this methodology which means that the benefits brought about one day matter
morally whereas the harm our decision caused the next day does not,
simply because we could not foresee it. Any line we draw because of a
lack of knowledge of the future can only be arbitrary (i.e. made
without good reason).

The difficulty with proportionalism is not only that people are not
omniscient but also that it relies on attempting to compare the incom-
parable (i.e. the incommensurable). The very reason we experience the
need to make choices is that we recognize that there are a range of
genuinely attractive benefits presented by the different options which
we have to choose between and that no single option will allow us to
realize all those benefits. For example, consider this simple choice:
should I stay at my desk and read or go out and see my friends? I sense
this as a choice because I recognize what is worthwhile in each option
and know that neither option allows me to pursue both these worthwhile activities. I recognize that the good in staying at my desk is that
my knowledge will grow, whereas if I see my friends I will enjoy the
good of my friendship with them. To say, 'well, choose the option
which will maximize your welfare or well-being' is unhelpful because
I recognize that knowledge and friendship are both distinct components of my welfare or well-being. If different possibilities for
choice produce benefits which have *distinct* values then these benefits

will be incapable of comparison in order to say, for example, that a choice which produces knowledge is better or more optimal than a choice which produces friendship. While there are a number of other problems with a proportionalist approach to ethics, it should already be sufficiently clear that it is a logically unworkable means of making moral decisions and, therefore, these further problems need not detain us further here.[13]

A modern realist ethic: where Aristotle meets Kant

At this point, it is worth turning to a more promising approach to ethics which has been produced and refined over the last thirty years by Germain Grisez, John Finnis, Joseph Boyle and other collaborators.[14] It seeks to bring together a tradition of ethics which finds its roots in Aristotle and adds refinements of the insights of great modern moral thinkers such as Kant. This approach begins by recognizing that it is just those distinctly worthwhile things, such as knowledge and friendship, which we seek to realize by our actions which provide the ultimate reasons which justify our choices.

If we ask ourselves, 'why do I do what I do?' about the various activities of our adult lives, until we can get no further answer, we will find that we have uncovered a series of basic (irreducible) reasons for action. These reasons point to those goals or objectives of human life which we find are worthwhile or valuable to pursue. If we reflect upon why we find these goals valuable, it is likely that we will recognize that it is because in pursuing and realizing them we gain a sense of well-being, or fulfilment. When we finally obtain some particular knowledge, for example, we feel a sense of satisfaction or wholeness. The fundamental similarity of human nature – in the sense that we are all living, knowing, feeling (emotional), reasoning creatures capable of interacting with and shaping our environment and interacting with others – means that we are all likely to produce a set of reasons coinciding in substance, even if not in exact description, for action. Finnis, Grisez and Boyle helpfully suggest a description of these reasons for action – or elements of human wholeness – as being essentially life; knowledge and aesthetic experience; some degree of excellence in the skills of work and play; friendship (community); self-integration (integration of different dimensions of the person, e.g. reason and emotions); and harmony with some more-than-human source of meaning and value. All of these inherently worthwhile activities can be pursued in a myriad of different ways and combinations. This is, in other words, a form of ethics which *explains*, rather than is challenged by, the fact of cultural diversity. This first stage of what can be described as a modern realist ethic represents an elaboration and refinement of Aristotle's approach to ethics.

Identifying the worthwhile goals and objectives of human life is, however, only the first step of ethics because the question remains as to which goals are to be pursued and how. Or, to put the question another way, what principles are to guide us as we seek to live whole (fulfilled) lives in community with one another? Providing reasons or principles which answer these questions is the task of *practical reason*. These principles will be the principles which are necessary for living a whole human life given

1   *the conditions of human existence* (i.e. that life is short and subject to unpredictable and disruptive occurrences, that human projects take time and resources, that there are finite resources and that many worthwhile things can only be realized in cooperation with others)
2   *human nature* (e.g. given that desires and emotions can be in tension with reason)
3   *the nature of practical reason itself* (i.e. that its purpose is to direct people in community towards human wholeness).

For example, given that life is short and that the human projects by which we might reach our worthwhile goals take time, a basic principle of practical reason will be that one should have some kind of life plan. In relation to determining what the other principles of good practical reasoning might be, John Finnis has observed that

> In the two millennia since Plato and Aristotle initiated formal inquiry into the content of practical reasonableness, philosophical reflection has identified a considerable number of requirements of *method* in practical reasoning. Each of these requirements has, indeed, been treated by some philosopher with exaggerated respect, as if it were the exclusive controlling and shaping requirement.[15]

This means that in determining what good practical reasoning involves we are wise to turn to moral philosophers such as Kant to help us determine what these principles might be. However, we need to do so with the awareness that the principle(s) they emphasize may be but one of a number of principles of good practical reasoning.

This is not the place to provide an exhaustive list and explanation of such principles and their origins, though the following, drawn from a list produced by John Finnis, in addition to the requirement to have a coherent life plan, may be worth noting to give some sense of the scope of these principles:

1 Do not leave out of account, or arbitrarily discount, or exagger-ate the goodness of other people's participation in human goods (put simply, do not discriminate between people or be unfair in your dealings with other people).
2 Do not attribute to any particular project the overriding and unconditional significance which only a basic human good (i.e. any inherently worthwhile human goal) and a general commit-ment can claim.
3 Do not waste your opportunities with needlessly inefficient methods, and do not overlook the foreseeable bad consequences of your choices.
4 Do not choose directly against any basic human good (e.g. do not intentionally harm or kill another person).
5 Foster the common good of your communities.[16]

In considering the dilemmas raised by modern scientific products, those principles which are of direct relevance will be discussed in more detail.

Altogether, this means that the subject matter of ethics is reasoning about the task of pursuing human wholeness in community. On this account, immoral decisions not only harm others by disfiguring their humanity, but also disfigure our own humanity by harming our human wholeness. From another perspective, this means that ethics is about becoming a community of virtuous people – of people who will act on the basis of a consistent set of reasons (which are integrated with their emotions and beliefs) for pursuing that mix of worthwhile goals which, as individuals and a community, they have chosen to seek. This approach is not a highly prescriptive form of ethics which dictates only one right answer to every choice which humans must make. There will be many morally acceptable courses of action open to individuals and communities. What this approach does hold is that being moral is being reasonable. On the other hand, being immoral is to choose to do that which is unreasonable – that which is contrary to the pursuit of human wholeness or well-being.

Before turning to consider some applied problems, it is worth recalling E.O. Wilson's observation that 'human behaviour – like the deepest capacities for emotional response which drive and guide it – is the circuitous technique by which human genetic material has been and will be kept intact. Morality has no other demonstrable function'.[17]

Yet what has clearly emerged is that morality demonstrably does have another function: it articulates the sound reasoning which humans use to pursue, in community with one another, human wholeness – a wholeness which is conceived of in terms which cannot, without the gravest misunderstanding or misrepresentation of the nature of morality, be reduced to the perpetuation of genes. If there is an integral relationship between science and ethics, it is based on the fact that they ultimately work towards the same goal – enhancing human life.

The ethical problems generated by scientific products

The most helpful place to begin the discussion of the ethical problems generated by scientific products is with the moral nature of the scientific products themselves. From the discussion of the nature of ethics, it should have become clear that ethics is concerned with the reasonableness of our proposed choices or purposes. This means that the actual products of science – whether a substance (e.g. a drug) or knowledge (which could be of something, e.g. a person's genetic make-up, or of a process, e.g. how to produce a particular chemical) – are themselves morally neutral. What matters is the purpose for which the product is used. The same drug, for example, could be used for therapeutic purposes, recreational purposes or lethal purposes. The morality of its use will depend upon the purpose.

The use of 'ill-gotten' gains

Perhaps the case when scientific products seem most to possess a moral quality in themselves is when they have been produced or obtained by an immoral process. A classic example of such a situation received wide media coverage a few years ago when a school in England refused to allow its pupils to be immunized against rubella because the vaccine was originally derived from material taken from an aborted foetus. A more universally recognized problem might be the question, 'what should we do with valuable therapeutic knowledge derived from non-consensual medical experimentation?'. There are no special principles for such situations. Rather, it is a matter of making sure

1   that one's purposes in using such products do not include that other people engage in wrongdoing
2   that we foresee no unfair side effects arising from the use of these products.

In relation to the two cases just mentioned, on the basis of criterion (1) there would be nothing unreasonable in using these products for the worthwhile end of improving human health. Given that these products actually exist, one's purpose need not (although it could) include that someone else successfully do something (gravely) wrong. In other words, in using the product we need not intend or desire that the initial wrong occur.

In considering these two cases from the perspective of our responsibility for foreseeable but unintended and undesired side effects, we would need to consider whether using these products was likely to create any risk of encouraging people to continue the immoral practices by which these products were obtained. If there is a risk of this occurring, we would need to consider whether it was fair to accept that risk. What constitutes fairness could be the subject of an entire discussion. For the present, it is sufficient to observe that it is classically expressed in the non-philosophical formulation of the Golden Rule: 'do unto others as you would have them do unto you'. In modern philosophical thought, the same essential insight has arisen from the requirement – derived from the logical need to use language consistently if it is to convey meaning – that one should be able to *universalize* one's judgements about what one ought to do. If I say, 'it is wrong for you ever to lie' but I then lie, and say, 'I was not wrong to lie', the result is that neither of my judgements is intelligible. When a person's judgements involve those things which they consider to be worthwhile, this requirement that one's judgements are universalizable makes a very similar demand to the Golden Rule.[18]

When, in making these judgements, we recognize that we share with others a common set of worthwhile goals in human life, we reduce the risk of unreasonable self-preference distorting our judgement.

In returning to the two cases at hand, the only risk would appear to be that of contributing to some general undermining of the importance of adhering to moral practices in scientific processes. We would have to ask whether we would accept this increased risk if it was us or our family or friends who would be subjected to the increased likelihood of suffering at the hands of immoral scientific practices. Given that this risk appears to be small, it is likely that we would accept it, especially if we thought we could minimize any such risk by explaining the reasoning behind our use of the product, including our strong objection to the means by which the product had been obtained.

Who has a right to know my future?

One of the products of modern genetic science is an ever-growing knowledge of our future. When this knowledge concerns our future health, others are likely to lay claim to an interest in it. These claims will give rise to disputes as to who has a right to this knowledge and its use. A way of focusing the discussion as to how these disputes might be settled is to ask whether health-insurance companies are entitled to knowledge about our future health prospects. A full answer to this question would require a much more elaborate discussion of the nature of justice and of social institutions and responsibilities than there is space for here. However, it is possible to suggest the essential form of an answer. When considering questions of justice, the realist moral theory outlined above begins by observing that *cooperation* between people (dividing tasks according to ability, working together, sharing burdens and so on) better enables the realization of human wholeness.[19] This gives rise to the principle of practical reasonableness that people *should seek to foster those conditions and institutions of cooperation (the common good) which advance the realization of human wholeness*. Justice, then, is a matter of determining the concrete implications of this requirement of good reasoning: what are the conditions and institutions which advance the realization of human wholeness?

When we move from the conditions best able to increase the common stock of assets (which are likely to include institutions such as private property and free and fair markets) to questions of distributing those increased resources (beyond those retained by individuals as return for their efforts), an important criterion will be needed. Mutual assistance in helping one another to sustain a threshold level of participation in those things which bring value into a human life is one of the most fundamental ways individuals in a community can support one another in their attempt to sustain well-being and further their human wholeness. Over time, societies have developed different mechanisms for providing such support. In modern times, these mechanisms have included state-provided health care and varying combinations of public and private health insurance.

Whether there should be any obligation to disclose one's genetic information to health insurance companies will depend upon the exact function which they perform in our society. If the state provides adequate health care (as it might be argued it does in the United Kingdom), then insurance companies are likely to be providing a service to those who seek a higher level of cover than that accepted by the community as sufficient to meet the requirements of distributive justice. In such a case, the state could legitimately (assuming it could meet confidentiality requirements) request knowledge of genetic information *if* such information would assist it with the task of meeting the health care needs of the community. Insurance companies could also request such information because the premiums they charge are calculated on the basis of the probability of various occurrences. Non-disclosure of information affecting these probabilities (such as knowledge of the high likelihood of suffering a particular disease) would mean other people paying higher premiums than they would otherwise need to pay. Only the non-economic criteria of distributive justice could justify people paying higher premiums.

Of course, in countries where the state does not provide adequate health care for all its citizens (such as the United States), then it can be presumed (on the basis that it is a basic requirement of justice) that insurance companies are an integral part of the community's mechanism for the provision of mutual assistance with health needs. In this case, there is a non-economic criterion (a requirement of justice) which actually requires the non-disclosure of such genetic information and the accompanying higher premiums. If this were not the case, many people's health needs would not be met, or they would only be met at a price far higher than the needs of other members of the community, despite their having done nothing to create the circumstances which gave rise to that difference. There would, in other words, be no good reason for such people to be treated differently when it came to the community meeting their basic health needs.

It is important to recognize that the legitimacy of claims for information about our future, based on knowledge of our genes, is dependent on the institutions expressing interest in this information and the role which they play in that particular society. This point can be highlighted by reflecting upon the rather different nature of the claim which employers might make for access to such knowledge.

Given the nature of work, it has become widely accepted that the application of the principle of fairness (in not discriminating) means that employers should only make decisions about who to hire on the basis of

1   a person's capacity to perform the work
2   the anticipated value of that work.

Illness with a direct genetic cause could, depending upon the circumstances, affect both a person's capacity to work and the value of their work. This will be the case particularly where illness requires a person to give up their job. In such situations, the extent to which the illness will affect the value of their work will be dependent upon the cost of replacing them, a cost which will include the outlay involved in finding an appropriate replacement and possibly in training them. There is, however, a 'natural' turnover of employees resulting from people seeking different work or leaving the workforce for non-health reasons, such as for early retirement, as well as leaving because of illnesses which do not have a direct genetic cause. In other words, the value of *all* work will be affected by replacement costs. The average effect on work value of this natural turnover will be something that employers, explicitly or implicitly, will always take into account when hiring employees. This suggests that an employer's legitimate interest in knowledge of an illness with a directly genetic cause only arises when it will result in a person's period of employment being significantly less than the average for an employee carrying out that employee's type of work. There may even be some cases where replacement costs are very low or natural turnover is very high, as in the case of some unskilled or semi-skilled jobs, where the employer will never have a legitimate interest in their potential employees' future health for the purposes of hiring them.

Before proceeding, it should be noted that where genetic knowledge is only about probable future illness, the employer could not fairly take account of such information in making employment choices if they did not also take account of those environmental or lifestyle factors (e.g. whether a person is a smoker or a heavy drinker) which could similarly affect the probability of a particular person becoming ill. If such requirements of fairness were respected, there would be cases where an employer would have a reasonable interest in a person's future health. This is not to say that an employer should make choices on these grounds, only that it would not be unreasonable of them to do so. However, given the propensity of firms to maximize profit aggressively, if firms had a *right* to knowledge about future health prospects there is a high risk that they would make choices on these grounds, even when the probability was that a worker would provide an average length of service. A balance of fairness could be struck by allowing employers the legal right to recover against employees who intentionally failed to disclose knowledge of *any* relevant factor affecting their future health prospects which created a high likelihood that they would not provide a reasonable (defined as average for that type of job) period of service. This would create a situation where people could not legitimately seek work for which they were otherwise well qualified. Care would need to be taken, therefore, in providing this right or any other right (such as an employer's automatic right to knowledge of future health prospects) which affected people's employability, to ensure that provision for their resulting needs was made.

Scientific intuitions and hypotheses as science products

In the discussion so far, we have focused upon subjects which are fairly obviously scientific products. They have been products which will have been produced by the application of careful scientific methodology. Such research projects will, however, have been guided by hypotheses and intuitions about their subject matter. Other scientists not directly involved in the projects are also likely to have had hypotheses and intuitions about the subject matter, perhaps even before it has become the subject of research. Those hypotheses and intuitions which are the product of scientists who have expertise in the particular field are very far from being mere guesses – they are best considered a form of science product. The extent to which they represent expectations of what is likely to be found is revealed by the fact that there are times when scientists with only these hypotheses and intuitions are prepared to act upon them. It is at this point that they may start to have a moral obligation to other people, especially if their actions are to avoid expected harms.

The case in Britain of the emerging connection between BSE in cattle and its human equivalent CJD which began in the 1980s provides a helpful illustration of this type of situation. There were a substantial number of scientists with aspects of knowledge bearing upon the problem (such as neurophysiologists, immunologists and biologists) who were sufficiently confident in the likelihood that their hypotheses and intuitions were correct that they took considerably greater precautions to avoid exposure to BSE than those recommended by the 'government scientists' and/or took them long before they were recommended. Similar cases arise in relation to hypotheses or intuitions about the health or environmental risks associated with various chemical products. Scientists who act upon the basis of such information have a range of responsibilities of fairness towards others.

Most significant of these responsibilities will be a responsibility to inform others of their hypotheses and intuitions. These responsibilities arise because when people rely on someone for something it is a form of unfairness to breach the trust that is involved in that reliance. So, for example, if a university college leads one of its students to believe that they will have accommodation for her in the following year and the student relies upon that belief (especially if it is with the knowledge of the college) then it is unfair if the college does not provide that accommodation. In the case at hand, one of the things that the community has been led to believe is that it can rely upon scientists to communicate scientific knowledge which might affect people's lives.

The nature of the responsibility of any particular scientist to communicate this knowledge will depend upon her position in the scientific community and the basis for her hypothesis or intuition. A relatively junior member of the community will always have a responsibility to inform her family and friends of an intuition strong enough for her to be acting upon it because these will be people with a personal reliance upon the scientist. If such a person has a theoretical basis for her hypothesis sufficiently firm to publish it in a scientific journal, she should certainly do so as part of her contribution to the scientific community, as a whole, meeting its responsibilities. If this junior member of the community considers the knowledge she has to be important enough (perhaps because many people's lives may be at risk) and the basis for holding it secure enough that she could effectively communicate it more publicly through the general media, she should also consider doing so. A more senior member of the scientific community (e.g. a university professor), upon whom the public relies more directly for the communication of scientific information, and whose views are understood to have authority because of her learning, has a responsibility to consider communicating any hypothesis or intuition concerning health which she is prepared to act upon.

The qualification 'to consider communicating' is important because of the side effects of such communications. These might concern the employment of the scientist. More generally, the release of even a speculation about a threat to health by a senior member of the scientific community can affect many people's livelihoods if it seriously concerns a sector of the economy. Because of this, the scientist needs to consider whether she would release this information if she or her family worked in or relied upon this sector of the economy. Where serious threats to health are concerned, it is likely that such a scientist will reason, 'even if my daughter's livelihood is harmed, I would rather that than risk her health being seriously harmed, let alone her dying'.

Ethics and science

If the problems such as those which we have been discussing are to be solved, then it will be necessary to abandon the notion that there is such a thing as 'science ethics' or, for that matter, 'medical ethics', 'business ethics' and so on. What the above discussion should have revealed is that solving ethical problems raised by the products of science essentially involves the application of principles derived from a general theory about ethics. Simply focusing upon a particular field of human activity encourages the notion that there is an ethic of that field which sets to one side the question of how best to do ethics whatever the field. Yet unless that prior question is resolved, there will be little hope of actually resolving the questions to which particular fields of human activity give rise. Instead of being questions as to whether the application of some sound principle is correct, these questions will, in fact, be theoretical disputes about the principles themselves disguised in the garb of practicality. In this chapter, we have sought to avoid that problem by defending the possibility, first, of there being ethics at all against the challenges of one of the important products of modern science and, second, of there being *any one* system of ethics. This is a system of ethics which, in its practical application, will hopefully have given flesh to its theoretical goal – a goal which, as we observed, goes hand-in-hand with that of science, namely enhancing human life.

Notes

1 My thanks to Jan Anderson for her careful editing and to Jeremy Green for checking the science.
2 John Gribben and Mary Gribben (1988) *The One Per Cent Advantage: The Sociobiology of Being Human*, Oxford: Basil Blackwell.
3 Ibid., p. 91.
4 Ibid., p. 93.
5 Ibid., p. 127.
6 Ibid., p. 128.
7 Ibid.
8 Richard Dawkins (1989) *The Selfish Gene*, new edition, Oxford: Oxford University Press, p. 201.
9 Gribben and Gribben, p. 93 (emphasis mine).
10 For the classic statement of this diagnosis of the state of modern ethical thought see Alasdair MacIntyre (1984) *After Virtue*, second edition, Notre Dame, IN: University of Notre Dame Press, pp. 1–22.
11 See, for example, R.M. Hare (1963) *Freedom and Reason*, Oxford: Clarendon Press.
12 John Finnis (1983) *Fundamentals of Ethics*, Oxford: Clarendon Press, p. 86.

13 For a more comprehensive statement of these and other criticism of proportionalism, see Finnis, *Fundamentals*, pp. 80–108.
14 This account is based upon their theory as it is articulated in Germain Grisez, Joseph Boyle and John Finnis (1987) 'Practical principles, moral truth and ultimate ends', *American Journal of Jurisprudence*, vol. 32, pp. 99–151; and John Finnis (1980) *Natural Law and Natural Rights*, Oxford: Clarendon Press, pp. 59–127.
15 Finnis, *NLNR*, p. 102.
16 Finnis, *Fundamentals*, p. 75. For a discussion of the content of these principles, see Finnis, *NLNR*, pp. 103–26.
17 E.O. Wilson (1978) *On Human Nature*, Cambridge, MA: Harvard University Press, p. 167.
18 R.M. Hare (1963) *Freedom and Reason*, Oxford: Clarendon Press, pp. 90–1.
19 For a more complete account, see Finnis, *NLNR*, pp. 134–97.

References

Aristotle (1985) *Nicomachean Ethics*, translated by Terence Irwin, Indianapolis, IN: Hackett.

Dawkins, Richard (1989) *The Selfish Gene*, new edition, Oxford University Press.

Finnis, John (1980) *Natural Law and Natural Rights*, Oxford: Clarendon Press.

Finnis, John (1983) *Fundamentals of Ethics*, Oxford: Clarendon Press.

Gribben, John and Gribben, M. (1988) *The One Per Cent Advantage: The Sociobiology of Being Human*, Oxford: Basil Blackwell.

Grisez, Germain, Boyle, J. and Finnis, J. (1987) 'Practical principles, moral truth and ultimate ends', *American Journal of Jurisprudence*, vol. 32, pp. 99–151.

Hare, R.M. (1963) *Freedom and Reason*, Oxford: Clarendon Press.

MacIntyre, Alasdair (1984) *After Virtue*, second edition, Notre Dame, IN: University of Notre Dame Press.

4

ENGINEERING ETHICS

Vivian Weil

Introduction

President Clinton issued a statement for National Engineers' Week of February 1999 that included the following comment: 'American Engineers have made numerous contributions to our society . . . Yet, for all of its influence on our modern world, the engineering profession remains a mystery to many Americans.'[1] This very brief comment makes two major points: engineers' work has significant impact and to many the engineering profession is almost invisible. These points provide the rationale for the overview that follows.

As engineers' contributions increasingly shape our world of everyday activity and work, they present perplexing questions and choices for citizens and policy-makers. How should aircraft producers, airlines and the government regulatory agency deal with wiring insulation problems that have surfaced? What will be the consequences of changing our pollution-control strategy? Suppose that instead of attacking outflow of pollutants at the pipe end, we target input at the 'front end'?

It is reasonable to think that engineers play a role in answering such questions and making such choices. But it is hard to see what that role might be as long as the engineering profession remains a mystery. To clear away the mystery, we ask how people with the necessary knowledge and skills have organized to solve technical problems in order to turn out engineering products. That question puts the spotlight on engineering problem-solving in context, in business organizations, highlighting how engineers make choices and decisions. In a great range of projects, such as designing a bridge or a Mars 'rover' vehicle, testing a heart monitor or a new aeroplane brake, or maintaining nuclear power plants, engineers must use their trained judgement to make choices and decisions.

Because their projects have consequences – sometimes momentous consequences – for the welfare of people and the environment, engineers' exercise of judgement must meet certain standards. How do engineers learn to make good judgements, and how are the standards determined? How do engineers come to know the standards and what supports their adherence to standards? How can engineers take account of foreseeable consequences in their decision-making in the workplace? These are questions driving our overview. The issues concern how engineers – individually and collectively – make and should go about making choices and decisions in designing, testing, producing and maintaining technological products.

The discussion to follow will show that there is an international profession of engineering. It has a history of about three centuries and it has long been concerned with ethics. Safety is a paramount ethical issue for engineers and, together with the concern for reliability of engineering products, it permeates the profession's outlook on other ethical responsibilities. Protection of practitioners' exercise of uncompromised judgement is a characteristic concern of professions. This concern has special force in engineering because of its link with safety and reliability. Other important ethical issues to be considered are loyalty, conflict of interest, confidentiality and intellectual property protection.

The claim that engineering ranks as a profession in a full sense may seem obvious, but some writers have challenged it.[2] They were captivated by a picture of professions that included certain patterns of professional control over territory or clients, e.g. physicians' authority in hospitals in decades past. Finding such patterns in medicine and law but not in engineering, writers concluded that engineering does not measure up as a profession. At issue, of course, are the defining features of professions and the stakes in being ranked as a profession. The thumbnail history and the examination of professionalism to come will show why engineering should rank as a profession and why that matters.

Thumbnail history

The knowledge, skills and standards – both technical and ethical – that come into play in contemporary engineering problem-solving have issued from roughly 300 years of development. This history of how certain occupational groups coalesced into a profession is marked not only by the creation of certain key institutions, such as engineering schools, curricula and professional societies, but also by the promulgation of technical and ethical standards.[3]

Experience in carrying out engineering projects, as well as formal research and scientific understanding, formed the basis for constructing tables, codes and standards that practitioners came to rely upon. For the protection of public health and safety, some of these codes were eventually incorporated into legal regulations.[4] A classic example is the American Society of Mechanical Engineers' Boiler Codes. The process of devising engineering codes and standards and of incorporating some in legal rules is ongoing, with continuing advances in technology and increases in technical knowledge.

Engineering projects are usually undertakings of significant scale. From the earliest production of military 'engines' by the French in the seventeenth century to the projects of subsequent centuries – mines, canals, steamboat boilers, telegraphy, locomotives, chemical plants, electrical and electronics products, automobiles, aircraft and nuclear plants – the scale and impact of products required systematic methods for reducing guesswork. Guesswork that could not be eliminated had to be dealt with. In the face of uncertainties, engineers had to design, test and maintain products for practical use. They needed strategies for handling uncertainties if they were to satisfy demands for reliability and safety.

In this light, we understand the effort during the eighteenth century in France to define an appropriate curriculum for training engineers. The aim was to produce people with the knowledge and skills to carry out projects that meet requirements of reliability and safety. The rise of formal, mathematically oriented engineering education at the end of the eighteenth century thus turns out to be a defining moment in the history of the engineering profession. With emphasis on the exact sciences and mathematics, this curriculum was first established at the Ecole polytechnique in Paris in 1794. It became a model for engineering education in other countries. In the present-day engineering curriculum in the US, this ancestry is still recognizable, especially in the calculus, physics and chemistry requirements.

In the nineteenth century in the US, engineering schools, conceived on the French model, were established, technical codes were formulated and promulgated and professional societies were formed. Civil (distinguished from military) engineering, mining and mechanical engineering formed separate specialities by roughly mid-century. In the latter part of the century, the growth of large industrial organizations brought a sharp increase in the number and specialities of engineers who were needed in projects featuring large capital investment. In this period, chemical and electrical engineering emerged as separate specialities.

Over the course of the twentieth century, new specialities emerged, professional societies for the new specialities were organized and the promulgation of technical and ethical codes has continued. In the aftermath of the Second World War, for example, nuclear engineering formed a new speciality, and, in subsequent decades, biomedical engineering became established as a separate speciality. Still unsettled is a debate of several decades about whether software developers should constitute a new speciality of engineering.[5] Genetic manipulation using recombinant DNA technology is often referred to as genetic engineering, but it is doubtful whether practitioners should be classified as engineers, except in a loose or metaphorical sense. That is because the training, practices, and routines of these practitioners do not sufficiently resemble those of engineering.

Because a rapid increase in the number of engineers and the growth of large business organizations employing them occurred in tandem in the late nineteenth century, we can say that engineers were born into large business organizations. These technically skilled employees nevertheless joined engineering societies, which continued to organize and grow. In this way, these employees showed their solidarity with one another and identified themselves as engineers although they did their work in different companies.

In Britain in the late nineteenth century, and in the United States and Russia in the early decades of the twentieth century, the engineering professional societies began to draft and promulgate codes of ethics, as well as technical codes. In the US the process of revising codes of ethics has continued through this century, punctuated by periods of relatively intense activity following each world war and in the period of social ferment of the late 1960s and early 1970s. The special ethical standards of professions set them apart from occupational groups that are subject only to the rough-and-tumble of the marketplace, to the law and to ordinary morality.

In this historical survey, we can discern the evolution of the modern profession of engineering or, more accurately, the evolution of an occupational group (or cluster of occupational groups) into a profession. Also discernible is the evolution of the ethics of the profession, the special standards binding upon members of the profession because they are members. It is reasonable to regard the ethics codes as articulating ethical concerns that tacitly underlie technical codes. The concern with safety is a prime example. Looked at this way, the codes form a continuum from the technical to the ethical. Integral to engineering work and a paramount ethical consideration is the concern with safety. It is distinctive of engineering, necessitating standards that support the profession's announced commitment to serve the public.

Ethical problems commonly arise for engineers in their daily work. Confronting uncertainties and risks, they must make judgements that are informed by their ethical and technical standards and grounded in their special knowledge, but not dictated by these underpinnings of judgement. For example, a question may concern a metal alloy engineers specify for use in automobile bodies. Certain properties of the alloy are critical to the vehicles' withstanding anticipated impacts, but the properties cannot be assumed to be utterly consistent from shipment to shipment. Inevitably, batches of the product vary somewhat, and engineers cannot be sure that the required properties are present in every batch. In their specifications, engineers must take such uncertainties into account in order to ensure adequate safety and reliability. Incorporation of a safety factor, an extra margin for error, is one strategy engineers use for coping with such uncertainty, and they exercise judgement in choosing the safety factor. This entrenched engineering heuristic illustrates how technical and ethical considerations are interwoven in defining and solving engineering problems.

The engineer's role

Through the three centuries surveyed, the engineering role itself has evolved, taking shape differently in different countries. Countries in which engineering emerged as an occupation in this period – France, Britain, Germany, Russia – have distinctively different socio-political systems and historical experience. Of course, differences among these countries are reflected in the situations of professions and in the status of engineers and other professionals.

For an example of stark contrast, compare the imprint of the communist regime's central command structure on engineering in the Soviet Union with patterns in the US. The formation of separate specialities became exaggerated in the Soviet Union, by comparison with the US. Communist party control, which eliminated engineers' independent management of their societies, destroyed these organizations as professional societies. Adding to the destruction of the profession was the conscription of engineers by coercion to participate in the Soviet Union's mammoth engineering projects.[6] A dramatically contrasting emphasis on freedom prevailed in the US. It is reflected in the

growth of engineering societies as voluntary associations independent of government. And it is manifest in the legal doctrine of
'employment at will' that has governed the workplace, supporting the
almost unlimited right of an employer to fire and hire and of an
employee to take up or end employment.

The differences among countries notwithstanding, the situation of
engineers in the US can serve as a standard model or template for the
purpose of understanding the professional role of engineers. The
main reason for concentrating on engineering as it has developed in
the US is that it has been well studied. Furthermore, engineers from
the US are heavily engaged in international engineering and business
projects and therefore are visible in other countries. We should not
take the US situation as the ideal, but rather as a model that can be
used for comparative study to illuminate the role of engineers in other
countries. That study should stimulate thinking about making
changes to improve that role, in the US and elsewhere.

To understand the notion of a role it is useful to look at examples.
A diverse set of instances comes to mind: parent, citizen, friend,
student, employee and professional. Each is characterized by a cluster
of responsibilities and privileges – some of them defined by law – in a
particular social context. Because the associated responsibilities and
privileges are not fixed for all time, it is important to look carefully at
the social context, which also changes. Noting interplay between the
role and social context, we may identify and take advantage of circumstances that favour modifications for improving the role.

In their positions in business organizations in the US, engineers
must manage a range of responsibilities from the narrowly technical
to the managerial. Because it is difficult to draw a bright line on the
spectrum between these poles of responsibility, debate about the
boundaries of the role of engineer continues in the workplace, in engineering education and professional bodies and among specialists in
ethics.

For example, in a well-known analysis of the Ford Pinto case,
Professor Richard De George argues for a narrow role for engineers.[7]
Pinto engineers had discovered a defect in the placement of the gas
tank, had come up with economically feasible alternatives that would
remedy the defect, had offered these options to their managers and
then had apparently acquiesced when the managers rejected those
alternatives. De George contends that when the Pinto engineers
deferred to their managers, they behaved just as engineers should. He
denies that engineers should have a role in decision-making once they
have submitted their technical assessments and options.

By contrast, Professor Michael Davis advocates a more robust engineering role in decision-making based on an empirical study of communication between engineers and managers. Those interviewed were drawn from ten companies varying in size and business. These engineers and managers characterized their decision-making as a joint process to reach agreement.[8] They put a high premium on deciding by consensus and on engineers holding their ground on issues of safety.

The very elasticity of the engineer's role produces puzzles about the scope of engineers' responsibilities. Moreover, the extent to which engineers have room to exercise independent judgement within the requirements for cooperation of business organizations is similarly elastic, depending on local circumstances. In spite of changes in structure in US business organizations in recent years – for example a flattening of hierarchy and a trend towards teamwork – the engineer's role in the US remains problematic. Elimination of middle managers and formation of teams containing a mix of specialities does not guarantee that the engineering role accommodates more adequately the exercise of independent judgement. The role continues to embody certain tensions linked to questions about the scope of engineers' responsibilities.

First is the tension between the engineer's fundamental concern with safety, highlighted in the brief history above, and the demands of business organizations. That tension may be evident when engineers are required to give approval for shipping out a product that they believe does not meet specifications bearing on safety. In the complexities of meeting schedules and accommodating other constraints in large sophisticated organizations, engineers must maintain a focus on safety. Smaller, entrepreneurial organizations may be less complex, but they too generate pressures under which engineers must keep their eyes on safety. While employers depend upon their engineers for meeting appropriate standards of safety, they require their engineers to accommodate the needs of the organization: staying on schedule, respecting available budgets and the like. For responding to the demands of the organization while fulfilling the obligation to protect the safety, health and welfare of the public, engineers need special preparation in their education.

They need to acquire the discernment to identify problems at early stages (before they ripen into conflicts) and to assess their importance. They must develop the capacity to deal with ambiguities in these situations. To head off or resolve conflict, they have to cultivate the skills of an advocate or negotiator. For example, an engineer may see ahead that she must specify a more costly material than managers and others on the team are expecting. Having determined that this is an issue worth pressing in the interests of safety, the engineer might circulate to managers and colleagues information about this material and its comparative advantages. She might follow up by circulating a rationale for using the material despite the higher cost. When the time for decision-making arrives, the engineer might find that, having fore-warned colleagues, she can persuade them to accept the material she recommends. In any event, her effort will have introduced the safety issue in a way that assures it a hearing and avoids confrontation.[9] The acknowledgement that such methods are part of problem-solving in engineering points to a broader conception of the engineer's role. It is a conception that blurs the boundary between the roles of engineers and managers and thus can help to reduce this tension.

Second is the tension between the independence (autonomy) of a professional and the demands of loyalty to an employer. For example, consider an engineer in a firm who receives instructions to endorse the marketing department's statement about a product, a statement that in his view goes beyond what he can confidently stand behind. Loyalty seems to require the engineer to comply, but that runs counter to his judgement that the marketing statement might be mis-leading. To the business organizations that employ most engineers in the US, all employees have duties of loyalty, some of which are pres-cribed by law. At the same time, employers need engineers' exercise of independent, professional judgement in order to achieve the goal of producing successful products for the marketplace.

As several writers have forcefully argued, professionals have good reasons, from their own personal perspective and the perspective of society, to resist the expectations of blind loyalty.[10] By analysing con-ditions in which expectations of loyalty exceed proper limits, these writers offer insight useful for assessing particular expectations of loyalty. For example, a request to sign a petition supporting legisla-tion the company favours goes beyond what it is reasonable to ask of a professional. It invades the sphere of the citizen. Full discussion of this idea of critical loyalty with engineering students in the classroom and promotion of this concept by professional societies might help to reduce this tension. In order to maintain critical loyalty, engineers need discernment, the ability to deal with ambiguity and the skills to persuade and negotiate.

A third tension arises from doing work that is evaluated by both technical and business criteria, such as cost and marketability. Technical criteria include not only the requirements of good design, such as those the Shiley heart valve satisfied by allowing dramatically improved blood flow. Also included among good design criteria are manufacturability, performance in testing (including field testing) and maintenance requirements. These latter are technical criteria the Shiley heart valve failed to satisfy.[11] This suitably broad notion of technical criteria narrows the gap between technical and business criteria.

There are good reasons to include as well such factors as resource requirements, costs and schedule. These factors should not be separated out for the attention of managers alone. It makes little difference whether we classify these additional factors under an even broader notion of technical criteria or regard them as business criteria engineers should satisfy as well. In either case, engineers should normally apply these criteria to their work, and they should be educated to do so.

Emphasis on a broader range of technical criteria and on embracing some business criteria that engineers should strive to satisfy may help to reduce this tension and improve the role of engineer. These changes would encourage a thinning of the manager's role, a trend already under way. The task of articulating a broader set of responsibilities for engineers should fall not only to people in business organizations, but also to engineering educators, professional societies and other professional bodies, and to those who write about the profession.

Professionalism

Characteristic features

To make good the claim that the role of engineer is a professional role it is necessary to look further into the notion of professionalism. A commonly acknowledged feature that distinguishes professions from other occupational groups is a body of knowledge and skills for which extended education is needed. At least as important is the occupational group's organizing as a profession with an expressed commitment to serve the public and standards appropriate to that commitment. These criteria the engineering profession satisfies, but without requiring postgraduate education.

Commonly cited as a defining feature of professions are admission standards that demand acquisition of a legal licence. Examination of this feature in engineering reveals ambiguity that requires explanation. A minority of engineers (estimated at most at 20–25%) are licensed. The majority of US engineers are *not* licensed by law as professionals nor are they formally inducted into the profession.[12]

Licensed engineers have the privilege and duty of 'signing off' on products by affixing their signatures to documents. In this way, they guarantee that the products satisfy appropriate technical requirements and meet a reasonable standard of care. By law, many products (skyscrapers and bridges, for example) cannot be made available to the public unless engineers have signed off. In the US, licensing is a state-by-state procedure; in most states, however, industries have succeeded in lobbying legislatures to pass a 'manufacturer's exemption'. The exemption allows industries to employ unlicensed engineers in many of their engineering positions. Consequently, graduates of accredited engineering programmes commonly obtain engineering positions without professional certification, without the title of Professional Engineer (PE). Unsurprisingly, many do not see a need to undertake the extra preparation necessary to acquire certification. Yet, lacking the legal title, they identify themselves as professional engineers.

In doing so, they have endorsement from the Accreditation Board for Engineering and Technology (ABET). An authoritative, but non-governmental, body, ABET evaluates and certifies programmes of engineering education according to stated criteria. The ABET statement includes the following sentence: 'To be considered for accreditation, engineering programs must be designed to prepare graduates for the practice of engineering at a professional level.'[13] With very few exceptions, engineering programmes and schools attach great importance to ABET accreditation. While putting great weight on ABET criteria and evaluation, these accreditation arrangements afford a form of certification of engineers. In the US, it appears, those who have graduated from accredited programmes of engineering education and hold engineering positions can be regarded as professional engineers (with a small 'p').

Accordingly, the graduates are eligible to become members of professional societies. They are bound by engineers' codes of ethics, which set out the special ethical duties engineers have as members of the profession. They are entitled to the privileges of practising their profession; in turn they incur special responsibilities. This state of affairs in engineering in the US exhibits professionalism that is voluntary. Professionalism is not necessarily or logically tied to legal certification. Historically, engineering professional societies took root and promulgated technical codes and ethical codes, offering a model of professionalism without licensing.

Examination of professionalism in engineering prompts consideration of another claim about professions that some have taken for granted. It is the notion that the dominant (if not the only) model of a professional is the 'consultant' model.[14] This model fits occupational groups whose members do their work independently of organizational employment and in a personal relationship with an individual client. Law and medicine were the prime examples. Features of performing work in those occupations at about the middle of the twentieth century came to seem essential to some who studied professions. Proponents of this view failed to emphasize a key feature: that the occupational group organizes itself as a profession with a commitment to serving the public and adopts standards appropriate to that commitment. In the US, engineering professional societies established themselves with that commitment as practitioners came more and more to be employees of large business organizations.

In recent decades, employment in large profit-making organizations has increasingly penetrated the professions of law and medicine. One result has been the weakening of the practitioner's tie with an individual client, a relationship that was thought to form the moral and ethical core of practice in those professions. These institutional changes force fresh attention in medicine and law onto the question of what constitutes the moral and ethical core of practice in the professions.

Ethical codes and ethics in practice

In the US, adherence to the ethical codes in engineering is generally voluntary; there is usually no apparatus for applying sanctions in response to violations. (In any case, sanctions would only bar engineers from full membership in the society applying the sanctions.) Some might question whether codes that are voluntary can play the important role claimed here. To answer, we recall that ethical codes become a strong binding force by conveying to individual engineers what members of the profession expect of one another. Individual engineers can perceive the advantages, to themselves, to those they care about and to society, of their adherence to their codes. They see that their own adherence helps to maintain the standards that should guide all engineers and strengthens the solidarity that supports engineers as professionals. Practitioners and students sometimes express these perceptions saying, 'it's just common sense.'

In addition, when engineers argue for their professional judgements and recommendations, they can appeal to their professional standards and need not fall back on merely personal standards or conscience.[15] Pointing to formulated, generally recognized standards – not personal standards that in their variability are more easily dismissed – engineers are in a better position to hold their ground. As employees of organizations, they claim standing as professionals on the basis of their special standards of ethics, as well as their technical standards, special knowledge and specific skills. That engineering codes of ethics are binding, though adherence is voluntary, is less remarkable when we recall that there is a well-entrenched conception of codes of ethics that distinguishes them from legal codes.[16] In this view, the ethics codes are conceived of as apprising engineers of considerations they must take into account as self-directed agents committed to maintaining an appropriate standard of care. The situation is similar with respect to technical standards that do not have the status of law.

That there is a link between professionalism and adherence to special ethical standards comes into question from another direction. Holding a familiar sceptical view about professions, some contend that the chief motivation for occupational groups to organize as professions is to promote the narrow self-interest of their members. According to the sceptics, professionals seek monopolistic control over the services they provide, in order to secure economic benefits and prestige. They insist upon self-regulation, in the sceptics' view, to prevent outsiders from interfering in their affairs. They protect their territory with the claim that only members of the profession are equipped to evaluate its activities and standards. According to this line of thinking, codes of ethics are suspect. They offer a façade to cover ordinary self-serving activity rather than a guide to serving society. When negligence or wrongdoing by professionals catches the public eye it seems to provide the sceptics with confirmation of their views. They contend that codes of ethics should not be taken at face value, that codes merely provide a cover for ordinary self-interest, and even wrongdoing.

The study of professions in recent decades by specialists working on practical and professional ethics has not buttressed the views of the sceptics. To be sure, those studying the professions have found serious gaps in professional education with respect to ethics, halting efforts by professional societies to support responsible conduct of practitioners and lack of sensitivity to ethical issues on the part of practitioners. Often, professionals appear to be unfamiliar with their codes of ethics, even uncertain whether they have actually encountered them.

Yet, probing examination of the ethics of professions has frequently come about when educators in professional programmes and specialists in ethics have collaborated to address newly recognized ethical quandaries. The engineering profession is not alone in having welcomed or invited ethics specialists from philosophy and other disciplines to consult or take part in ethics initiatives in education and in the professional societies. Practitioners have often provided the most forceful voices in favour of strengthening the ethics component of engineering education. They have participated in projects with academics to promote attention to ethics in professional education and in professional societies.

Some of the orientation towards ethics in the professions, which specialists from outside encounter, probably results from or is enhanced by their involvement. However, there is good evidence in the engineering profession in the US that ethics has been a genuine concern for a long time. For instance, the National Society of Professional Engineers (NSPE), which, as its name suggests, has an overriding concern with professionalism, established its Board of Ethical Review (BER) in 1958, well before the clamour for professional accountability in the US in the mid-1970s.

The BER meets regularly to discuss problematic cases that practitioners submit in order to get an opinion about what would be an ethical and professionally appropriate response. In its opinions, the BER bases its judgements on the NSPE Code of Ethics, without attempting to assess the code or suggest modifications. Taking care to handle cases so as to protect the anonymity of sources and parties involved, the BER regularly publishes sanitized cases together with its opinions. It includes dissenting opinions when there is disagreement. The purpose of the BER's effort is educational; it has no capacity to investigate the facts or enforce BER judgements. Members aim to model and stimulate ethical discussion. Attesting to the seriousness of their enterprise is the sophistication about engineers' ethical issues that members and former members of the BER acquire.[17]

Unfortunately, the great majority of published BER opinions concern cases submitted by engineers in private practice in engineering firms, not employees of large business organizations. Because the BER has not received many cases from the latter, it has not addressed the tensions in the engineer's role to the extent one might wish. However, the BER remains an energetic enterprise. Engineers employed in large organizations may yet become sufficiently aware of this resource to begin contributing their cases.

A more recent initiative is the NSPE's creation of the National

Institute for Engineering Ethics (NIEE), which was spun off from the NSPE. It is currently supported by a number of engineering societies, including the NSPE, and individual and organizational members as well. From the outset, the NIEE has maintained on its governing board at least one outside specialist in ethics, usually a philosopher. One of its first efforts was to produce an award-winning film, *Gilbane Gold*, widely used in teaching engineering ethics in the US and abroad. The engineer in this film is a company employee. The NIEE has produced and updated a *Resource Guide* for teaching engineering ethics, publishes the periodical *Engineering Ethics Update* and is preparing for a second film. Looking at the NIEE, along with initiatives to promote ethics by other engineering societies, we see continuing (but occasionally interrupted) commitment and incremental growth, and occasional spurts of creative energy.

To counter the sceptics about ethics in the professions, these initiatives suggest an additional consideration. It is the advantage of taking at face value – without denigrating them – professions' claims to being bound by special, ethical standards. Taking the claims at face value is more likely to encourage ongoing efforts and new initiatives aimed at supporting members' adherence to ethical standards. Legal codes and rules cannot cover or anticipate many important choices professionals must make when they are not monitored. If occupational groups see to it that professional standards – not only the marketplace, law and our common morality shape their provision of services – everyone can benefit. The public benefits from being able to trust professionals in matters which outsiders are not equipped to judge for themselves. Members of the professions benefit, as we have noted, by being able to count on one another to meet an appropriate standard of care.

It is not yet clear whether the role of engineer in the US is evolving towards a configuration that better accommodates ethically responsible conduct of professionals. Engineers continue to occupy positions which span technical and managerial responsibilities and incorporate participation in marketing and sales. Quandaries about the role of professionals in business organizations have not yet galvanized interest – in the workplace, in professional education or in the literature on professional ethics. Yet two developments may favour a shift, however small, towards allowing engineers more scope for their professional judgement.

One is ABET's promulgation of its latest criteria – *ABET 2000* – for accrediting engineering programmes. Normally, ABET is required to publish proposed changes to its criteria for a review and comment period of one year before adoption. In this instance, ABET extended the review and comment period to two years. This latest statement from ABET is to replace the original statement of 1933, which, with subsequent amendments, was the basis for accreditation until 2000. The latest statement is to be used for accrediting programmes beginning in 2001.

ABET 2000 specifies, among other requirements, that 'engineering programs must demonstrate that their graduates have: '(d) an ability to function on multi-disciplinary teams; . . . (f) an understanding of professional and ethical responsibility; . . . [and] the broad education necessary to understand the impact of engineering solutions in a global/societal context'.[18] The 'Professional component' of *ABET 2000* requires that students have a 'major design experience' that incorporates 'engineering standards and realistic constraints', including 'economic, environmental, sustainability, manufacturability, ethical, health and safety, social and political'. This list, the product of a committee, is not systematic, but the factors included effectively convey increased emphasis on ethics and social responsibility and a broadened conception of the technical responsibilities of a professional engineer. ABET has embraced a more robust conception of what it means to be a professional engineer along the lines suggested in the discussion above of the engineering role.

Changes in the structure of business organizations that reduce hierarchy and provide room for experiments with teamwork offer new opportunities for small shifts in the engineer's role. The fresh approach to teamwork in the NASA Mars Pathfinder Mission – encouraging engineers to 'grow out of the box' – might offer a model to engineers and those to whom they report.[19] Incoming engineers, educated in programmes shaped by *ABET 2000* and sensing support from professional societies, may be better able to notice and take advantage of changes in organizations. They may carve out roles more accommodating to independent professional judgement.

Responsibilities of engineers

It is useful to sort engineers' responsibilities, as do their professional codes, into four types of obligation: to the public, to employers, to clients and to other engineers and the profession as a whole. In each of these areas of responsibility, protecting engineers' exercise of uncompromised professional judgement is at stake. What is the foundation of engineers' responsibilities? The answer is our common morality, the law and consensus in the profession.

Ethical standards of the professions must be compatible with our common morality. Indeed, the code of ethics of a profession in part interprets our common morality for the specifics of practice of that occupational group. For example, Section II.3.a. of the NSPE Code captures a duty of our common morality, the injunction against lying, by stating, 'Engineers shall be objective and truthful in professional reports, statements or testimony.' As we shall see, the codes contain provisions that go beyond interpreting our common morality for the circumstances of practice. The law sometimes shapes professional obligations by narrowing the reach of codes, as occurred when a US Supreme Court decision eliminated a prohibition against advertising. Consensus in the profession is expressed in standards that engineers have written into their codes of ethics. As that consensus evolves, engineers amend their codes to take account of responsibilities that have emerged, such as (in recent years) responsibilities to the environment.

Responsibilities to the public

In the US, engineers have agreed and announced in the codes of most of their professional societies that their obligations to the public are paramount. The earliest engineering codes in the US emphasized personal honour and engineers' obligations to their employers (to legitimate enterprises), giving less importance to obligations to the public. After mid-century, engineering societies in the US began to revise codes of ethics to put greater emphasis on obligations to the public. By the mid-1970s, most engineering societies in the US had adopted as Canon 1 in their codes: 'Engineers shall hold paramount the safety, health, and welfare of the public in the performance of their professional duties.'[20]

As unequivocal as this commitment appears to be, when we try to spell out what Canon 1 requires of engineers we face puzzling questions. Does the responsibility to the public always take priority? How should engineers regard the other types of obligation in light of the apparent priority provision of Canon 1? Who is the public? It becomes clear that Canon 1 stands in need of interpretation.

We note that the priority provision, coming first, provides context for the obligations that follow. By the order of these canons, the codes indicate priorities. The obligation to the public takes precedence; engineers should give greater weight to protecting the public than to duties to employers and clients. That means engineers must meet a threshold obligation to protect the public before factoring in other considerations.[21] To read provisions in context in this way is part of interpreting a code.

Essential to interpreting Canon 1 is an answer to the question of who is the public. We might think that the public includes everyone, encompassing everyone in the society, in the region, downwind or wherever. This interpretation is unacceptable insofar as it directs engineers to guard against dangers that affect everyone more or less equally. That reading is too undiscriminating. Many dangers threaten differentially, posing harm to some – for example, infants, children, the aged – and not others. This interpretation makes no room for taking account of groups that are especially vulnerable. Guided by this interpretation, engineers would not sufficiently protect the public from the consequences of their work.[22]

Alternatively, we might interpret 'public' as referring to anyone in the society, region and so on. Insofar as this interpretation directs engineers to equate holding public safety paramount with avoiding harm to anyone who might be put at risk by their activities, this interpretation also is unacceptable. It would rule out most engineering projects. Building a chemical plant, producing a heart valve, testing and even maintenance create risks of harm to some.

What engineers need is an interpretation invoking some relevant factor that enables them to pick out as the public the vulnerable parties who need protection. Michael Davis suggests that what makes people members of the public in this sense is their ignorance and consequent helplessness in the face of dangers created by the work of engineers.[23] People unknowingly exposed to the dangers of fiery explosions from the Pinto's gas tank placement would constitute the public whose safety Pinto engineers were obliged to protect. Engineers' colleagues at Ford who knew about the dangers of the Pinto and could make purchasing decisions accordingly would not be included, but the innocent prospective consumers, passengers and others would be.

Until someone proposes a better way to identify the public, this suggestion is the leading option, and it has much to recommend it. In ordinary, non-technical discussion of such episodes as the Pinto case, the *Challenger* disaster or the 1974 DC-10 crash over Paris, we speak of the innocent passengers, of the unknowing astronauts and schoolteacher. A very well-recognized condition for deeming risks acceptable is the informed consent of those exposed. This condition is intended to ensure that those endangered are neither unknowing nor trapped. The suggested interpretation also comports well with US product liability law. Lawyers look to whether risks have been identified and efforts made to eliminate them, or at least that appropriate safeguards have been installed or, failing that, that those at risk have been properly warned. Ford released the Pinto after design modifications were rejected, with neither a safeguard against fiery explosions of the gas tank nor a warning about the hidden danger. Pinto engineers apparently failed to hold paramount the safety of the public.

Responsibilities to employers and clients

In most current US codes, obligations to the employer do not appear until Canon 4. The ABET code (along with most other codes) states the obligation to the employer as follows: 'Engineers shall act in professional matters for each employer or client as faithful agents or trustees, and shall avoid conflicts of interest.' In principle or in the abstract, there is no conflict between Canon 1 and Canon 4. In actual practice, what an employer requires of engineers as faithful agents – in the name of loyalty – may be (or appear to be) at odds with holding paramount the safety, health and welfare of the public. Clients too may make problematic demands.

The observation that tension or conflict between Canons 1 and 4 arises from the circumstances of practice suggests two important considerations. One consideration concerns what it means to act as a faithful agent. Some tend to read Canon 4 as requiring employees to do whatever they are lawfully instructed to do. However, Canon 4 also requires interpretation. The code of ethics is intended to guide engineers' use of judgement. To determine what are their obligations as faithful agents, engineers must exercise judgement, as they do with respect to other obligations. Hence acting as a faithful agent does not mean automatically doing whatever an employer or client asks that is not in violation of law.

Critical loyalty, mentioned above, might lead an engineer to ask whether an employer's instruction that seems to conflict with the duty to the public actually does serve the interests of the employer. For instance, that question should occur to the engineer who has been instructed to endorse a marketing claim she thinks is misleading. Investigation might convince her that, as part of looking out for her employer's interests, she should contest the instruction to endorse the marketing claim, and perhaps contest the claim itself.

The second consideration is the possibility for reforms, especially changes in organizations, that reduce the likelihood of circumstances that produce tension or conflict. Modifications in processes of decision-making might have such an effect. For example, widening the practice of decision-making by consensus as described above might alter the roles of engineers and managers and thus reduce tension. A complementary reform in engineers' education would provide preparation for the processes of discussion and argument that are part of decision-making by consensus.

As things stand, conflicts that engineers face between their duties to the public and their duties to their employers or clients present the most difficult cases. Figuring out how to give priority to their duty to the public while avoiding causing injury to their employers or clients and jeopardizing their jobs and careers is a major and recurring ethical task for engineers. It is a task involving ethical claims that in the circumstances have come into conflict. The codes do not offer specific steps for individuals as they thread their way through these tangled circumstances, but they do close off certain options, for example lying.

To understand and implement steps, professional engineers need certain capacities and skills in addition to technical and reasoning skills. They must be able to imagine in a context those who will use or be affected by their work. Recognizing the importance of foresight to responsible behaviour, engineers must cultivate that capacity as well. Skills on ABET's list – communications, social and political – are critical to dealing with ambiguity, making allies, persuading others and negotiating. These skills are also essential for engineers to respond to the changing dynamics of circumstances as they pursue options, not necessarily one at a time.

In extreme cases whistleblowing becomes the choice of last resort. This occurs when the engineer confronts very serious wrongdoing within the organization or the threat of very serious harm, when the consequences are imminent and when other options appear to be closed off. Whistleblowing itself is morally and ethically complex. Almost all of us understand that complexity if we recall painful instances from childhood of acting as tattletales or being reported on. Even when approached carefully, whistleblowing almost always causes injury to the whistleblower, to colleagues and to the employer. Instead of forcing attention to the perceived wrongdoing, it almost always results in turning the spotlight on the whistleblower.

In view of the high costs of this option and the discernment, carefulness, courage, inner strength and luck that whistleblowers need in order to succeed in remedying matters, whistleblowing should be a rare occurrence. However, we cannot reject this option altogether. That is because much important activity in the professions and business has to proceed without monitoring. Devious people can engage in serious wrongdoing and cause severe harm. We have too many instances in which we are indebted to whistleblowers for bringing serious wrongdoing to light. Accordingly, a number of writers have considered what conditions must be satisfied for whistleblowing to be ethically justified and under what conditions it may even be obligatory.[24]

The high costs associated with this option argue for investing effort in educational preparation and workplace strategies for engineers that will reduce the need for whistleblowing. That effort should include emphasis on making and keeping careful records of situations that seem to have the potential for ripening into occasions for whistleblowing. This is one device that may help to manage these situations and perhaps obviate the need for whistleblowing. If the engineer, nevertheless, must resort to whistleblowing, careful documentation may make a critical difference to the effectiveness of the whistleblowing and the fate of the whistleblower. According to Roger Boisjoly, the engineer who is known for revealing the story behind the *Challenger* disaster:

> I was the only one who had real-time notes on the [pivotal] meeting that took place . . . When I turned in my memos, the whole complexion of the investigation changed. They could no longer just look at the technical causes. They had to go and address now what kind of management tomfoolery had been going on.[25]

We should observe that this strategy exhibits the interweaving of the practical and ethical that is characteristic of engineering problem-solving.

A feature of whistleblowing that has just begun to receive attention is its sensitivity to social and historical context.[26] In Russia, long experience under a totalitarian regime has produced strong negative attitudes towards reporting on others. By threats and rewards, the regime induced people to report to employers, police and other authorities on the behaviour of colleagues, supervisors, fellow employees, friends, acquaintances, neighbours and family members.[27] Looked at from within the Russian context, whistleblowing at this time seems hard to defend as an ethical response.

Responsibilities to clients are primarily the concern of engineers in private practice, generally civil engineers. Serving clients directly, their mode of practice approximates that of lawyers and doctors, who seem to exemplify the traditional professional–client model. Engineers in private practice have to be alert to issues concerning fair treatment of clients. For example, the NSPE Code (III.10.b) states, 'Engineers using designs supplied by a client recognize that the designs remain the property of the client and may not be duplicated by the Engineer for others without express permission.' At II.4.b, the NSPE Code directs engineers not 'to accept compensation . . . from more than one party [client] for services on the same project' without the informed consent of all interested parties. Engineers in companies also may have responsibilities to clients, usually to clients of their employers. In these situations, engineers may find that serving the employer's client may come into tension with serving the employer. These engineers have to take care to avoid coming between their employers and the employers' clients and causing harm to one or both parties.

The trust essential to relationships with clients can be threatened by conflicts of interest. This is a hazard not only for engineers in private practice, but also for those employed in companies, in relation to their employers, as well as to clients of their employers, customers, suppliers and vendors. As noted above, Canon 4 includes mention of conflicts of interest; this issue will receive attention in its own right below.

Responsibilities to other engineers and to the profession

Responsibilities to other engineers and to the profession as a whole were touched upon in the earlier discussion of codes of ethics. Michael Davis has suggested thinking of engineers' obligations as arising from a convention among engineers.[28] In organizing as a profession, engineers contract, so to speak, with one another to serve the public and to adhere to standards in support of that ideal. They owe it to one another conscientiously to uphold the ethical standards of the profession as expressed in the codes.

That engineers should act on behalf of the profession itself is the leading idea of the Fundamental Principles of the ABET code, which begins thus: 'Engineers shall uphold and advance the integrity, honour, and dignity of the engineering profession by' and follows with the four Fundamental Principles. In Fundamental Principles III and IV and Canons 5, 6 and 7 of the ABET code, obligations to the profession – to individuals and to the aggregate – receive attention.

Fundamental Principles III and IV affirm ideals: engineers increasing the competence and prestige of the profession and supporting their professional and technical societies. In question are activities by individuals that enhance the profession as a whole. Canon 5 deals with an ethical obligation of fairness. It addresses engineers as individuals, enjoining them to build their careers on the merit of their services and not to compete unfairly with others – in the interest of engineers individually and of the profession as a whole. The NSPE code specifies unfairness, directing engineers not to try to gain employment, advancement or professional engagements by untruthfully criticizing other engineers or by other improper or questionable methods (III.7).

ABET's Canon 6 returns to the leading idea, directing engineers to uphold and enhance the honour, integrity and dignity of the profession. Canon 7 directs engineers to continue professional development throughout their careers and adds the duty to 'provide opportunities for the professional development of . . . engineers under their supervision', a directive included in the NSPE code at III.11.a to III.11.e. The concern of the provisions in this section is the welfare of engineers, individually and as an aggregate. Sceptics might read these provisions as self-serving; to some extent they surely are. However, self-regard is not in itself objectionable. Moreover, the codes' emphasis on integrity and honour seems credible in the light of such specifics as the directive to foster the professionalism of engineers one supervises.

Specific issues

Conflict of interest

Consider an engineer employed by a company who notices that a relatively new composite material that she specifies with increasing frequency has been especially well received. As she records an unusual number of favourable reports from customers about the material, she begins to think she might benefit from buying stock in the company that manufactures the material. At first, this seems a good opportunity, an advantage of holding this engineering position. However, this engineer should think further and realize that buying the stock is likely to create a conflict of interest (COI).

Three conditions must obtain for a COI to arise. A professional (or any person) must be in the position of acting on behalf of another party. That party reasonably expects competent, reliable (i.e. uncompromised) judgement. The person or professional has some attachment, investment, loyalty, affiliation, interest, relationship or the like which might compromise judgement.[29] From these conditions, we can see why COIs can arise in all the professions, indeed in any situation in which someone is expected to render reliable judgement on behalf of another party. These problems are significant because professionals are depended upon for uncompromised judgement, not only for their knowledge and skills. The example above indicates how easily COIs can arise in engineering. Moreover, professionals may fail to be alert to COIs. For these reasons, COIs are worth discussing although they are not specific to engineering.

Engineers cannot always avoid involvements that threaten reliable judgement. In all innocence, an engineer might inherit stock that creates a COI. However, to act with an unacknowledged COI betrays the trust of the company or client on whose behalf the engineer renders judgement. That party is deceived, not realizing that reliable judgement is under threat. These are moral reasons why the ABET code mentions COI in Canon 4. Like other professionals, engineers must cultivate wariness; they must be on the lookout for COIs. And they need to know what to do about them.

For anyone who has a COI, there are three ethically defensible options. Which one to use depends on the circumstances. One is to acknowledge the situation, to disclose the COI to the party depending upon one's reliable judgement. In some instances the parties who are informed will choose to proceed at their own risk. At least their trust is not violated, and they are not deceived. A second option is to withdraw from rendering judgement, to recuse oneself. In many instances, mere disclosure is not enough; the professional must refrain from rendering judgement. The third option is to divest oneself of, to get rid of, the investment or attachment that might compromise judgement.

For the engineer in the example above, the first two options are not appropriate, for it appears that she is regularly depended upon for specifying such materials. She should not invest in the company that manufactures the composite material as long as she is in a position that regularly calls for specifying such material. The threat the investment would pose to reliable judgement is enough to rule out investing. Neither she nor anyone else could ever be sure whether her investment actually biases her judgement, either by prompting her to specify the material or to bend over backwards to avoid it. That uncertainty is damaging to trust.

It may seem that the conditions constituting a COI are clear enough and that the options for dealing with COIs are straightforward enough to prevent confusion and enable engineers to avoid or deal responsibly with COIs. In the classroom and in practice, however, people have to work hard to get a good understanding of what a COI is, why it is wrong to render judgement with an unacknowledged COI and what to do about it. Attempts to distinguish between apparent and actual COIs often breed confusion. It is good policy to assume there is no distinction because an apparent COI can equally damage trust.

Confidentiality and proprietary protection

After six months in his position at a young company, Telecron, Inc., engineer Alan Ortiz receives a memo from Telecron's engineering director. It is an invitation to a meeting to discuss improvements affecting the weight of a line of cell phones in production. In his position with his previous employer, Computrola, a large, well-established international company, Ortiz had made useful contributions to the development of a lightweight cell phone. He had a good grasp of some of the innovations that had led to the success of the product. In his exit interview at Computrola, Ortiz was reminded of the employment agreement he had signed in the hiring process three years earlier. At that time, he had promised not to disclose any confidential information – either directly or indirectly – to competitors for a period of one year after leaving Computrola. When Ortiz came to Telecron, in a move up to an exciting position, he explained the agreement he had made with Computrola. The person with whom he discussed the prior agreement has left Telecron. The prospect of the upcoming meeting makes Ortiz uncomfortable.

The legal duties of a faithful agent (Canon 4) require an employee of a business organization not to act adversely to the employer's interests. This means that there is a curb on disclosing information; engineers are obliged to withhold information they obtain through their positions as employees. Included are confidential information given to the engineer expressly because of his position, and information discovered in the course of work. The ABET code does not refer explicitly to duties of confidentiality; they are implied by Canon 4. The NSPE code, however, includes, in a discussion of professional obligations, III.4: 'Engineers shall not disclose confidential information concerning the business affairs or technical processes of any present or former client or employer without his consent.'

In view of the value we place on propagating knowledge and the emphasis in engineering codes on honest and full reporting, the requirement of confidentiality at first may puzzle engineers. And they may wonder why they cannot simply use the 'knowledge in their heads' to advance their careers and the spread of technology. In a business organization, however, an engineer is not merely a person with information 'in his head' to circulate as he pleases. Engineers employed in companies are agents, with access to companies' (the principals') confidential information and documents. Often, they are privy to proprietary information, i.e. trade secrets and information restricted during the patent-application process.

In spite of the value in the US of the free flow of information, the employer's right to restrict information that confers a competitive edge is well recognized. It is a ground rule of business competition in the US that 'all projects, data, notes, etc. made by the engineer' during the period of employment and 'directly related to his field of work are property of the principal [the employer].'[30] A company may succeed with legal action against a former employee if it can show that that employee passed company documents to a new employer. Confusion and controversy have surrounded the issue of engineers' right to use knowledge and observations acquired at one company to advance their careers at another company. How should engineers distinguish the knowledge and observations they can legitimately bring to a new employer from what is prohibited?

The Ortiz case with which we began involves an employment agreement, a part of the employment contract. During the time of the engineer's employment, an agreement that is not excessively restrictive has the support of law, professional ethics and our common morality (keep your promises). The claim that the agreement covers subsequent employment can be defended if the restricted information is well specified and limited, if the length of time and geographical distance are reasonable and if options for future employment are not unduly restricted. In Ortiz's case, these conditions seem to have been satisfied. That being so, Ortiz should deal with his discomfort and his ethical problem by discussing with an appropriate person at Telecron the employment agreement he signed with Computrola. He might try to get consent from Computrola to use the information at Telecron.

For determining their responsibilities – whether or not in situations covered by agreements, explicit requests for confidentiality and so on – engineers may lean on the distinction between generic and specific information. It is legitimate to share generic information and very difficult to prevent its disclosure. The general understanding behind particular products and processes cannot easily be kept secret for long. Promotion of products to attract customers reveals information to rivals. Details of product and process technologies tend to be of a location and organization-specific nature and therefore can be protected more easily – for a time. Proprietary protection of such information is justified on the grounds that it provides incentive to innovation. Companies can reap the benefits of innovation if competitors do not get a free ride, if rivals must make their own investment in specific processes to implement new knowledge.[31] Making reasonable employee agreements and requests for confidentiality and respecting those agreements and requests builds an environment of trust.

Conclusion

In preceding sections, we have concentrated on how ethical standards, technical standards and the circumstances of practice do and should shape engineers' conduct. Only passing references to legal constraints on engineers' conduct were made. There is a little more to say about the role of legal constraints on engineers' conduct before turning to consider engineers' freedom.

Government regulation began to circumscribe engineers' activities in the US about 150 years ago.[32] Licensing, legal codes, standards, regulations and lawsuits resulting from injuries produced by engineered products form the legal context of engineering practice. A prominent engineering writer, Samuel Florman, has argued that this legal framework should give the public adequate protection.[33] Where the framework is lacking, it can be added to or amended. In his view, educating students and practitioners about the importance of professional ethics in engineering is misguided. As long as engineers and their employers respect legal limits, engineers should be free to follow their employers' instructions and their own creative paths. Florman feared that emphasis on engineers' ethical standards might interfere with ongoing development and enforcement of legal standards.

This line of reasoning overlooks important considerations. Laws, regulations and lawsuits come about after injuries and damage have occurred. The legal response inevitably lags behind the experience of those on the scene. Responsible engineers in the workplace can anticipate problems and take measures to avoid or reduce harm. Furthermore, they acquire knowledge that is needed for producing appropriate legal rules. Indeed, certain issues of responsibility for individual engineers concern duties in relation to the regulatory framework. The regulatory structure provides significant support but not a substitute for the independent judgement and responsible conduct of engineers.

Having emphasized limitations to the conduct of engineers – government regulations, technical standards, codes of ethics and circumstances in the workplace – we turn to the freedom of engineers. The ABET code's ideal of advancing the integrity, honour and dignity of the profession offers a goal for the aspirations of engineers, not merely restrictions. ABET's First Fundamental Principle states that engineers serve that ideal by 'using their knowledge and skill for the advancement of human welfare'. The code here shows a way in which the freedom Samuel Florman sought for engineers can find expression. Not by rationalizing that whatever they are assigned to do somehow advances human welfare do engineers pursue these aspirations. Rather, it is by giving thought to how to conduct their careers to make things better for some actual people and then making it happen.

An exemplar is Fred Cuny, an engineer who began his career with a role in the construction of the mammoth Dallas–Fort Worth airport and then turned his attention to disaster relief. Through the firm he founded and headed, Intertect Relief and Reconstruction, Cuny responded to destruction in the wake of civil war in Biafra, Sri Lanka and Lebanon; to earthquakes in Guatemala and Armenia; to refugee crises in Cambodia and the Sudan; and to famines in Ethiopia and Somalia.[34] Eschewing 'vaporous good intentions', Cuny and his associates refined an approach that emphasized technical competence.

From the beginning, Cuny was amazed that the standard response to international disasters was to fly in doctors and medicines rather than engineers and piping. In every crisis, he had to ask officials why they did not give priority to, say, fixing the sewage system instead of trying to relieve the results of breakdown of sanitary conditions. Cuny's principle for approaching breakdown and chaos was, 'In any large-scale disaster, if you can isolate a part that you can understand you will usually end up understanding the whole system.'[35]

One of Cuny's last enterprises before his death was to bring relief to Sarajevo, then (1993) under bombardment and sniper fire. One of the highest priorities, he and associates determined, was water. The modern water retrieval and filtration system was not working because of the absence of electricity. Cuny reasoned that there must be an old system that could be reactivated. With local help, he found a network of cisterns and channels still in working order. To deal with polluted river water, Intertect managed to construct and fly in a filtration plant to be reassembled in Sarajevo. From the renovated system, one third of the population remaining would have running water part of each day without having to go to the river and risk sniper fire.[36]

The questions with which we began, one concerning wiring insulation problems in aircraft and the other a shift in pollution-control strategies, should now seem less daunting. Engineers in the aircraft company, the airlines and the regulatory agency all have responsibilities related to resolving the insulation problems. All will have to use the wide range of skills discussed above to arrive at a plan of action that 'holds paramount the safety . . . of the public' and then accommodates as well as possible the needs of each organization. Engineers in the private sector and in the EPA at the federal and state level can take advantage of new ideas and techniques for dealing with pollution in a preventive mode at the 'front end'. New approaches might, as in some past instances, turn out to be profitable as well. Moreover, engineers, inspired by a vision of clean production processes, may find opportunities to pursue their ideal to 'enhance human welfare'.

This century has been marked by destructive wars, most of them featuring weapons and delivery systems that represent the most sophisticated work of engineers. Engineers were essential to producing these products and cannot escape association with them. These observations help to explain the point of those who argue that the technical and the social are intimately connected and that engineers, without noticing, make social decisions.[37] Taking stock at the end of the old or the beginning of the new millennium, engineers might concentrate on how to become associated with projects inspired by a vision of peace, not war.

Notes

1 Remarks reprinted in aseeaction@asee.org, 15 January 1999. National Engineers' Week was founded by the National Society of Professional Engineers, the US engineering society most concerned with professionalism.
2 For a recent example, see Robert Zussman (1995) *Mechanics of the Middle Class: Work and Politics Among American Engineers*, Berkeley, CA: University of California Press, p. 222.
3 A fuller account of the history is found in Michael Davis (1998) *Thinking Like an Engineer*, New York: Oxford University Press, pp. 18–30.
4 The history of the earliest regulations for health and safety in the US is found in John Burke (1966) 'Bursting boilers and the federal power', *Technology and Culture*, vol. 7, no. 1, pp. 1–23.
5 Davis, *Thinking Like an Engineer*, pp. 38–40.
6 A full account of the history is found in Loren Graham (1993) *Ghost of the Executed Engineer*, Cambridge, MA: Harvard University Press.
7 Richard De George (1981) 'Ethical responsibilities of engineers in large organizations: the Pinto case', *Business and Professional Ethics Journal*, vol. 1, no. 1, pp. 1–14.
8 Davis, *Thinking Like an Engineer*, pp. 124–41.
9 This scenario is based on the report of a former student, Jerry Von Haten. Somewhat older than most undergraduates, he had considerable workplace experience and provided this example of one of his strategies for behaving responsibly. He is co-author with this author of an as yet unfinished joint paper on preventive ethics.

10 Marcia Baron (1984) *The Moral Status of Loyalty*, Chicago: Center for the Study of Ethics in the Professions, IIT, pp. 1–32. Reprinted in part in Deborah Johnson (ed.) (1991) *Ethical Issues in Engineering*, Englewood Cliffs, NJ: Prentice Hall, pp. 225–40; Charles E. Harris, Michael Pritchard and Michael Rabins (1995) *Engineering Ethics: Concepts and Cases*, Belmont, CA: Wadsworth Publishing Company, pp. 286–90.

11 John Fielder (1993) 'Getting the bad news about your artificial heart valve', *Hastings Center Report*, vol. 23, no. 2, pp. 22–8.

12 The source for this conservative estimate of the percentage of licensed engineers in the US is R.L. Greene, member, National Council of Examiners for Engineering and Surveying, in 'An Update on Professional Ethics and the NCEES' (1999) at the International Conference on Ethics in Engineering and Computer Science, Case Western Reserve University, Cleveland, Ohio.

13 ABET Board of Directors (1995) *Engineering Criteria 2000: Criteria for Accrediting Programs in the United States*, Engineering Accreditation Commission, Baltimore, MD.

14 Michael Bayles (1981) *Professional Ethics*, Belmont, CA: Wadsworth Publishing Company, pp. 9–10.

15 For this point and others concerning the authority and function of codes of ethics, I owe much to the work of and discussions with Michael Davis. See Davis, *Thinking Like an Engineer*, pp. 47–60.

16 Mark Frankel (1996) 'Developing ethical standards for responsible research', *Journal of Dental Research*, vol. 75, pp. 832–5.

17 Serving on the board of directors of NIEE for some years, I have become acquainted with several former and present BER members.

18 ABET *Criteria 2000*.

19 A persuasive account was presented by Richard Cook, Mission Manager, NASA Pathfinder Mission, in the session 'Teamwork and Responsibility in the Era of "Faster, Better, Cheaper"', at Ethics and Success: Lessons from the Pathfinder Mission, a conference at Illinois Institute of Technology, Chicago, IL, October 1998. He emphasized how he recruited people with strong backgrounds who did not necessarily have specific experience relevant to the project. He brought them to the same location and gave them room to extend their mastery and accept responsibility from 'cradle to grave' in cooperation with others on the team. He weeded out those who failed to measure up.

20 Interestingly, in Russia in 1910, the *Electrical Engineering Society's News* published Osadchiy's 'The issue of engineers' professional ethics'. The essay originated in a presentation by Professor Osadchiy earlier that year at a convention of graduates of the Electrotechnical Institute of Emperor Alexander II. Osadchiy objected to the action of the Fifth All-Russian Electrical Engineering Convention of 1909 in approving an ethics code for discussion based on a US code for electrical engineers. He argued that the US code made responsibilities to the owner of the enterprise and loyalty to the owner's interests the most important values and ignored the engineer's responsibility to society. This information is in Irina Alexeyeva (1997) 'Discussion of engineering ethics at the beginning of the twentieth century in Russia', in I. Alexeyeva and A. Sidorov (eds) *Engineering Ethics: History, Context, and Significance*, vol. 1, Academy of Innovations

Management, Moscow, pp. 23–7. English translation available from this author. In proposing that responsibility to the public is paramount and contributing to discussion of this principle, Osadchiy was many decades ahead of members of the engineering profession in the US.

21 Harris *et al.*, *Engineering Ethics*, p. 278, who acknowledge their debt to Michael Davis (1988) 'Explaining wrongdoing', *Journal of Social Philosophy*, vol. 20, pp. 74–90.

22 This analysis of 'the public' draws heavily from Harris *et al.*, *Engineering Ethics*, pp. 109–10 who, in turn, draw upon Michael Davis (1991) 'Thinking like an engineer: the place of a code of ethics in the practice of a profession', *Philosophy and Public Affairs*, vol. 20, no. 2, pp. 150–67.

23 Davis, *Thinking Like an Engineer*, pp. 57–8.

24 Richard De George (1981) 'Ethical responsibilities of engineers'; and Gene G. James (1980) 'In defense of whistleblowing', in Deborah G. Johnson (ed.) (1991) *Ethical Issues in Engineering*, Englewood Cliffs, NJ: Prentice Hall, pp. 263–78; Sisela Bok (1980) 'Whistleblowing and professional responsibilities', *New York University Education Quarterly*, vol. 2, p. 4.

25 Vivian Weil (1996) 'Whistleblowing: what have we learned since the *Challenger*?' NIEE's *Engineering Ethics Update*, vol. 6, no. 2, pp. 1–3.

26 Vivian Weil (1998) 'Comments on "The psychology of whistleblowing" and "The voice of experience"', *Science and Engineering Ethics*, vol. 4, no. 1, pp. 29–31.

27 Irina Alexeyava and Alexei Sidorov, colleagues in Russia, made this point in personal conversation in Moscow in May 1997 at an NSF-funded Conference on Engineering Ethics in Russia and in an article co-authored with Elena Shklyarik, 'Ethical environment of Russian business', *Business Ethics Quarterly* (forthcoming).

28 Davis, *Thinking Like an Engineer*, p. 50.

29 Michael Davis (1982) 'Conflict of interest', *Business and Professional Ethics Journal*, vol. 1, no. 4, pp. 17–27.

30 These words are attributed to Professor Osadchiy in Alexeyeva, 'Discussion on engineering ethics in Russia', and are as accurate today as in 1910.

31 Vivian Weil (1996) 'Owning and controlling technical information', in James A. Jaksa and Michael S. Pritchard (eds) *Responsible Communication*, Cresskill, NJ: Hampton Press, pp. 235–6. The discussion there, as here, draws from Richard Nelson (1989) 'What is private and what is public about technology?' *Science, Technology, and Human Values*, vol. 14, no. 3. pp. 229–41.

32 Burke, 'Bursting boilers'.

33 Samuel C. Florman (1978) 'Moral blueprints', *Harper's*, October, pp. 30–3.

34 'Saving Sarajevo from below' (1993), in 'The Talk of the Town', *The New Yorker*, 22 November, pp. 1–2.

35 Ibid., p. 1.

36 Ibid., p. 2.

37 Langdon Winner (1986) *The Whale and the Reactor*, Chicago: University of Chicago Press.

5

ETHICS IN CONFLICT

Brad Hooker

Ethical systems

I shall follow the prevailing practice of taking 'ethical' and 'moral' to be synonymous. An ethical (or moral) system is a system of principles or values determining right and wrong. Such a system indicates what people must not do, what they are allowed to do and what they must not fail to do. It might also indicate how people ought to feel in certain circumstances – for example, it might hold that people are right to resent other people's doing certain things and that they ought to feel guilty if they themselves do these things.

We can debate what distinguishes an ethical system both from a legal system and from the conventions of etiquette. Whatever the distinguishing marks are of ethical systems, we cannot plausibly hold that the legal and the ethical are always exactly the same. Something might be legally required without being morally required, and vice versa. Likewise, the ethical and the polite are not always the same. Something might be polite without being morally required, and vice versa.

Here we are interested in ethical (moral) requirements. The most important of these might coincide with legal requirements. However, our focus here is on the ethical dimension.

Let me now survey some of the most important ethical systems. One of these, perhaps the limiting case of an ethical system, is egoism. This is the view that each ought always to do what is best for himself or herself. But if each person always does what is best for himself or herself, the consequences are likely to be far worse for all. Without restrictions limiting the pursuit of self-interest, each person would have to spend virtually all his or her time and effort on self-protection. As Hobbes (1651) put it, without a system protecting people from one another, life would be 'solitary, poor, nasty, brutish, and short'. Egoism thus seems very unattractive as an ethical system.

Other ethical systems involve restrictions on the pursuit of self-interest. These restrictions must at least provide for enough social harmony to prevent the society from tearing apart. All the systems I shall describe below seem to promise social harmony.

One such system would be comprised of the Kantian principle that each person should act only on principles that she or he could will to be universally followed – that is, followed by everyone always (Kant 1785; see also Herman 1993; Hill 1992; Korsgaard 1996; O'Neill 1989; Paton 1947). This system clearly prohibits one person's or group's free riding on the self-restraint of others. Kant also claimed that we must treat others never merely as means but always also as 'ends in themselves'. What is it to treat people as ends in themselves? One prominent way of interpreting this injunction is as requiring us to treat people according to principles to which they can freely consent. This idea has been developed into the social contract view of ethics.

There are a variety of views that might be thought of as social contract theories of morality. The social contract view that is most prominent in philosophical circles understands morality as an *ideal* or *hypothetical* social contract. In this view, what matters is *not* whether rules and social arrangements have *actually* garnered the consent of all parties. What matters instead is whether these rules *would* be consented to by all free and equal beings, or by everyone concerned to find rules that everyone must reasonably accept. The social contract referred to in this view is thus *ideal* or *hypothetical*, not necessarily actual. (For discussion, see Barry 1995; Gauthier 1986; Hampton 1986; Kavka 1986; Nagel 1991; Rawls 1971; Richards 1971; Scanlon 1982; and the papers in Vallentyne 1990.) Admittedly, the moral rules and social arrangements that are currently accepted in any *actual* society have for the most part *not* arisen from contracts struck between free and equal beings, or between beings with equal concern to find rules which everyone must reasonably accept.

Before I say more about the idea of hypothetical social contracts, let me say something about the ethical system that focuses on *actual* social agreements. In this view, right and wrong are understood not as the outcome of a hypothetical contract, but as the upshot of real social agreements, be they implicit or explicit.

One attractive feature of this view is its connection with the thought that what really matters morally is not what people might hypothetically agree to, but rather what people actually have agreed to. Certainly there are many everyday cases in which our *actual* agreements with one another generate moral obligations. That purely *hypothetical* agreements ever generate obligations is not so clear (Nozick 1974, pp. 94–5).

Another attractive feature of this kind of contractualism is that the view easily accommodates the differences in moral practices found in different societies. If when in Rome you should do as the Romans do, this view can explain why. What is morally right in one society might not be right in another, if the two societies have in fact arrived at different agreements.

Relativizing morality to actual social agreements is plausible, however, only so far. We quickly run into areas where such relativism seems terribly wrong. Suppose you need some medicine very badly, and the only way you can get it in time is if I drive you to the pharmacy. And suppose, cold-hearted cad that I am, I agree to drive you there only if you agree to work hard for me for the rest of your life at subsistence wages. Suppose you do agree, because the alternative is dying. But could this agreement really establish a lifelong moral obligation? Or take a case where the agreement is between groups rather than between two individuals. Suppose one group comes to the rescue of another only on condition that those in the group needing rescue then become subsistence-wage employees for the rest of their lives. How could this *legitimately* fix subsequent moral obligations for the rest of people's lives?

To be sure, egoistic bargaining can shape subsequent moral arrangements, but we need to know the conditions under which agreements are morally binding. One of these conditions seems to be that the parties to the agreement gave their consent freely and rationally. At the minimum, this means that the consent was elicited without coercion or deception. We may need to add additional conditions when we are thinking about an agreement that will establish the very ground rules for society. Taking a line from John Rawls (1971) we might say that in order for agreeing to something to determine moral obligations, the circumstances in which the agreement was struck must have been fair. If one group would agree to terms offered by another group only because the first group was in a weak bargaining position, then the unfairness of the initial disparity in bargaining position might be inherited by the deal struck between the parties in those unequal bargaining positions. Unfair bargaining conditions often lead to unfair contracts.

There are two obvious questions for any social contract view that insists on fair initial conditions for the negotiation of the social contract: Can we specify fair conditions for negotiating a social contract? And even if we can, will *any* arrangement agreed to under these conditions be morally right? These questions have bedevilled social contract theory for more than thirty years; I won't try to resolve the issues here. (See Daniels 1975; Hooker 1995; Kymlicka 1991; Rawls 1971, 1993; Scanlon 1982.)

Instead, I shall turn to consideration of rival ethical systems. One is consequentialism, although perhaps this is best thought of as a family of systems. A theory is a member of the consequentialist family if and only if the theory assesses acts and/or rules (or motives, social codes, ways of life and so on) in terms of nothing but how much good (intrinsic value) results. What is this good? Virtually all consequentialists would say that it is constituted in large part, if not entirely, by aggregate well-being. Aggregate well-being is to be calculated impartially, i.e. in the sense that benefits or harms to any one individual are to be counted the same as similarly sized benefits or harms to any other individual.

Consequentialists disagree among themselves about what counts as well-being. Such things as pleasure, enjoyment, the fulfilment of desires, autonomy, knowledge, friendship, achievement and the perfection of our distinctively human capacities have each been thought the sole determinant of well-being. A different kind of view of well-being is one that takes well-being to be composed of a plurality of things. These might be autonomy, knowledge of the most important truths, friendship and achievement. Pleasure and enjoyment would of course have to be added to this list. But the pluralist idea is that the other things on the list are not just conducive to but constituents of well-being. In other words, they *constitute* benefits to us independently of whether they bring us pleasure or enjoyment, and independently of whether they are tied to capacities that are distinctively human. To be sure, autonomy, knowledge, friendship and achievement can bring us enjoyment, but when they do, the enjoyment is an additional benefit.

Whatever the correct view of well-being, consequentialists can disagree about whether other kinds of value can be important independently of their effects on aggregate well-being. Fairness, for example, might be thought valuable even when it produces less overall benefit. Some consequentialists are not only pluralists about the goods that constitute well-being, but also pluralists concerning well-being and other values.

Much of the discussion of consequentialism and utilitarianism can proceed, however, without resolving the debate between the main consequentialist views about value. This is because normally people get pleasure out of the fulfilment of their desires, and they desire autonomy, knowledge, friendship and achievement. In *practice*, the main views about well-being usually coincide in their recommendations. Conflict between fairness and aggregate well-being is perhaps more common. But even here the two values usually go together rather than conflict.

More important than disagreement among consequentialists about what has value is the disagreement among them about the relation between good consequences and right action. One sort of consequentialist believes that the right act is always the one that would either actually maximize value or would maximize expected value. This kind of consequentialism claims that the rightness of any particular individual act must be determined by that individual act's actual or expected consequences. The usual name for this kind of consequentialism is *act-consequentialism*. It now gets more attention from philosophers than any rival form of consequentialism.

Act-consequentialism can be formulated in terms of the act that would *actually* have the best consequences, or in terms of the act with the highest *expected* value. From the point of view of an agent deciding how to act, expected value seems a better focus than actual consequences (Pettit 1994, p. 11; Regan 1980, p. 265, n. 1). The expected value of a possible act is calculated by multiplying the probability of each possible consequence of the act by the value or disvalue of that consequence if it came about. Typically some of the possible consequences will be positive and some negative. Furthermore, both positive and negative consequences will range from very unlikely to certain (as in the case of cost incurred by the purchase of a lottery ticket).

Let me describe an example. Suppose I am deciding between two alternative acts, with only the possible consequences listed in Table 5.1. The expected value of Act 1 is $1.9 - 1.5 = 0.4$ and the expected value of Act 2 is $4.1 - 3.9 = 0.2$. So the act with the highest expected value is Act 1.

Table 5.1 shows a relatively simple case. Given all the possible variables, in many cases the calculation would be bewilderingly complicated. But sometimes this sort of calculation can be done fairly easily. Indeed, in our everyday lives we frequently rely on rough calculations of expected value. For example, we reason that parking in the middle of a busy road during rush hour in order to look at the buildings has a high expected disvalue.[1]

Act-consequentialism has a number of things going for it. For one

Table 5.1

Different possible outcomes			*Positive and negative expected values*
Act 1			
Possible positive outcome: 3 units of good @ 10% probability	Possible positive outcome: 2 units of good @ 70% probability	Possible positive outcome: 1 unit of good @ 20% probability	0.3 + 1.4 + 0.2 = 1.9
Possible negative outcome: –2 units @ 10% probability	Possible negative outcome: –1 unit @ 70% probability	Possible negative outcome: –3 units @ 20% probability	–0.2 + –0.7 + –0.6 = –1.5
Act 2			
Possible positive outcome: 2 units of good @ 10% probability	Possible positive outcome: 3 units of good @ 70% probability	Possible positive outcome: 9 units of good @ 20% probability	0.2 + 2.1 + 1.8 = 4.1
Possible negative outcome: –1 unit @ 10% probability	Possible negative outcome: –4 units @ 70% probability	Possible negative outcome: –5 units @ 20% probability	–0.1 + –2.8 + –1 = –3.9

thing, it crystallizes the idea that doing what produces the most good overall cannot be wrong (Foot 1988, p. 227). For another, it proposes that morality is grounded in benevolent concern for others (Smart and Williams 1973, p. 7).

For yet another, act-consequentialism gives us a way of dealing with situations in which different considerations pull us in different directions. Suppose, for example, that you find yourself able to help someone but only by breaking a promise to someone else. Here kindness and trustworthiness seem to conflict. Act-consequentialism resolves the conflict. If the way to maximize the expected good is by breaking the promise, then that is what you should do. If the way to maximize the expected good is by keeping the promise, then that is what you should do. Of course it often is difficult to calculate which act has the highest expected value, but the moral principle involved is simple: choose the act with the highest expected value.

There are, however, serious problems with act-consequentialism. For example, it tells us to harm some innocent people if this would benefit others more and thus maximize aggregate value. Now there might be cases where a disaster of such horrible proportions looms that someone might *rightly* be willing to harm some innocent people if this is the only way to prevent the disaster befalling very many others.

Actually, even this is controversial (Anscombe 1958, p. 16; Dostoevsky 1880 [Penguin Books, 1993, p. 282]; Le Guin 1980; Thomson 1990, pp. 167–9). Nevertheless, the claim that act-consequentialists make seems very counterintuitive. For they claim that harming innocent people is morally required *whenever* this will maximize expected good – even if the good produced by harming an innocent person will be *only a little* more than would be produced by an alternative act that did not involve harming anyone.[2]

Another common objection to act-consequentialism is that it requires us too often to pass up opportunities to benefit those to whom we have some particularly close connection. It requires us to pass up these opportunities so that we can instead benefit those to whom we have no special connection. The act with the highest expected value, calculated absolutely impartially, is very often not the act best for yourself, or your family, or your client. To be sure, morality does restrict the pursuit of self-interest, as well as what you are allowed to do in order to promote the interests of others such as family or clients. But act-consequentialism requires that you do *not* do what benefits yourself or your family or your friends or your neighbours or your clients, on any occasion when you could instead produce larger benefits by helping people with whom you have no special connection (Hooker 2000a, chapter 7). Even if acting in such a relentlessly impartial way is possible, for a theory to require it seems unreasonable.

I indicated that there are two main kinds of consequentialism. So far I have been discussing act-consequentialism. The second kind of consequentialism is rule-consequentialism. There are different ways of formulating rule-consequentialism. But I will take the liberty of formulating it in the way that seems most plausible to me. Rule-consequentialism holds that an act is permissible if it accords with the code of rules whose general internalization has the greatest expected value (or if two or more codes come out equal in terms of expected value, then the one closest to the conventionally accepted morality).

Detailed explanation and defence of rule-consequentialism appears in Hooker 2000a, but let me note here a few of the theory's attractions. Consider the moral code whose acceptance by society would, as far as we can tell, result in the greatest overall good, impartially calculated. Should we not try to follow that code? And consider the familiar question, 'what if everyone felt free to do what you are doing?' Rule-utilitarianism is one way of spelling out the idea behind this appealing and familiar moral test.

Another attraction of rule-consequentialism is that the theory seems to agree with our beliefs both about when we can, and when we cannot, do normally forbidden acts for the sake of the overall good. It claims that acts of murder, torture, promise-breaking and so on can be wrong even when they result in somewhat more good than not doing them would. The rule-consequentialist reason for this is that the general internalization of a code prohibiting murder, torture, promise-breaking and so on would clearly result in more good than general internalization of a code with no prohibitions on such acts.

Another rule whose general internalization would be desirable is a rule telling us to do what is necessary to prevent disasters. This rule is relevant when to break a promise or do some other normally prohibited act is necessary to prevent a disaster. In such cases, rule-consequentialism holds that the normally prohibited act should be done. I mention this rule about preventing disaster because its existence undermines the objection that rule-consequentialism would, in a counterintuitive way, prescribe mindlessly following rules when this would result in disaster.

One more ethical system should be mentioned. This is what might be called virtue ethics. Virtue ethics claims that right action is to be explained in terms of virtuous character. To be more specific, virtue ethics claims that what is right is what a virtuous person would do. This view holds that there are a number of virtues – kindness, honesty, fairness, loyalty and so on – and that we need a unity of these in order to act rightly. This view is normally contrasted with, first, the Kantian injunction to act only on maxims we can will to be a universally followed rule, second, the contractualist injunction to act on rules no one could reasonably reject and, third, the act-consequentialist injunction to do the act with the highest expected value.

What is not so clear is how far virtue ethics contrasts with rule-consequentialism. Rule-consequentialists make the rightness of acts depend on the expected value of rules, and the expected value of a rule is the expected value of people's internalization of that rule. The most important part of internalizing a rule is becoming disposed to follow it. For rule-consequentialists, therefore, the rightness of acts depends on the expected value of people's becoming disposed in certain ways. It remains for virtue ethicists to explain how they decide which dispositions are virtues, and whether their theory has implications that are as plausible as rule-consequentialism's.

Metaethics

What exactly is a moral judgement? Is it the expression of a belief? What else could it possibly be, you might ask. Well, moral judgement might be thought to be the expression not of a belief but of some other mental state. The most prominent versions of this idea are that moral judgement is the expression of a sentiment, attitude or commitment.

Non-controversial expressions of belief are 'wood burns' and 'this chair burns'. Non-controversial expressions of non-cognitive states are 'boo robbers' and 'hooray cops'. The view that moral judgements express non-cognitive states has sometimes been called the 'boo/hooray' theory of ethics.

The theory may well be untenable, but it is certainly an improvement on another theory which might seem similar. This other theory – usually called naive subjectivism – is that our moral judgements simply state (or describe) what we feel. My judgement that 'polygamy is evil' simply states that I hate polygamy, according to naive subjectivism. But what if you say back to me, 'polygamy is not evil'? On naive subjectivism, you and I are not really disagreeing. You are stating something about yourself, and I am stating something about myself. If this were the right analysis of the situation, our judgements about polygamy would no more contradict one another than your stating that you are hungry and my stating that I am not.

The 'boo/hooray' theory avoids this absurd position; it holds that two apparently conflicting moral judgements do not state facts about different things, but instead express different attitudes about the same thing. Furthermore, the boo/hooray theory has the appealing feature that it links moral judgement with human motivation (given that attitudes are linked to motivation). A theory that construes moral judgements as expressing beliefs that purport to describe the external world might have trouble explaining why sincere moral judgement seems to bring with it motivation and commitment. (Beliefs about the external world do not normally seem so tightly connected to motivation and commitment.)

But perhaps the connection between sincere moral judgement and motivation is only this: judgements about what morality requires are judgements about what moral code would be best (as far as we can tell) to have internalized by society. This is close to saying that moral judgements are about what people should be motivated to do.[3]

Moreover, if people generally failed to have motivations that went along with their moral views, society itself would be threatened with disintegration and chaos. In a healthy society, by contrast, most people have not only moral beliefs but also corresponding moral motivations.

Over the last thirty years much of the discussion in metaethics has shifted from questions about the nature of moral judgements and the metaphysical status of moral properties to the question of what makes one normative moral view better than another. John Rawls and many of his followers have developed a view called the method of reflective equilibrium. This method involves searching for the best possible fit among our judgements about what has moral relevance, our judgements about what would be right in particular cases and our more general moral principles (Rawls 1971, pp. 19–21, 46–51). The idea is that we seek principles whose implications match the considered beliefs we have about particular cases; when we have a set of principles that does well against this test we modify whatever beliefs we have about particular cases so that they cohere with the best set of principles we can find. We work back and forth, modifying from both ends so as to reach a consistent whole.

This method has been subjected to fierce attack. The method seems to take our initial moral beliefs as starting points. In the light of this point, the method may seem at bottom to be merely 'reshuffling our prejudices'.[4]

Another objection is that the method seems to have severely relativistic implications, since some people's initial moral beliefs might be quite different from other people's.

These objections have bite. But on the other side we should note that it is very difficult to see what grand moral theory or abstract and general moral principle could really overturn some of our most confident moral beliefs. That torturing innocent babies for fun is wrong, for example, is a judgement that seems more secure than any theory we might come up with that conflicts with it. Likewise for the judgement that morality does not require, at least of an average person in average circumstances, a life of *relentless* self-sacrifice. There seems little point in putting forward any moral theory that conflicts with either of these (or many other) moral beliefs. For a proposed moral theory or principle to be plausible, it must be one we can really believe, i.e. one against which there is no obvious counterexample.

Which ethical system is most plausible, i.e. fits best with our considered beliefs? As a matter of fact, I think rule-consequentialism best, as I have argued elsewhere (Hooker 2000a, 2000b). However, to argue for one particular ethical system is not part of my task in the present chapter. So let me close this section by simply encouraging others to consider rule-consequentialism as a theory about what distinguishes right from wrong.

Practical versus theoretical

Moral philosophy is primarily theoretical, in the sense that it seeks the most general moral truths, truths that should be reapplied in any number of particular cases. Some moral truths can be complicated, as can moral arguments. And many moral principles employ concepts with vague borders. For example, consider the principle that you should not be dishonest. What counts as dishonest? Of course there are clear cases of honesty and clear cases of dishonesty. But there also seem to be cases where the concept 'honesty' seems vague. Moral vagueness is something that moral theorizing can accommodate. Indeed, it had better – if we confidently think that any conception of morality that completely eliminated vagueness from ordinary moral life would be implausible for that very reason.

But sometimes we need immediate help with moral problems, help with deciding what to do in difficult moral circumstances. In such circumstances, vagueness and complexity can be deeply unwelcome. For this reason, the law and professional codes often try to *specify* the interpretation of concepts so as to put sharp edges where there might have seemed to be only vague boundaries. Of course new cases can arise that expose vagueness unnoticed before. Life perpetually throws up new problems. There is no perfect prophylactic against this.

The need to act versus the need to be ethically correct

Action of course often involves taking risks. We do not know for certain what many of the consequences of an act will be. And if the consequences turn out some ways, we will deeply regret what we did. We may not only regret our decision but also feel horribly guilty.

Suppose you could build a bridge across a very deep ravine. Given the materials you have at hand, the bridge will be risky – it may break with people on it and cost them their lives. Focusing on the chance that the bridge will crash may keep you from building it. You may think that the way to avoid staining your moral record is to avoid acting.

If there is no great good in prospect, then of course you should not take serious risks with people's lives. But, for the sake of argument, suppose that, if you do not build this bridge, people on one side of this ravine will probably starve to death. So building the bridge has a non-negligible risk of costing lives, but not building the bridge also has this risk.

Suppose the probability of people dying as a result of the bridge's not being built seems greater. In such circumstances, it is hard to see how you could stay entirely innocent if you refused to build it. True, you might well feel guilty if you build the bridge and then it drops people into the ravine. You might well feel guilty even if you did everything you could to make the bridge safe. You took a risk and the unfortunate happened.

Sometimes circumstances are such that there is just no time to do further studies about safety (or anything else). Risk can be paralysing, but in some cases letting it paralyse you cannot be right (even if the trauma of having had to make a life-and-death decision can mitigate later criticism). The level of risk it is appropriate to accept may depend on the circumstances and what is at stake. But certainly it is sometimes right to take risks for the sake of protecting or benefiting people. In the face of uncertainty (as in other contexts) courage in pursuing the right ends is a virtue.

Resolving moral disagreements

Many interpersonal conflicts are not really moral conflicts. Suppose you want the building we are commissioning to face west, because you think the view will be best in that direction. Suppose I want the building to face south, for the same reason. We may fight bitterly over the matter. But, absent special circumstances, to construe this as a moral matter is to stretch the concept of morality too far.

Resolving such non-moral conflicts can be immensely important. Often an important first step in taking the heat out of the conflict is to point out that the conflict is not a moral one.

Of course many conflicts *are* caused by moral disagreement. Moral disagreements can in turn have different sources. Some arise from disagreements about what the empirical facts are. Some arise because of disagreements about which proposed moral principles are right. Some arise because of disagreements about how to apply agreed principles.

If we disagree about which moral principles are correct or relevant, we will probably disagree about exactly which empirical facts are morally relevant. This is because moral principles determine which empirical facts are morally relevant. Even if we agree about the relevant moral principles, however, we may well disagree about which particular act would be morally right in the circumstances. We may in turn disagree about what the empirical facts are.

To take a prosaic example, suppose we agree that morality requires us to do what is best for some group. You think the group could and would benefit enormously from the construction of a new road; I think the group would not use the road but would use a new building, which I therefore favour. We disagree about the extent to which the group would use the road and therefore disagree about what to do. But we do not disagree here about the relevant moral principle.

Let me offer another example to illustrate this important point. Many people who agree on the principle that capital punishment is justified only if it deters murder, nevertheless disagree about whether it is in fact justified. This is because they disagree about whether capital punishment really does deter murder. A disagreement about an empirical question leads here to a moral disagreement among people who agree about the relevant moral principle.

Consider instead a proposed change to society – e.g. legalizing divorce in Ireland, or instituting legal recognition for same-sex marriage in the UK. For almost any large-scale change to society, there will be many people who oppose it on the grounds that it will lead to social disintegration. Virtually everyone may agree that no change should be made that *would* lead to social disintegration, but people disagree about whether certain changes would have this result.

Let me offer one more example, this time from a professional context. Suppose you and I agree on the moral principle that (given certain parameters) professionals should be paid the market rate for their work. But suppose you think that my work is slow compared to that of others in my profession, and thus that the market rate for me would not be high. Suppose I, on the other hand, arrogantly think my work is relatively swift, and thus should command large payments. In this case, we disagree about what I should be paid, though we agree on the moral principle that (given certain parameters) I should be paid the market rate.

Because many moral disagreements can be traced back to empirical disagreements, we can resolve many moral disagreements if we can resolve the empirical disagreements that cause the trouble. And often we can do just that. We poll the group to ascertain how many would regularly use the road we could construct. We compare the murder rates in highly similar communities, one of which uses capital punishment and the other of which does not. We try some social change – perhaps initially not throughout all of society, but only in selected areas as a pilot scheme – and see if it leads to social disintegration. We agree upon some way of ascertaining whether my speed compares favourably with that of others in my profession. In these cases and countless others like them, empirical research can lead to agreement about what agreed upon moral principles require.

What about disagreements at the level of moral principles? Many of these can also be resolved – with sufficient patience. Suppose I articulate some moral principle that you reject. For example, suppose I say that you should do unto others what you would want them to do unto you. You might try to talk me out of this principle, or at least talk me into thinking the principle needs revision. You might, for instance, ask me whether I believe that I ought to give you all my money. I answer, 'of course not'. You then ask whether I would like for you to give me all your money. 'Yes, of course', I reply. You then point out that, since I would like for you to give me all your money, the 'do unto others' principle seems to require me to give you all my money. Once I see this, I see I must agree with you in rejecting (or at least modifying) the 'do unto others' principle. Another clear example of arguing against a principle by pointing to its implausible implications was presented earlier in my sketch of objections to act-consequentialism.

In fact, this is the usual way of arguing about moral principles. One person argues against another's principle by describing circumstances in which the principle clearly has implausible implications. Especially when this is done is a cooperative and friendly manner, we can often find ourselves coming to agree that a principle that had been causing a moral disagreement between us is much more compelling than some of us thought it was.

I suggested that seeing the implausible implication of a principle would push us sometimes to reject the principle and sometimes to modify it. Especially if we can point to an impressive range of cases in which a principle clearly has the right implications, we might be more inclined to modify the principle. But once we see that it needs modification – once we see that it cannot rightly be mechanically applied in all the cases that we had thought it could – then we need to ascertain whether a particular case in front of us is one in which it should apply or one in which it should not. How can we do this? One traditional method, often referred to as casuistry, involves looking at a range of cases, starting with paradigm cases of how and when a given general principle should be applied. As we consider new cases, we look for analogies but also disanalogies with the paradigm cases. The goal of this exercise is to ascertain the morally relevant similarities and differences between cases. Though the term 'casuistry' never recovered from Pascal's attack on it (in his *Provincial Letters*, 1656), the method of reasoning is widespread in practical ethics.

Despite all the ways of resolving moral disagreements I have summarized here, some moral differences are notoriously recalcitrant. With respect to some of these recalcitrant differences, we might be willing to agree to disagree. With respect to others, we must keep arguing.

But what about situations in which there is some deadline for a decision? Sometimes we cannot put off making some decision until everyone agrees which side wins the moral argument about what to do. In such cases, we are pushed back to the moral question of what to do in the face of ongoing moral disagreement.

There is likely to be at least partial agreement about how to deal with moral disagreement. All parties can agree, for example, that they should continue trying to find a course of action that leaves everyone happy, or at least that respects everyone's deepest moral convictions. All parties should also agree to try to consider the matter from the other's point of view, and perhaps from the point of view of an arbitration tribunal. All parties should also be brought to agree that resources – not only money, but also time, attention and effort – are limited. We cannot give to each valuable endeavour all the resources that, considered just on its own, it might seem to deserve. Compromises between competing valuable things are inevitable. Also inevitable is some degree of risk. Such observations may seem platitudinous, but they can be helpful in resolving moral disagreements with those of a particularly idealistic bent.

An empirical approach to ethical systems

An empirical approach to ethical systems might be thought to focus on the question 'what works?' There are different interpretations of this question. For example, 'what works?' might be thought of as asking what makes people on the whole better off. Or it might be thought of as asking what proposals people actually support.

However, 'what makes people on the whole better off?' is not a purely empirical question. Admittedly, if we agree what consequences would be best, then we can focus on the most efficient means to achieve these consequences, and the risks involved in aiming for the best consequences. But we must not lose sight of the fact that what makes people better off is not an entirely empirical question; the question has an irreducibly evaluative component. It is also not an empirical question whether what makes people better off must necessarily be morally right. The question is an entirely evaluative one.

Nor can we turn ethics into a search merely for what people will support. People might be in the grip of superstitions or oppressive ideology. We can all have misguided concerns as well as mistaken beliefs about how best to serve our concerns. So what people will support is not necessarily right.

Still, there is a place – a very important place – for empirical questions about ethical systems. For it must matter what the consequences would be if this or that moral code were established in society. By 'established' I mean *internalized* by almost everyone in society, and by this I mean that the code would be reflected in the beliefs and dispositions of the people. We need to ask questions of the form 'if people felt free to do such-and-such, what would be the long-term consequences?' For example, in some scientific contexts, we need to ask what the long-term effects will be on the amount of innovative research that gets done if people feel free to make money from their scientific discoveries, and what the implications are for the sort of people who will be attracted into this research. In engineering contexts, we need to ask what the long-term effects are likely to be of professionals being held morally and legally liable for this or that sort of consequence. We might well think that better consequences would result if, for example, the moral code imposed on engineers a strong duty to 'blow the whistle' when they see their employers or clients cutting corners in a way that endangers others.

Notes

1　Would that more people were aware of the fact that buying lottery tickets has, in purely economic terms, net expected *dis*value.
2　See W.D. Ross's discussion of promise-breaking in Ross 1930, pp. 18, 34–5.
3　This is related to a view developed in Copp 1995.
4　This is the objection mounted by Brandt 1979, pp. 21–2.

References

Anscombe, Elizabeth (1958) 'Modern moral philosophy', *Philosophy*, vol. 33, pp. 1–19.

Barry, Brian (1995) *Justice as Impartiality*, Oxford: Clarendon Press.

Brandt, R.B. (1979) *A Theory of the Good and the Right*, Oxford: Clarendon Press.

Copp, David (1995) *Morality, Normativity, and Society*, New York: Oxford University Press.

Daniels, Norman (1975) *Reading Rawls*, Oxford: Blackwell Publishers.

Dostoevsky, Fyodor (1993 [1880]) *The Brothers Karamazov*, translated by David McDuff, Harmondsworth: Penguin Books.

Foot, Philippa (1988) 'Utilitarianism and the virtues', in S. Scheffler (ed.) *Consequentialism and its Critics*, Oxford: Oxford University Press.

Gauthier, David (1986) *Morals by Agreement*, Oxford: Clarendon Press.

Hampton, Jean (1986) *Hobbes and the Social Contract Tradition*, Cambridge: Cambridge University Press.

Herman, Barbara (1993) *The Practice of Moral Judgment*, Cambridge, MA: Harvard University Press.

Hill, Thomas, Jr. (1992) *Dignity and Practical Reason in Kant's Moral Theory*, Ithaca, NY: Cornell University Press.

Hobbes, Thomas (1651) *Leviathan*, London.

Hooker, Brad (1995) 'Rule-consequentialism, incoherence, fairness', *Proceedings of the Aristotelian Society*, vol. 95, pp. 19–35.

Hooker, Brad (2000a) *Ideal Code, Real World: A Rule-Consequentialist Theory of Morality*, Oxford: Clarendon Press.

Hooker, Brad (2000b) 'Reflective equilibrium and rule consequentialism', in B. Hooker, E. Mason and D. Miller (eds) *Morality, Rules, and Consequences: A Critical Reader*, Edinburgh: Edinburgh University Press, pp. 222–38.

Kant, Immanuel (1785) *Groundwork of the Metaphysics of Morals*, translated by H.J. Paton (1953) as *The Moral Law*, London: Hutchinson.

Kavka, Gregory (1986) *Hobbesian Moral and Political Theory*, Princeton, NJ: Princeton University Press.

Korsgaard, Christine (1996) *Creating the Kingdom of Ends*, New York: Cambridge University Press.

Kymlicka, Will (1991) 'The social contract tradition', in P. Singer (ed.) *A Companion to Ethics*, Oxford: Blackwell Publishers, pp. 186–96.

Le Guin, Ursula (1980) 'The ones who walk away from Omelas', in *The Wind's Twelve Quarters*, vol. II, St Albans: Granada Publishing, pp. 112–20.

Nagel, Thomas (1991) *Equality and Partiality*, New York: Oxford University Press.

Nozick, R. (1974) *Anarchy, State, and Utopia*, Oxford: Blackwell Publishers.

O'Neill, Onora (1989) *Constructions of Reason*, Cambridge: Cambridge University Press.

Paton, H.J. (1947) *The Categorical Imperative: A Study in Kant's Moral Philosophy*, London: Hutchinson's University Library.

Pettit, Philip (1994) 'Consequentialism and moral psychology', *International Journal of Philosophical Studies*, vol. 2, pp. 1–17.

Rawls, J. (1971) *A Theory of Justice*, Cambridge, MA: Harvard University Press.

Rawls, J. (1993) *Political Liberalism*, New York: Columbia University Press.

Regan, D. (1980) *Utilitarianism and Co-operation*, Oxford: Clarendon Press.

Richards, D.A.J. (1971) *A Theory of Reasons for Action*, Oxford: Clarendon Press.

Ross, W.D. (1930) *The Right and the Good*, Oxford: Clarendon Press.

Scanlon, T. (1982) 'Contractualism and utilitarianism', in A. Sen and B. Williams (eds) *Utilitarianism and Beyond*, Cambridge: Cambridge University Press, pp. 103–28.

Smart, John Jamieson Carswell and Williams, Bernard (1973) *Utilitarianism: For and Against*, Cambridge: Cambridge University Press.

Thomson, Judith Jarvis (1990) *The Realm of Rights*, Cambridge, MA: Harvard University Press.

Vallentyne, Peter (ed.) (1990) *Contractarianism and Rational Choice: Essays on Gauthier*, New York: Cambridge University Press.

6

A SOCIAL CONTRACT?[1]

Andrew Reeve

In this chapter, I do not wish to review the history of the idea of a social contract, nor do I want to endorse the view that the model of a social contract is the best way to consider issues broadly surrounding the questions of what we owe one another, and what political implications are generated by the answer. Instead, I want to use the idea of the social contract as an organizing thread to explore how contemporary political theorists have tried to set about answering those questions. To do so, I outline what might be called the classic view of the social contract – and of some of its problems – in Section I. In Section II, I turn to the most significant – but by no means only – application of a contractual approach in contemporary political theory, namely its application to justice, paying equal attention to the critical perspective. In Section III, I draw these threads together in an attempt to define the parameters of the problem, if not the answers.

Evidently, to ask what we owe to each other, or what our rights, duties and responsibilities with respect to other persons are, is to ask about the content of morality. Our enquiry has to be narrowed to matters of political concern: perhaps the content of political morality.[2] The relationship between morality as a whole and political morality is not, however, straightforward, not least because what counts as specifically political is a contested issue. For example, a Benthamite utilitarian could specify fundamental moral principles, and then attempt to apply them to the political domain,[3] but another thinker might start from a consideration of the nature of politics, attempting to derive principles applicable in the light of its special characteristics, without hoping to specify the content of morality in the round.[4] So there might be an attempt to explain the content of morality as the result of a contract, to which specifically political arrangements might be referred, or an attempt to explain the contractual origins of political arrangements within the framework provided by a more general morality.

I

The device of a social contract, in general terms, is intended to explain and justify particular institutions by reference to what persons in more or less hypothetical conditions might be taken to have agreed to. The idea of a social contract, unsurprisingly, has a long history.[5] In its recent – seventeenth-century and later – form it is associated with the development of the modern state, and also with modern doctrines of natural law and natural rights.[6] In particular, the social contract has been invoked to answer the challenge posed by an attachment to freedom. Such a challenge arises most profoundly in two guises: what, if anything, could justify the claims of those who wish to rule over me? and what, if anything, could justify the claims of those who wish to limit my access to the resources of the world? Seventeenth- and eighteenth-century doctrines of natural law, natural rights and the social contract have been described as exhibiting three features: rationalism, radicalism and individualism.[7] The shape and content of the social contract and its role in political argument have been variously conceived. Some exploration of these points will help to locate the attractiveness and the limitations of the social contract as a way of illuminating the problem of what, if anything, we owe each other in politically relevant ways. It is useful to begin with a brief account of the social contract as it appears in the works of Hobbes, Locke and Rousseau, writers chosen because comparing their approaches enables us to think about what is contractual about society, and what is social about contract.[8]

In his masterpiece, _Leviathan_,[9] Hobbes used the device of a social contract to consider what sort of political subjection men who lived without a 'power able to over-awe them all'[10] would be prepared to accept. In his view, life without such a power would be intolerable: individuals competing for scarce resources, especially for power, would be engaged in a war of all against all, or at least they would be permanently disposed to fight.[11] Crucially, Hobbes held that the state of nature, or state of war as it would inevitably be, was incompatible with society.[12] Social life required a sovereign, to remove the rational distrust of one another that men would otherwise experience and respond to. It was obvious, Hobbes thought, that in the absence of anything worthy of the name 'society', there could be no property, since no one could have any confidence in his ability to maintain his connection with resources, however acquired. The contract to create Leviathan, the sovereign, or, in modern terms, the state, was therefore emphatically not a contract to determine the political arrangements to be adopted by men already enjoying a settled social existence; rather it was a contract to create political power which was the pre-condition of any social life at all.[13] Each individual rational calculator was to be thought of as agreeing with every other individual in pair-wise covenants to relinquish his right of self-government, to the extent that others were willing to do so, to a designated sovereign; that sovereign was not a party to the contract, although he benefited from it.[14] Hobbes's thought was clearly rationalist and individualist; its rad-icalism is perhaps less obvious, since it might seem to license an extremely powerful, unaccountable and authoritarian ruler. But it was radical in trying to locate the duties of subjects and the legitimate powers of sovereigns not by reference to Scripture or tradition or history, but by appeal to the prudential reasoning of self-interested individuals concerned above all with their own preservation and, perhaps, salvation. So for Hobbes society was contractual, in the sense that men might be understood to have contracted to bring it into existence, and the contract was social in the sense that society existed by virtue of each man's undertaking to subject himself to one common ruler. The sovereign, having been authorized to act on behalf of each, represented in his own person a unity which disparate individuals could not otherwise possess.[15] The answers to the question 'on what terms would you (a rational self-interested prudential indi-vidual) be prepared to enter society?', and to the question 'on what terms would you (similarly identified) be prepared to live in political subjection?', were in this sense one and the same.

John Locke's thought approaches the social contract in a different way. For Locke, men would be capable of a social life in the absence of the state – or of 'civil society'.[16] Although it is controversial just how extensive the institutions of that acephalous condition were,[17] and although there is some ambiguity about the extent to which they would be capable of obeying the (God-given) law of nature without government, Locke clearly conceived them to be living in a recogniz-ably social condition (but one lacking a positive legal system) in a way rejected by Hobbes.[18] The law of nature regulated the emergence of private property from the common state in which God had given it to Man, and individuals entered political society to protect their prop-erty. Their social contract, therefore, was not to make society possible, but to express an agreement on how it was to be governed: a *political* society was thereby created, and power entrusted to particular persons to legislate for the good of all. One of Locke's central concerns was to differentiate civil society from any other relationship, to explain why it could not be conceived on the model, for example, of the family, or of despotic slavery.[19]

Rousseau's *Social Contract*[20] is famous as an expression of the moral claims of direct democracy, under which the people give legislative expression to the general will. As part of his attempt to make his theory consistent, Rousseau conceptualized the social contract in a different way to the authors already considered. His contract was not of each with each, like Hobbes's, but of each with all – for Rousseau this made his political society an association rather than an aggregation of persons.[21] He also thought that individuals, in contracting, surrendered natural liberty but acquired moralized liberty – the capacity to govern themselves collectively by decisions coming from and applying to all equally.[22] And he identified liberty, in part, as freedom from obedience to the impulse of appetite, suggesting that we are truly free only when our higher rational or moral sense has subjugated base desire.[23]

Even this very brief glance at the use to which the idea of a social contract was put by three historically prominent authors is sufficient to explain one of the complaints of an equally prominent critic of the idea, David Hume. Hume analysed the origins of private property and of political society by reference to the idea of convention, the emergence of a set of arrangements over time. He had a number of criticisms of the contractarian analysis of political society, one of which is particularly relevant for present purposes.[24] He was concerned about the variety of questions which were allegedly answered by reference to the idea of a contract, and we can see the force of his point in the light of the three examples of contractarian thinking just given. Of course, authors might envisage the terms and conditions of the contract in different ways, but they also applied it to multiple purposes as a result. For Hobbes, a social contract was the solution to the problem of distrust and enmity which precluded any social life. For Locke, it was the source of a uniquely political society, in which legislative, executive and judicial functions were to be exercised for the public good. For both, the contract defined the nature of political power and of political authority – the right to rule – but also set their limits, and thereby the proper extent of political obligation – the obligation of subjects to obey their rulers. But insofar as the contractors might bestow authority on others, they might be thought to have obligations to each other as a result of their agreement; those empowered might also have obligations to the ruled. For Hobbes and Locke, but less clearly for Rousseau, the framework for action was provided by a theory of the laws of nature and of natural rights.

Apart from Hume, two of the most trenchant critics of an individualistic social contract were Burke and Hegel. Burke's political society was the result of history, and questions of legitimacy were to be settled by the custom and practice established through centuries of experience. He wished to talk of the rights, not of Man, but of Englishmen (or Frenchmen, and so on). He conceded that society indeed rested on contract, but he made two reservations.[25] It was, in the first place, not a contract between discrete individuals, but a contract between generations. It subsisted through time, and those here today were to consider those who had gone before and those who were to come after. This doctrine he applied to property and to political society. In the second place, he vehemently denounced a parallel between a social contract and commercial agreements. The latter were temporary agreements for private gain and lacked the majestic significance of an intergenerational political settlement. These 'reservations' have the effect of substantially undermining an analogy between a contract, as ordinarily understood, and a social contract, for there is no obvious way in which collectivities like generations can be understood to contract with each other, except in the behaviour they adopt.

G.W.F. Hegel generalized Burke's second point in insisting on a sharp distinction between 'civil society' and the 'state'.[26] Civil society was the sphere of contingent economic interaction, in which individuals pursued their self-interest by contractual, market, arrangements. It extended the freedom conferred on those who externalized their personalities by the acquisition of property, because it possessed some universality: everyone participating in the network of market relations was brought into some connection with every other participant. Just as Burke criticized the assumption that political society could be seen as an expression of temporary and self-interested concern, so Hegel denounced those who could not envisage the state except on the model of civil society. The state, for Hegel, was necessary to the realization of freedom: it provided a sphere in which the public good could be articulated and acted upon. Both its necessity and its purpose precluded the notion that it had a contractual origin, and although Rousseau was right to identify the moral possibilities of political community, he was to be condemned for supposing that a social contract could account for them.[27]

From Hobbes to Hegel we have moved from the view that the social contract is necessary if any society is to be possible to the view that the highest expression of self-conscious freedom is to be found by acknowledging the conceptual impossibility of the contractual origins of political community. Nevertheless, we have identified a number of considerations which re-emerge in the context of modern political theory.

II

The focus of much contemporary work in political theory is on the nature of justice. Justice is essentially a distributive issue, and can be conceived of more or less narrowly. For example, David Miller has pointed out that the most ecumenical formulation of the requirements of social justice is *suum cuique*, to each his due; but of course this leaves open the basis on which the 'due' of any person (or group) is to be calculated. Miller suggested that three crucial and potentially conflicting bases of assessment were rights, desert, and need.[28] But the distributive issue can be posed more generally still, to ask, in the words of the philosopher whose work has been central to debate over the last twenty years, John Rawls, what is 'to be the proper distribution of the benefits and burdens of social co-operation'?[29] The question is more general in two senses. First, it is concerned with the resolution of the potential conflicts just mentioned. Second, it locates the 'problem' of justice so that it applies not to the distribution of this or that good in particular, but to the fundamental constitutional and political arrangements of a given society. Rawls's project is then to work out a conception of justice which may be applied to the most fundamental constitutive elements of a common life, and results in reflections on civil disobedience, the just economy and so on.

The question posed is, for most thinkers, the most urgent we need to confront. But it contains three controversial references: to the nature of a 'common life', to relevant 'benefits', and to relevant 'burdens'. Rawls himself tried to clarify these notions by hypothetical contractarianism.[30] He invited us to consider what principles of justice we would be prepared to accede to if we had no knowledge of our place in society, no knowledge of our skills, talents or disadvantages. This knowledge, we were to imagine, is denied to us by a veil of ignorance, which also obscured from our view our own conception of the good life and how we should wish to pursue it. The contract for justice, defining the critical principles to be applied in the assessment of the actual arrangements of any real society, was therefore to be drawn up in conditions of uncertainty. Not only would actors not know their attitude to risk, but they would also experience the uncertainty caused by the unavailability of information about the probability of their occupying any particular social role. They could not, therefore, take a chance, by reference to their attitude to risk, of being well placed: neither their assessment of risk-taking nor the probabilities involved in taking that chance would be available to them. Rawls proposed that in such uncertain conditions, each contractor should choose as if his position in society was to be allocated to him by his enemy. This would lead, he claimed, to a general concern with the position of the worst-off representative person in society: for that person might be me (or you).[31] The contractors should therefore, he argued, adopt principles of justice which ensured that the position of that worst-off representative person was maximized. Maximizing that position would be one of two conditions laid upon any departure from equality, the other being that positions to which advantages were attached should be open to all under conditions of fair equality of opportunity. The various principles of justice were to be arranged in a lexical order, so that the principle at the top of the list was to be fulfilled to the greatest possible extent before the succeeding principle came into play. This has the effect of ruling out trade-offs between potentially conflicting principles. Rawls concluded, then, that the principles of (social) justice which would be agreed upon, under the specified conditions, were:

- each should enjoy the maximum system of equal basic liberties
- departures from equality are legitimate if they are attached to offices or social positions available to all under conditions of fair equality of opportunity
- they are to the benefit of the worst-off representative person in society.

The literature spawned by Rawls's theory is enormous,[32] but major positions can be located by reference back to the three problematic issues of the characterization of social cooperation, or a common life, the explanation of the relevant benefits and the account of the relevant burdens. Each raises issues which exist, at least putatively, in the accounts of the proponents and opponents of the social contract mentioned in Section I.

What is a 'common life'? From a Rawlsian perspective, it clearly cannot involve a shared commitment to a particular conception of the good life, because it is the very variety of such conceptions which has to be accommodated within the framework provided by a theory of justice. In a sense, it is a weakly empirical or historically contingent issue: it matters less how we came to be living together than how we are to regulate the conditions of that common life. It is not that we contract to create society, but that we contract to define the nature of a just society so that we can publicly justify the benefits and burdens which attach to any particular position in it. But in truth the idea of a common life is radically ambiguous. Mutual involvement may arise from common political subjection, from economic interdependence, from shared pursuits or from contingent contiguity. Historically, these categories were explored through the notions of the state, the market and the community;[33] but also through the idea of a common humanity. The notion of communality, in its thinnest sense, may refer only to the fact that all are human, all can suffer, all have moral potential, all are born and all die. In its richest sense, it supposes a particular quality in human relationships, available only to those who can treat their neighbours as part of a family, or who can share common aspirations or even a common conception of the good. (The connection between quality of relationships and size of community is obviously crucial.) And that contrast is linked to another: between the potential universalism of a focus on common humanity and the potential exclusiveness of community. Communities exist in part by definition of their membership, by reference to insiders and outsiders. 'Members only' may be applied to political society and to communities, to clubs and to associations, but less readily to markets. So ideas of a 'common life', the nature of social cooperation, cover a huge range, drawing on disparate ideas: the quality of relationships, their voluntarism or contingency, their inclusive or exclusive character.

The second of these considerations, about voluntarism and contingency, is pressed most avidly by libertarians of a certain stamp. Why should anyone have obligations to other persons, they ask, unless they have agreed to them? And even then, they might recommend that we never agree to some arrangements. More formally, they hold that the only obligations which can legitimately be forced upon a person are those which follow from respect for others' rights, or those which are voluntarily acceded to. This position can be contrasted with that which holds that legitimately enforceable obligations may arise from other sources: most notably, participation in a common practice which creates expectations in others, or receipt of benefits from others' activities or forbearances.

A deeper consideration of the questions surrounding the 'benefits' and 'burdens' of a common life, associated with libertarianism, brings to light the central issues in the contemporary debate about justice. First, is it appropriate to begin from natural rights? The tradition of thought associated with natural rights has been subjected to substantial criticism. Critics have alleged that insofar as natural rights theories attribute rights to persons simply as a result of their humanity, they provide no explanation of why persons should have rights; that in a secular morality, natural rights have no grounding; that proponents of such rights commit the naturalistic fallacy of deriving a prescriptive proposition from a descriptive one; that there has been no agreement on the specific content of such rights; that their apparent universalism is incompatible with our ordinary feelings that our obligations are strongest towards those with whom we are most closely associated.[34] It is notorious that Robert Nozick begins his libertarian – and deeply anti-Rawlsian – tract, *Anarchy, State, and Utopia*, with this claim: 'Individuals have rights, and there are things no person or group may do to them (without violating their rights).'[35] But he does not explain the origin of these rights, he simply proceeds as if this is already established.

Even if Nozick does not explain why persons have natural rights, a question remains about the purpose of rights. Thinkers have generally given one of two answers. The first sees rights as protecting choices, the second as securing especially important interests. Since the first presupposes the capacity for choice in the right-holder, it appears to limit the range of right-bearing entities to those persons who have that capacity, at least beyond some qualifying threshold. The location of that threshold, and indeed whether that capacity is uniquely human, are highly controversial issues. The status of foetuses, young children and animals, especially higher primates, is problematic. The second theory, by contrast, can treat any entity capable of important interests as a right-bearer. For example, environmentalists bitterly dispute whether the planet might be said to have 'interests' which are independent of those of the persons who pro tem inhabit it. Of course, this second theory only serves to raise in turn disputes over the content of those interests which are 'sufficiently important to be treated as rights'. In the absence of this sufficiency condition, the language of rights becomes inflated and devalued as any momentary and partial interest is turned into a right-claim.

Although both theories have been taken to provide a foundation for natural rights (for example, every person has the (God-given?) capacity of rational choice, or every person has an important interest in self-preservation), the content of the rights thus derived differs markedly. Whereas the first theory is more congenial to the traditional civil and political liberties, the second is more congenial to 'welfare' rights. Even if we are concerned not with natural or human rights, but with social or legal rights, the same point applies. An important distinction between natural rights and social rights is that the former are claimed universally, whereas the latter can be referred to the circumstances of time and place. For example, even if there were a natural or human right to medical care, such a right might nevertheless be linked to the technological and material development of the social provision of medicine in its more specific recognition. Even if human or natural rights are constitutionally entrenched through bills of rights, the issue of interpretation in the light of technical and social change is ever present, as illustrated clearly by the experience of the USA and the activities of its Supreme Court. Whether constitutional entrenchment, leaving decisions on controversial issues of interpretation to judicial authority, or political action, leaving decisions to everyday political processes, is to be preferred, is certainly debated. None of these issues is readily resolved, whether conventional rights are thought of as being created by a social contract, or whether that contract is taken to confirm precedent natural rights. The crucial issue remains the content of a coherent set of rights which is sensitive to social change. The appeal to natural rights and the appeal to a social contract are ways of structuring the debate about the content of that set, but they are not a substitute for it. Continuous debate and public justification of rights-claims is indispensable.

For *libertarians*, the most significant right (or perhaps bundle of rights) taken to exist is that associated with 'self-ownership'. This has proved to be a very troublesome idea. It appears, in one form, of course, in John Locke's political thought. His justification for private property rests on the assertion that individuals have a property in their persons, and consequently in their labour.[36] And in a fundamental sense, the idea of self-ownership seems to express a commitment to equal freedom, the rejection of slavery. No man may own me: I am my own man, I have self-ownership. Even those who are sceptical of the uses to which the idea of self-ownership may be put when it is presented in a more extended form accept this foundational sense of self-ownership (but may nevertheless complain that it is a misleading way of putting a point which can be more clearly expressed in other language).[37]

The more controversial application of the 'self-ownership' notion arises from the contested nature of the object of the ownership to which it refers. This has been seen as a source of incoherence, in that the subject and object of ownership must be distinct entities for 'ownership' to have conceptual purchase.[38] In Locke's thought, an agent is conceived to own his person and his labour; in Nozick's, his talents and the rewards arising from their use. But for Rawls, as we have seen, a person's talents are morally irrelevant; in that sense, he or she has no greater claim to them (or to a reward for their superior character, or superior earning power) than anyone else. For libertarians, this amounts to a violation of self-ownership as it appears to allow the legitimacy of others' claims on (part of) a person. And this problem has a mirror image: Rawls's dismissal of the relevance of *desert* to the claims of talent can be applied to the undeserved nature of handicaps (including low earning power). For Rawls, a scheme of justice demands, in a sense, that 'luck' be neutralized; or, more carefully, that inequalities due to luck be neutralized or shown not to be detrimental to the interests of the least advantaged. For Nozick, persons seem to bring their (good and bad) luck into the world with them. Although the whole project of 'luck neutralization' has been said to be misguided, because allegedly based upon a unsustainable notion of responsibility,[39] a great deal of contemporary political theory has been concerned to explore exactly what it involves – work which has produced answers at variance with Rawls's own proposed solution.

The second major problematic arising from consideration of the Nozickian libertarian position is its treatment of property. It is an analytic feature of natural rights that the spatial–temporal location of any individual is irrelevant. The natural rights enjoyed by one generation must be equally available to all, without distinction of time or place. Any argument which aims to substantiate a natural right to property needs to face this issue squarely, and a libertarian argument which aims to do so has to explain how self-ownership and associated claims to property may equally be enjoyed by all. A recognition of this has led thinkers – both historical and contemporary – to distinguish between claims to natural resources and claims to produced resources, to limit the content of (private) ownership and to worry about the rules governing transmission of property via inheritance and bequest.[40] Rawls himself tried to handle this issue by proposing a contractual solution: crudely, what rules of justice would anyone agree to, if ignorant of his or her particular location in the temporal existence of a particular society?[41]

More generally, concerns with exhaustible resources, pollution, sustainable growth and so on have more recently led to an attempt to work out the content of intergenerational and international justice. These 'applications' of the idea of justice, or these components of the principles of justice, raise once again the issues of identifying the relevant benefits and burdens and the nature of a common life. Rawls's two principles were put forward on the assumption of a (conceptually) closed political society. Cosmopolitan aspirations, and certainly natural rights theories, cannot stop at the borders of states: their foundation of commonality is universalistic.

The Rawlsian contract for justice has been attacked for a different failure to identify the nature of the common life, by emphasizing the status of individual (prudential?) rationality in determining the outcome, in circumstances when the choosers have such limited information. It is a standard problem of all contractualist theories that in a sense the outcome – the content of the contract – is determined by the assumptions made about the circumstances in which the contract is made. For example, the willingness of a Hobbesian contractor to submit himself to the extensive power of Leviathan depends heavily on the bleakness of what Hobbes alleges to be the only alternative: the state of nature. And the notion in Rawls, that individuals deprived of all the information discussed earlier would proceed on the assumption that their enemy was assigning them their place in society, seems to make the maximization of the position of the worst-off representative person not only 'rational', but also a matter of prudential self-interest. Rawls's own view is that self-interested choice under fair conditions is a useful test of the requirements of justice. This has led many to doubt whether the requirements of *morality* can be captured by such a device. As Brian Barry has written,

> The possibility is thus opened up that the requirements of morality might run counter to those of even the most sophisticated long-run self-interest. As T.M. Scanlon has put this idea, the moral motive is 'the desire to be able to justify one's actions to others on grounds they could not reasonably reject', where the basis on which others decide whether or not they can reasonably reject the grounds one offers is given by *their* 'desire to find principles which others similarly motivated could not reasonably reject.'[42]

This characterization of the moral motive, and its link to the idea of public justification, seems the most helpful to adopt in our present enquiry.

III

Let us return to the central idea that a purpose of a theory, or a social contract, is to explain the proper distribution of the benefits and burdens of a common life, and ask how some of the major issues involved are related to developments in science and technology. A full reply needs a theory which can explain how risk, uncertainty, reward and responsibility are to be related in social practices: a theory which is not yet available, although the arguments we have reviewed in Section II all surround this problem. Do our talents deserve reward? To what extent am I responsible for my own fate, and to what extent should I be able to call upon others? To what extent do different social practices constitute sufficient of a 'common life' to justify the view that participation in them requires the acceptance of mutual claims and obligations? Historically, the advent of 'industrial society' led thinkers to explore the relationships between the individual, civil society (often conceived as 'the economy'), community and the state in their attempts to answer these questions in the light of the fundamental changes they thought were wrought by developing industrial society.[43] Although concern with community has been renewed, contemporary writers have added the third sector – neither the market nor the state – in the guise of non-profit-making organizations,[44] and treated civil society as a domain not merely of the economy but also of voluntary association.[45] And, of course, the very idea that political power, or individual national economies, or the activities of charitable organizations, are best analysed with reference to national borders is under constant challenge from theorists of globalization. The 'common life', from that perspective, extends to all those on the planet.

Nevertheless, some of the reports of the death of the state and the decreasing importance of the domestic economy seem highly exaggerated. From the point of view of most citizens, the state remains the most important locus of political power or authority in their lives, and the domestic economy, regulated by the government of that state, remains the most important determinant of their life chances. Opportunities for welfare[46] depend not only on initial endowment – talent, ability – but also on the institutional arrangements which control access to resources, employment, education and so on, and provide the social context in which the very idea of talent – and indeed, of low earning power – has meaning.

In exploring the idea of a social contract, we have encountered in both Sections II and III two major problems: what is the domain or scope of the 'social'?, and what is the domain or scope of the 'contract'? Different responses to these ground-level questions are linked to different reasons for invoking the idea of a social contract. These need elaboration because the social contract has been taken also to include quite specific institutional and policy implications. This move from the general to the specific clearly depends on an agreed answer to the general question, and even then the attempt to derive very specific implications might be construed as misguided: perhaps we are asking too much of the device. Nevertheless, what is common in all applications of the idea is the notion that the putative contractual explanation is a *justifying* device.

The first foundational issue of the domain of the social involves contested sets of contrasts between social and political, social and natural, social and individual, political and private, society and community, state and economy. All of these contested distinctions are linked inextricably to fundamental disputes about the connections between, and obligations arising from, the distribution of risk, reward and responsibility. The more narrowly 'social' is construed, the more these obligations will be outside the foundational contract; conversely, the broader the view of 'social', the more they will fall within it. For example, Rawls has been vehemently criticized by Nozick and others for what is, from their viewpoint, construing the benefits and burdens of social cooperation too broadly. On the other side, Nozick has been criticized for losing sight of the social in his emphasis on individual rights. So, for example, whether economic or welfare concerns should be included in the foundational contract is furiously contested. The risks, rewards and responsibilities covered, in the narrower view, are those of political life, narrowly construed, not those attached to everyday economic experience.

These issues – about the scope of the social – are linked inextricably to disputes over whether the very idea of a contract is at all relevant because, as we have seen, Burke and Hegel, and indeed contemporary communitarians, see something deeply repugnant in what they take to be the reduction of the defining features of human sociability merely to contractual obligations between discrete individuals: such an approach vitiates the proper expression of humanity. The fully shared life cannot sensibly be reduced to contractual arrangements.[47] Quite apart from this wholesale rejection of the very idea of a contract, there are continuing and unresolved difficulties about the nature of the contractors. The rational individualism – however interpreted – of contractors might in itself be seen to load the whole exercise in a particular direction, whether radical, in the sense of subverting community, or rationalistic, in the critical sense of neglecting profoundly important forms of human experience.

The very idea of a social contract, however, might be rational in one fundamental and ideologically liberal sense: that we want to be able publicly to justify our practices to one another, and that justification must transcend simple appeals to narrow self-interest. Indeed, doubts about whether there can be a *social* contract on those terms might be taken to support Rousseau, among others, who vehemently protested that the social contract was different from everyday contracts precisely because of those features of publicness. Public justification transcending immediate self-interest presupposes democratic institutions and political education coupled with commitment, but whether a contract is the best or only expression of that justification remains contestable.

Leaving aside all these particular niceties, we might ask this basic question: what would a reasonably well-informed person, capable of even minimal impartiality, be concerned about, when rationally assessing the desirable distribution of risk, reward and responsibility – especially if that person were a citizen and also a 'scientist'? As a citizen, those concerns might include the typically political ones: the fundamental constitutional arrangements governing political power and authority; property regimes; and the provision of welfare.

Let us take each in turn. The most fundamental political issue is the space which is left to each individual to pursue his own conception of the good life, in circumstances where his survival is not precarious. Following from that are questions of individuals' rights against each other and particularly against governmental and state agencies. This must generate thought about a public/private divide, the distinction being made even more complex by changing technology. So, for example, pornography on the World Wide Web, CCTV in city centres and elsewhere, reproductive technologies and euthanasia all force us to rethink the nature of this distinction as it has been transmitted to us, and to rethink the appropriate distribution of rights between individuals, for example in the conflict between the right to free speech and the right not to suffer harm or offence.

Similarly, in the context of property regimes, globalization and resource depletion, we would again be led to question transmitted views about political boundaries where risks, rewards and responsibility seem, at most, only contingently connected. An example is the decision by the French company Renault to close its Belgian plant against the strongly expressed wishes of French, Belgian and European Union political elites. And, of course, to state what is now obvious, pollution respects no political frontiers. Acid rain does not fall only on those responsible for its generation. With this globalization, the loci of economic responsibility are elusive and perhaps impossible to control.

A specific area in which most people would expect to be exposed to some combination of risk, reward and responsibility is in the labour market. At one extreme, particular views of that combination are used to justify competitively low wages or, alternatively, competitively high remuneration packages for international executives. Workers typically face both risk and uncertainty, the degree of which is determined in many ways by technological change. Work is more or less hazardous,[48] continuing employment more or less uncertain, according to the speed of technological change and the resources devoted to health and safety provision. Those who bear the risks are not always those who benefit from their existence, and may well be responsible neither for the existence of the risk nor for their exposure to it.

Familiar justifications for welfare provision – whether it be private or public, however defined – are rendered less prominent by advances in medical technology, with all their demographic implications, and globalization. These familiar justifications include: expressions of solidarity and responses to need within national communities; the protection of the vulnerable by redressing the burdens of uncertainty; compulsory insurance schemes within particular legal jurisdictions; and a hypothetical contract between the members of a particular polity.[49]

Even if education is to be justified by its economic contribution in a globally competitive economy, its contribution to self-development and cultural enrichment would have to be considered essential within any framework of public justification of the kind with which we are concerned. After all, the contractors are to be reasonably well informed, capable of impartiality and able rationally to assess the proper distribution of risk, reward and responsibility.

Although the notion of public justification might be seen as intrinsically and exclusively 'liberal', it is not necessarily bound to generate liberal conclusions or a liberal social contract. Those embedded within very different social practices might very well be able to provide a public justification, at least one internal to their community or way of life, even if that justification is unpersuasive to outsiders. But the point of Scanlon's characterization of the moral motive, and therefore of any contractual application of it, is that each participant wants to engage with reasonable citizens anxious to find common reasons for action, or principles, which are not reasonably rejectable, and this constrains the sorts of justification which can be advanced. Scanlon's characterization appears to remind us of the importance of the separateness of persons and therefore, in contrast to utilitarianism, insists that *each* individual has rights which limit the scope of acceptable *common* reasons. Nevertheless, even if it were to be agreed that the social impact of scientific and technological developments should be publicly justified, reference to a social contract is simply one possible way of providing a justification.

The risks, rewards and responsibilities for scientific or technological developments should be seen as part of the domain of the social and, even if they do not lie within the domain of the social contract, scientists owe a public justification of their activity transcending immediate self-interest, both within their own community and to the wider society; in their capacity as citizens, scientists' public justification of those activities might indeed be a political justification, which will have to take account of the arguments sketched above. Such a justification requires that, as far as possible, they engage with others equally concerned to justify public or social practices on grounds which are not reasonably rejectable; this enterprise is fundamentally egalitarian, in the sense that it seeks to exhaust the conversation of any power inequalities based upon differential access to information, understanding or special expertise, while bringing such differential access to bear for the general good.[50]

Notes

1 I am grateful for comments from John Cunliffe, Andrew Williams and the editor.
2 David Gauthier (1986) *Morals by Agreement*, Oxford: Clarendon Press, addresses the general issue. Joseph Raz (1994) *Ethics in the Public Domain*, Oxford: Clarendon Press, takes the view that political morality 'is concerned primarily with protecting and promoting the well-being of people' (p. v).
3 Jeremy Bentham (1982 [1789]) *An Introduction to the Principles of Morals and Legislation*, edited by J.H. Burns and H.L.A. Hart, London: Methuen, famously states the principle of utility (p. 11) which James Mill claimed (in 1820) committed the utilitarian to support for representative government. Mill's essay, and the subsequent debate, are explored in J. Lively and J. Rees (1978) *Utilitarian Logic and Politics*, Oxford: Oxford University Press. J.J.C. Smart and Bernard Williams (1973) *Utilitarianism For and Against*, Cambridge: Cambridge University Press, and Geoffrey Scarre (1996) *Utilitarianism*, London: Routledge, provide accessible accounts of modern versions of the doctrine – and criticisms of them. Armatya Sen and Bernard Williams (eds) (1982) *Utilitarianism and Beyond*, Cambridge: Cambridge University Press, remains a valuable collection.
4 This is particularly true of the 'realist' tradition, which suggests constraints on 'moral' possibility imposed by the nature of politics and power. Machiavelli and Hobbes are frequently considered in this way.
5 Michael Lessnoff (1986) *Social Contract*, London: Macmillan, provides an overview. Brian Skyrms (1996) *The Evolution of the Social Contract*,

Cambridge: Cambridge University Press, distinguishes two 'traditions' –
one which asks what individuals would agree to in a state of nature, and
one which asks how 'the existing implicit social contract' can have
'evolved' (p. ix). The claim that some sort of social contract is *implicit* in
our social practices may have its difficulties, but it is less vulnerable than
the first 'tradition' to scepticism about the historical reality of any actual
contract. Nevertheless, the contrast should not be overstated, since many
writers in the first 'tradition' treated the contract as hypothetical.

6 A.P. d'Entreves (1970) *Natural Law*, second edition, London: Hutchinson.
7 D'Entreves, *Natural Law*, p. 52.
8 Sir Ernest Barker (1947) *Social Contract: Locke Hume Rousseau*,
London: Oxford University Press, remains a useful collection of extracts
and includes Hume's critical response.
9 Thomas Hobbes (n.d. [1651]) *Leviathan*, edited by Michael Oakeshott,
Oxford: Blackwell.
10 Ibid., p. 81.
11 Ibid., p. 82.
12 Ibid.
13 Ibid.
14 The disputable coherence of Hobbes's argument has, of course, fasci-
nated scholars. See, for example, S. Beackon and A. Reeve (1976) 'The
benefits of reasonable conduct', *Political Theory*, vol. 4, pp. 423–38. For
a sophisticated modern treatment employing the resources of game
theory, see Jean Hampton (1986) *Hobbes and the Social Contract
Tradition*, Cambridge: Cambridge University Press.
15 *Leviathan*, p. 113.
16 John Locke (1988 [1690]) *Two Treatises of Government*, edited by Peter
Laslett, Cambridge: Cambridge University Press.
17 Cf. Richard Ashcraft (1987) *Locke's Two Treatises of Government*,
London: Allen and Unwin, especially pp. 143–7; C.B. Macpherson
(1962) *The Political Theory of Possessive Individualism*, Oxford:
Clarendon Press; and James Tully (1980) *A Discourse on Property*,
Cambridge, Cambridge University Press.
18 Locke, *Two Treatises*, II, section 123.
19 Ibid., II, chapter VII.
20 Jean-Jacques Rousseau (1913 [1762]) *The Social Contract and Discourses*,
edited by G.D.H. Cole, London: Dent.
21 Ibid., pp. 11–13.
22 Ibid., p. 25.
23 Ibid., pp. 12, 15 and 85–6.
24 See Barker, *Social Contract* and David Miller (1981) *Philosophy and
Ideology in Hume's Political Thought*, Oxford: Clarendon Press,
pp. 78–80.
25 Edmund Burke (1969 [1790]) *Reflections on the Revolutions in France*
edited by Conor Cruise O'Brien, Harmondsworth: Penguin,
pp. 19–25; see also C.B. Macpherson, *Burke*, p. 45 for discussion of this
conception of a contract.
26 See Jack Lively and Andrew Reeve, 'The emergence of the idea of civil
society: the artificial political order and natural social orders' in Robert

Fine and Shirin Rai (eds) (1997) *Civil Society: Democratic Perspectives*, London: Frank Cass.

27 G.W.F. Hegel (1952 [1821]) *The Philosophy of Right*, edited by T.M. Knox, Oxford: Clarendon Press, section 258.

28 David Miller (1976) *Social Justice*, Part I, Oxford: Clarendon Press.

29 John Rawls (1971) *A Theory of Justice*, Oxford: Clarendon Press, p. 4.

30 'My aim is to present a conception of justice which generalizes and carries to a higher level of abstraction the familiar theory of the social contract as found, say, in *Locke, Rousseau, and Kant. A Theory of Justice*, p. 11.

31 *A Theory of Justice*, for example, p. 80.

32 Good places to begin an exploration are C. Kukathas and P. Pettit (1990) *Rawls*, Cambridge: Polity; and N. Daniels (ed.) (1989) *Reading Rawls*, Stanford, CA: Stanford University Press.

33 Cf. A. Reeve (1997) 'Community, industrial society and contemporary debate', *Journal of Political Ideologies*, vol. 2, pp. 211–25.

34 The following provide helpful coverage of the issues involved in rights discourse: Peter Jones (1994) *Rights*, London: Macmillan; Jeremy Waldron (ed.) (1984) *Theories of Rights*, Oxford: Oxford University Press; Jeremy Waldron (1987) *'Nonsense Upon Stilts': Bentham, Burke and Marx on the Rights of Man*, London: Methuen; Richard Tuck (1979) *Natural Rights Theories: Their Origin and Development*, Cambridge: Cambridge University Press.

35 Robert Nozick (1974) *Anarchy, State, and Utopia*, Oxford, Blackwell, p. ix. This is the first sentence in the book. For critical reaction, see Jeffrey Paul (ed.) (1982) *Reading Nozick*, Oxford: Blackwell; and Jonathan Wolff (1991) *Robert Nozick*, Cambridge: Polity Press.

36 See, for example, Andrew Reeve (1986) *Property*, London: Macmillan.

37 Attracta Ingram (1994) *A Political Theory of Rights*, Chapters 1 and 2, Oxford: Clarendon Press. Cf. G.A. Cohen (1995) *Self-Ownership, Freedom and Equality*, Cambridge: Cambridge University Press.

38 J.P. Day (1989) 'Self-ownership', *Locke Newsletter*, 20, pp. 77–85.

39 Susan Hurley (1993) 'Justice without constitutive luck', in *Ethics*, edited by A. Phillips Griffiths, Royal Institute of Philosophy Supplement: 35, New York: Cambridge University Press.

40 Cf., for example, Hillel Steiner (1994) *An Essay on Rights*, Oxford, Blackwell; Stephen R. Munzer (1990) *A Theory of Property*, Cambridge: Cambridge University Press; James O. Grunebaum (1987) *Private Ownership*, London: Routledge and Kegan Paul; J.W. Harris (1996) *Property and Justice*, Oxford: Clarendon Press, especially Part II. For earlier writers, see the essays by John Cunliffe (1988) 'The liberal rationale of rational socialism', *Political Studies*, 36, pp. 653–62; *idem* (1990) 'Intergenerational justice and productive resources', *History of European Ideas*, 12, pp. 227–38; and *idem* (1990) 'The neglected background of radical liberalism: P.E. Dove's theory of property', *History of Political Thought*, vol. 11, pp. 467–90.

41 Rawls, *A Theory of Justice*, pp. 137–9.

42 Brian Barry (1989) *Theories of Justice*, Berkeley, CA: University of California Press, p. 284. There is a more elaborate exploration of the

application of Scanlon's position to theories of justice in Brian Barry (1995) *Justice as Impartiality*, Oxford: Clarendon Press.

43 See note 33.

44 Alan Ware (1989) *Between Profit and State*, Princeton, NJ: Princeton University Press.

45 See the editors' introduction to Fine and Rai (eds) *Civil Society*.

46 The phrase emerged in the debate about what egalitarians should aim to equalize, in which issues of responsibility, reward, desert and luck are central. See Richard J. Arneson, 'Equality', in *A Companion to Contemporary Political Philosophy*, ed. Robert E. Goodin and Philip Pettit (1993), Oxford: Blackwell, and references there.

47 Stephen Mulhall and Adam Swift (1996) *Liberals and Communitarians*, second edition, Oxford: Blackwell.

48 See Robert Sass (1986) 'The workers' right to know, participate and refuse hazardous work', *Journal of Business Ethics*, vol. 5, pp. 129–36.

49 See Norman Barry (1990) *Welfare*, Milton Keynes: Open University Press, for an introduction.

50 Bruce A. Ackerman makes extensive use of the device of a dialogue exhausted of power in *Social Justice in the Liberal State* (1980) New Haven, CT: Yale University Press.

7

BIOLOGY, ENGINEERING AND ETHICS

Raymond E. Spier

The issues

Living organisms have a special place in our picture of the world. While not constituting a major portion of the mass of the Earth (the biosphere weighs about $1/10^{10}$ of the Earth's mass), life is certainly a rugged and determined survivor of some four billion years' existence on this planet. Based on the chemistry of the nucleic acids, which make up our genes, all life forms engage in processes of growth and replication. Additional features such as perception, cognition and memory give some organisms the ability to contemplate themselves, to begin to appreciate their nature and to understand the processes that made them the way they are. Standing on this foundation, humans have recently learned that they can acquire the ability to change the nature and functioning of the life forms occupying planet Earth, including the humans themselves. The issue, which this presents, is to determine how we might make the best use of such understandings and abilities. This in turn requires that we have a sense of the direction in which we should progress: a view of what would be beneficial and some sort of human-wide consensus that this is indeed the way to go.

Genius is a quality which both fascinates and terrifies. It may have its origin in the jinn of Arabian literature.[1] These demons were capable of perpetrating both good and bad deeds when interacting with humans. Modern engineers have been credited with abilities which would, in the ancient world, have been associated with these mythical entities who, among other things, were held to be responsible for the building of the Temple of Solomon at the turn of

127

the first millennium BCE.[2] The interactions between engineers and living organisms probably began with the origins of settled agriculture some 13,000 years ago in the Indus Valley. The continual selection of the seeds of the most advantageous plants, coupled with the controlled mating of the most desirable animals, has led to the high-yielding and high-performance plants and animals of the modern world. In deliberately controlling marriage partners, humans have been attempting to engineer the quality of the resulting children. Indeed, the practice of eugenics has been undertaken from time to time within the present century, with the intent of improving the quality of the 'human stock' of the society.[3] These limited and, for the most part, unsuccessful efforts to improve the human germ line have been augmented by a range of engineering capabilities which have emerged within the last twenty-five years. This battery of techniques includes the ability to

- fertilize human ova *in vitro*
- clone human embryos
- separate human sperm into those with the X or Y chromosome
- read the sequence of the bases which make up the human genome
- identify defective genes whose expression is likely to cause severe disease
- alter the genetic composition of somatic cells and germ-line cells.

We have also to consider a future when it may be possible to insert new genes into the human genome so that specific characteristics will be enhanced[4] and then to take advantage of that situation by cloning the enhanced individuals. The deliberate fabrication of newly designed hominid species is also a practical possibility.

Ethics constitutes verbally expressed guidelines intended to modulate human behaviour in a manner which promotes the survival of humans as individuals and communities (see also chapter 1). The emergence of the new capabilities delineated above requires us to devise appropriate ethics so that we might behave in a manner which turns these powerful tools to uses which we would consider beneficial. This, in turn, means that we have to know in advance, or devise a suitable mechanism to determine, which uses may result in benefits and which cause damage. There are several ways this need may be satisfied. Some would assert that their personal reactions or the teachings of their conscience would tell them how to proceed. Others demand some measure of consensus, be this a majority among those consulted, a uniform acceptance by a nominated committee or acclaim by the media. If 'mob rule' is rejected, recourse may be made to one or other of the ethical systems.

It would appear that one ethical system, selected from those available, is probably most applicable under a particular set of circumstances. Mechanisms for associating a unique circumstance with a particular ethical system need to be elucidated. While some might contend that scriptural or divinely inspired texts provide the basis for ethical guidelines for all circumstances, it is obvious that these ancient documents have not been designed to cope with the exigencies of the new engineering capabilities of the modern world. Contemporary hermeneuts may struggle to provide relevant messages based on archaic directives, but the basic premises for the directives themselves are coming under an ever-increasing challenge as the mysteries of our origins (matter, universe, earth and biota) recede before the advance of modern knowledge.

In the opinion of this author, we may seek benefit by choosing to ground our ethics on three foundations. The first comes from the basic message of the four-billion-year history of the evolution of living organisms, which is that their most basic objective is to survive. The second, for humans, is the way this survival may be achieved via the association of individuals into groups whose size and complexity is determined by the specific circumstances which pertain at that time. A third component of the survival approach to ethics is that it is most likely to be successful if it is both prudent and pragmatic. That is, we carefully and responsibly investigate the possibilities open to us and then choose options that potentially afford maximum benefit with the prospect of minimal concurrent harm. Again, this trial-and-error, or empirical, approach can be refined by using theoretical notions, coupled with rational deductions or predictions of which directions are most likely to be beneficial. But in the final analysis, we must determine the way ahead by the adoption of an experimental approach, which means that 'we learn through experience'.[5]

This chapter will deal with the issues thrown up by the emergence of a suite of new engineering tools that can modify biological entities or the way we deal with problems in biology such as infertility. Matters which relate medical doctors to patients and which were once satisfied by adherence to the Hippocratic code of conduct[6] will only be considered where new techniques are in evidence. Thus many of the issues pertaining to the autonomy of patients (realized through the need to acquire informed consent), their beneficial and nonmaleficent treatment and their just or fair handling, which are adequately covered in recent books of bioethics,[7] will not be examined here.

The structure I will follow will lead us along the path of evolution from the viruses, bacteria and other microbes to the plants, followed by non-hominid animals and then humans. I will set out some of the ethical issues that have been engendered by the application of modern engineering tools and techniques to these entities and, as appropriate, indicate how a prudent, pragmatic survivalist might approach the questions which arise.

Viruses, bacteria and other microbes

In this section I will outline the nature of the organisms involved and the kinds of product they generate. This will lead to a discussion of the ethical issues which have been raised in the media and literature as a result of the construction and use of the genetically engineered varieties of these entities.

Microbes and their uses

Most viruses may be described as one or many molecules of nucleic acid (the viral genes are some five to 1,000 in number with each consisting of a twisted ladder-like or spiral structure where the rungs of the ladder are made up from a pair of chemicals called 'bases'. There are only five such bases, and they can only pair in two ways: adenine with either thymidine (making DNA) or uracil (making RNA) and cytosine with guanine. They are surrounded by a protein shell. This may or may not be contained within a capsule or outer coat of lipid, protein and carbohydrate. Techniques developed in the last thirty or so years have enabled us to determine the sequence of bases on the viral genes and define the composition of the proteinaceous materials of the virus. This leads to a description of the way the virus enters a cell, sheds its protein coat(s) and replicates its nucleic acid. Then, having expressed the genes which code for the new protein coat, it reassembles and leaves its cellular host in such a state of disarray that the cell is normally killed. Additionally, it is possible to engineer new viral genes and to use viruses as vectors which can be used to carry and insert genes into the genomes of other cellular entities. We presently see such uses of these capabilities in the manufacture of new virus vaccines and in the efforts to find a vector which will infect selected human somatic cells. As viruses, such as the foot-and-mouth disease virus, which infects cloven-hoofed animals, and the measles virus, which infects many mammals, are the most infectious agents known, their modification to become agents of biological warfare cannot be overlooked. So the engineering of baculoviruses to carry genes whose expression results in the production of materials toxic to some insect pests has been used to attempt to control infestations of moths[8] and the cabbage looper.[9]

Bacteria are more complex than viruses in that they are surrounded by a cell membrane which enables them to control the parameters of their internal environment within tight limits notwithstanding the wild swings in the conditions of the external world. A typical bacterium might possess some 1,000 genes held on a single circular chromosome with additional genetic elements (plasmids) present in the cytoplasm. Although bacteria can be the purveyors of disease they can also be used industrially to produce fermented products (yoghurts), organic acids, antibiotics, vaccines, insecticides, fertilizers and enzymes, to prevent ice-crystal formation on strawberries and to digest oil spills and they may provide agents (anthrax bacteria, bubonic plague bacilli or botulinum toxins) to wage biological war. Resulting from the widespread use of antibiotics in animal feedstocks as well as their liberal prescription for curing bacterial infections, the development of bacteria that are unaffected by the majority of antibiotics has become a problem of growing proportions.

The simplest cells that contain a nucleus also hold within their cytoplasm a colony of tens to hundreds of degenerate bacteria called mitochondria. While the nucleus might host some 6,000 genes, each of the mitochondria retains about thirty to forty genes. These fungal cells, of which yeast is an example, are also used for antibiotic production (*Penicillium*) as well as the fermentation of a wide variety of carbohydrates with the production of alcohol. Other products from fungi include citric acid and aflatoxin, which may be used as a biological weapon.

Each of the organisms described above may be modified by making changes to the number or nature of the genes which they contain. This causes the properties of the organism to change. We may then ask a number of basic (generic) and specific questions as to how we may most beneficially apply the modified organism. A presentation and discussion of the questions raised will be dealt with in the next section.

Ethical issues contingent on the production and use of genetically modified microbes

The media is replete with sensational and over-hyped articles which evoke the image of the entity created and deserted by the fictional character Victor Frankenstein as conjured up by Mary Shelley in 1818. This entity was a conglomeration of oversized human parts which, as a result of a lack of courage and understanding on the part of its creator, caused a number of fatalities before remorse set in, which led to its demise. The genetic modification of micro-organisms is often alleged to be about to give rise to a doomsday bug which, through an all-pervasive plague, causes the end of humanity (a fictional representation of this was portrayed in Michael Crichton's *The Andromeda Strain*). Such fears were generated when the genetically modified *ice-minus* bacterium *Pseudomonas syringae* was sprayed onto a field of strawberries to protect them against the physical damage caused by ice crystals formed in sharp frosts. Although we do have viruses (the human immunodeficiency virus (HIV) and rabies) and bacteria (pertussis, tuberculosis) which cause terrible and lethal illnesses, it would be futile to attempt to convert them into the ultimate biological weapon by genetically engineering them to enhance their infectivity, transmissibility or pathogenicity. We have effective vaccines or drug treatments for three of these agents and it is likely that the same will apply to HIV as we improve our prophylactic and therapeutic armamentarium.

It is easy to beat a drum to the tune of the unforeseen disaster. The future is unpredictable because we do not have, nor will we ever have (because of Heisenberg's uncertainty principle of 1927) all the necessary knowledge to make the required calculations. Asteroids, earthquakes, volcanic eruptions, tornadoes and sunspot cycles all provide unpredictable elements of *major* consequence to life on earth. By contrast, we have, more or less, been able to cope with the translocation of various biological species to new habitats.[10] This includes the introduction of the rabbit to Australia, the potato to the eastern world, water hyacinth into Papua and Aswan and Africanized killer bees into the Americas. In each of these cases the newly introduced organism became a pest; our response has been to find another biological organism which can limit the growth of the pest without itself becoming a nuisance.

Naturalness has, for some, become a guiding principle. Such individuals criticize genetically engineered organisms for being 'unnatural'. But is this the case? I would assert that 'nature' has been doing genetic engineering for as long as living organisms have existed. Viruses act as transportation systems, shuttling whole genes from one organism to another. (This process may account for rates of evolution vastly in excess of what could be achieved by single-base mutations which are held to provide the minute variations called for in Darwin's theory of evolution by natural selection.) The key difference which distinguishes the human genetic engineer from natural processes is that in the case of the former there is an attempt at achieving a deliberately designed end, whereas in the latter case nature does not have a particular end in view. However, the insertion of a particular gene into a cell is fraught with uncertainties as to where that gene will become incorporated in the genome. Such position effects are crucial to the timing and efficacy of the expression of the exogenous gene. So engineers resort to the selection, from a number of engineered cells, of the particular cell which gives the result closest to the objectives sought. This increases the rate of production of novel organisms that have desirable (at least to a human perspective) properties. But it can hardly be called an unnatural process, relying as it does on the same kinds of biochemical components and reactions that have been changing and evolving for the last four billion years.

Genesis tells us that God created a man, a woman, the animals and the plants. Are we not usurping a function of the Deity by deliberately making changes to that which was 'created in his image'?[11] But many men shave their beards, cut their hair and are circumcised (as commanded); women have used make-up and pared their fingernails since recorded history. The dogs, cows, horses, camels and turkeys we have today are not like their historical progenitors of 10,000 years ago. Indeed, if we accept the alternative story to account for the origin of humans by the process of evolution, we have to envisage that some four to eight million years ago the ancestor of the modern human would have looked like a member of the ape/chimpanzee/bonobo assemblage. Some 750 to 1,500 mutations later *Homo sapiens* emerged. It would be difficult not to envisage a similar, if not greater, change taking place over the next four or so million years. The origination of a new species of hominid is not inconceivable, given our ability to use genetic vectors (based on modified viruses) to alter the genome of contemporary humans. A new suite of ethics is needed to handle such an event. It would be the most challenging task that has ever been presented to the human species. Perhaps this is what God intended. There is little doubt that the creation of a being with human properties would result in those abilities leading to the development of the next stage of evolutionary progress.

When all other arguments fail, it would seem that protest groups adopt the argument that the main beneficiary for the genetically engineered organism is the company which produces it. Is this something whose ethics need examination? Industry's functions include the need to survive, to provide a workplace for its employees and profits for the shareholders. Should this be objectionable then there would be dissension against all industrial activity and not just at that fraction which deals with genetically engineered organisms. That industry seeks to obtain monopoly positions should also not be surprising. The patent system represents that objective and provides limited-period monopolies for inventions. Any transformation of this system requires a radical overhaul of the basic political structure of our societies – a task which is beyond the scope of this chapter.

The four ethical issues above (the doomsday monster and its unpredictability, unnaturalness, usurpation of a function of a deity and benefit to industry) are commonly levelled at all developments in which the deliberate modification of genomic structures is undertaken. Other issues, dealt with below, may apply to one or more biological products derived from genetically engineered microorganisms.

How safe are genetically engineered products? Is the insulin made from genetically engineered bacteria and which is injected daily throughout the life of a diabetic patient a safe product? How safe are the new vaccines based on genetically engineering the avipox virus which have been shown to have encephalitic effects several orders of magnitude less than the successful vaccinia vaccine? The avipox virus is a relative of the vaccinia virus which was used to totally eradicate human pathogenic smallpox from the world in 1979. Hepatitis A vaccine is made from a formaldehyde-inactivated virus, as are the currently used inactivated polio vaccines; are they safe? In answering these questions it is crucial to appreciate that 100% safety (that is, zero damage) in relation to any human action is a goal which can never be achieved.

We are then left with the question of how much benefit we can achieve for how little cost, as each and every health-improving intervention will have its own cost. As a result of such incidents as the teratogenic effects following the use of Thalidomide, and the infection of vaccinees with imperfectly inactivated wild-type polio viruses in the Cutter incident, regulatory agencies in the USA and elsewhere were established. They have required new pharmaceuticals (of which the genetically engineered products are but one category) to pass stringent tests of safety, efficacy and consistency of production. Such tests commonly take three to ten years and may cost between $200 million and $800 million. This cost is passed on to the health care system in the form of a highly priced vaccine or therapeutic. Do we need to spend so much to make the risks of being damaged by the product so slight that they may not even be measurable by empirical methods? Might it not be more ethical to spend one tenth of the amount on testing and have a product that might cause one or two extra cases of damage per million product applications? This could mean a cheaper product, which would reach more individuals who might not have been able to afford the more highly priced and marginally safer product. The overall increase in the health of these people could more than balance out the increase in the relatively small number of adverse effects that might occur.

The field release of a baculovirus that was engineered to contain a gene, whose expression would result in the production of the toxin of the scorpion sting, has been tested. While it was effective against the target organisms, the cabbage looper, it was also held to have killed some rare and related species of moth in neighbouring fields. The public opprobrium which this generated has curtailed further uses of this technology. Otherwise the field release of genetically engineered ice-minus bacteria, and the use of a bacterium which was engineered to be able to metabolize the wide range of organic substances found in oil spills, have been able to proceed without serious dissent. By using a genetically engineered pox virus there has been a considerable success in the control of rabies in Belgium and surrounding countries following the field distribution of a fox bait containing an engineered virus that contained an immunogenic gene from the rabies virus. And there are extensive field trials with modified live bacteria which can be used to control the diarrhoeal diseases of neonates. These bacteria will enter the environment as they flow through the guts of the vaccinees but, as they are vaccine strains, they can only benefit people who become infected by them subsequently. Much of the initial concern about the potential of a genetically engineered organism to transform into a doomsday bug has largely dissipated. Each application is now judged on a case-by-case basis and those that have gone forward have achieved considerable successes. This prudent and pragmatic approach to the use of these new organisms for human and animal benefit has, therefore, become the dominant ethic in this area.

It is important to note that it is often possible to obtain a patent for a genetically engineered organism when the new organism expresses some surprising and novel trait. Indeed, this does give the patentee a monopoly on the use of that living organism for a period of some sixteen to twenty years depending on the patent authority and the time taken from patenting to the obtaining of a licence to manufacture and sell. Such a monopoly over the use of a living organism cannot be held to be contrary to ethical teachings as a purchaser of a cat, dog, bird, horse or farm animal has similar rights to those living organisms that a patentee has to the novel organism that s/he has created.

The commonest causes of death of some four million neonatal children annually in the developing world are diarrhoea, respiratory illness and malaria. In each of these cases vaccines which are genetically engineered are promising candidates for inexpensive and orally administered products. Were such deaths to be prevented one might expect that there would be an increase in the population of the world. However, while death rates have been decreasing in recent times, the rate of increase of the population has also been decreasing. For example, figures that may be culled from an UNICEF publication indicate that in 1960 the number of children born to a woman in the developing world (which encompasses some 70% of the total world population) throughout the period of her fertility was 6.06. This figure dropped to 3.75 by 1994.[12] So the supply of decontaminated water and genetically engineered vaccines is not necessarily a recipe for an increase in the world's population. The opposite, a decline in fertility, may ensue from a decrease in the need to have so many children because the survival of those that are born is enhanced.

We have been living in a technology-driven world since the origin of the steam engine by James Watt in 1765. Other remarkable advances include

- the distribution of electrical power (Faraday and Henry 1831)
- the camera (Daguerre 1839)
- the elevator (Otis 1853)
- the telephone (Bell 1876)
- light bulbs (Edison 1878)
- the petrol engine (Daimler and Benz *c.* 1885)
- radio (Marconi 1896)
- the aeroplane (Wright brothers 1901)
- vaccines (Jenner 1798, Pasteur 1860s, Salk and Sabin 1950s)
- antibiotics (Fleming 1927, Florey and Chain 1940s)
- nuclear power (Fermi 1942)
- computers (Turing 1940s)
- transistors (Shockley, Brattain and Bardeen 1948)
- DNA structure (Watson and Crick 1953)
- the contraceptive pill (1956)
- genetic engineering (Cohen and Boyer 1975)
- humans in space flights (Gagarin 1961).

So much so, that we have come to believe that all our problems may be solved by the application of the appropriate technology. Even behavioural problems can be obviated by the use of technical solutions. For example, sexual relations in humans have become more prevalent following the developments of antibiotics (to cure gonorrhoea and syphilis), the contraceptive pill (to prevent unwanted pregnancies) and vaccines (to protect against the sexually transmitted disease of hepatitis B). Thus ethical problems which involve people behaving differently can be circumvented by the use of the apposite technical fix.[13] Whether the appropriate ethic is to design a technical fix where a behavioural change would achieve the purpose of, say, preventing a disease, needs to be examined further.

For example, the infectivity of HIV is dependent on sexual intercourse or the exchange of bodily fluids. The disease would be eliminated were infected people to abstain from unprotected (condom-free) sexual activities, intravenous drug delivery (involving shared needles) and providing blood for transfusions. In the efforts expended to invent a drug-based therapy or a vaccine, society has determined that it is futile to attempt to change the behaviour of infected individuals. Rather we can meet the need to decrease the prevalence of this disease by using a technical fix: a drug or vaccine based upon a genetically engineered virus or subcomponent thereof. Perhaps this is a cost-effective way of dealing with this issue. We could, for instance, compare the costs of a continuous and sustained public relations programme to decrease AIDS, such as that which has decreased cigarette consumption in developed countries, against the costs of the development, licensing and use of a vaccine protective against AIDS. On the other hand we have to consider those who would ignore such a campaign but who might be denied access to socially provided facilities in the absence of a valid vaccination certificate. Presently we seem to be reacting to this situation with a combination of responses. As this disease is most prevalent in sub-Saharan Africa and in Asia we can expect expensive therapeutic approaches to dominate in developed countries. But to get a world-wide solution we would have to have an inexpensive vaccine. If one ethic may be seen to emerge from this, it is that as a result of a trial-and-error, or pragmatic, approach we can adopt a variety of strategies to contain this disease, each one of which may be particularly applicable in a specific set of circumstances.

Vaccines also provoke a further suite of ethical concerns.[14] These prophylactic approaches to disease control and eradication require whole populations to become vaccinated. In this way a 'herd effect' is generated whereby the weight of infection across the society is lessened to such an extent that even those who have either not been vaccinated or whose immune systems do not respond to vaccination (the immunocompromised) are protected from infection. As each vaccine may cause some, generally slight, reactions, some people wish to opt out of the vaccination programme. (There were severe cases of encephalopathies with smallpox vaccines in 1 in 10^6 vaccinees and some (1 in 2.5×10^6) cases of polio from the live virus vaccine.[15]) The ethical question which this poses is, should the autonomy of individual members of the society be infringed in order to better protect the rest of the society? As the rights of the individual, enshrined in the concept of autonomy, require that the individual is provided with a 'free' choice as to whether s/he will engage in any medical practice, how do we proceed to obtain compliance for society-wide vaccination campaigns? If we evoke those ethics which pertain to pragmatic survivalism, we can seek to convince individuals that it is one of their social responsibilities to play their part in helping the society control or eradicate a disease. Otherwise, one could argue that if responsibilities are spurned, then the rights of the individual might be correspondingly curtailed. The pragmatic approach would seek to explore every voluntary avenue to obtain compliance, for to effect these ends by compulsion would have drastic and deleterious effects on the social fabric. In proceeding in this way, we do not provide the individual with a free choice. Rather we (as society) adopt the role of a guardian, and seek to influence the decision of the patient to play their part in the social effort to rid the society of a debilitating disease, even if that were to mean that the patient is exposed to some risk of slight discomfort or side effect of the vaccine. There is also the untested possibility that people who opt out of vaccination opportunities be required to pay a tax which would compensate the society for the extra risks which have to be accepted and for any disease-related costs incurred by the individuals who have spurned the vaccination.

Birth control may be achieved by doping a water supply with an agent based on a genetically engineered bacterium. Salmonella bacteria (the normal agents of food poisoning), when both attenuated not to produce disease and engineered to express a protein which is found in the zona pellucida of the egg, will, following oral administration, immunologically sterilize the imbibing animal.[16] Clearly the composition of society's drinking water is a matter for determination by the society as a whole. The treatment of domestic drinking water with oxides of chlorine to reduce bacterial counts and the addition of fluoride (hotly contested in some communities) to strengthen teeth are present examples of the way we have chosen to control the composition of what we drink. May we not also choose to add a birth-control material to this essential supply? It may be that the society, having been fully informed, consents to the addition of the birth-control material to the water supply at concentrations that will, for example, decrease the number of people in the society by 10% over a period of twenty years. On the other hand, what if a group of people or a single individual decides, in the absence of comprehensive consultation, to do the same task? Clearly individual autonomy is impugned. Depending on the circumstances prevalent at the time (conceivably a desire for a decreased population or a runaway increase in the rate of population growth) one or other of the birth-control strategies outlined above could be brought into play. The birth-control tool, which has been fashioned out of a genetically engineered biological entity, can be used with care and discretion to increase the well-being of a society. It is also clear that its application needs to be controlled and accountable so that an excessive deployment can be prevented before harm has occurred.

Dumping an infected human down the well of an enemy, catapulting a plague-infected corpse into a fortified town under siege or soaking blankets in smallpox pustular juices before providing them to American Indians about to journey to their newly delineated reservations are all methods which have been used historically to achieve the objectives of people at war.[17] Genetic engineering tools may enable us to make micro-organisms, which are already damaging to humans, more effective as biological weapons.[18] But it is not just humans which are the targets of biological warfare. Crop plants, particularly monocultures, are especially susceptible to destruction by a biological agent. (Genetically engineered fungi that are toxic to the opium poppy have been made and may well be spread over such crop plants in countries which have failed to take action against the production of heroin and opium.)[19] While we may regard the production of such biological warfare agents with disapproval, we cannot guarantee that one or other of our potential adversaries or a group of terrorists would be equivalently inhibited from seeking to gain an advantage through the use of such agents. (This is notwithstanding the many conventions which seek to limit and control the production and use of biological and toxin weapons.) So, to seek to achieve our own survival, we have to be knowledgeable of the organisms and their variants that might pose a biological hazard.

Additionally, it is incumbent on us to develop the means to combat such threats and have the mechanisms to deploy the appropriate vaccines and antidotes at short notice. (While this manuscript was in

preparation President Clinton announced such a state of prepared-
ness was to be acquired *vis à vis* biological agents by the USA.[20]) To
what extent does the society as a whole have to be involved in this
move–countermove activity? It is to nobody's advantage to cause
unnecessary alarm, or to disclose to a potential enemy the state of
one's knowledge and capability. The crucial factor in whatever is done
is that there are representatives of the society engaged in overseeing
the response. If they hold that the resources of the society are misused
or, alternatively, if they consider that insufficient resources are
deployed to counter such threats they may bring forward the appropriate recommendations.

Genetically engineered microbes have been with us for some
twenty-five years. During that time they have provided adequate supplies of high-quality insulin, blood clot dissolving agents, new
vaccines (hepatitis B), ice-crystal preventers, bacterial rennin to make
cheese, yeast which make enzymes to clarify beer and other products
and their uses. Along with such powerful additions to the human
armamentarium of products and capabilities has come the need to
rethink some aspects of the way we behave. A new ethics which
enables all these new developments is in process of formulation. As
yet this has to be incomplete, as new and more potent agents burst
upon the scene. But from the cases that have been presented above it is
clear that we need not fear these developments, but rather that we
should welcome them and the associated ethical challenges. For from
the debates which this situation engenders may come a new ethical
synthesis which will provide stable and assured guidelines which we
may adopt with confidence. Notwithstanding this situation, the
issues raised by the genetic engineering of plants present a suite of
different problems.

Genetic engineering with plants

Almost every plant used in agriculture is presently undergoing genetic
modification. Some such modifications alter the nutritional, taste or
storage life of the vegetable foods, while others affect the economics
of production by decreasing the losses in the field due to insect
destruction or inefficiencies in the utilization of fertilizers and herbicides. Further modifications to extend the range of soils used and the
climatic conditions that can be tolerated are also in hand. Additional
attention is focused on the use of harvestable crop plants for the production of biopharmaceuticals including oral vaccines. As may be
expected, each such modification has ethical implications which are

currently under discussion. This section will elaborate on the engineering and ethical aspects of these genetically modified plants. (A thorough and clear presentation of many of these issues may be found in a report of the Nuffield Council on Bioethics.[21])

Transforming plants

Genes may be introduced into plants by using the transportation system afforded by a piece of DNA called the Ti plasmid of *Agrobacterium tumefaciens* that may have been engineered to incorporate exogenous genes. An alternative method involves coating small spheres of colloidal gold or tungsten with the DNA of the desired gene and then 'shooting' the plant cells with a gun to propel the coated gold spheres into the plant cells. This gun is powered by an explosion, gaseous helium or electrical forces (hence the term 'biolistics'). Genetically modified viruses may infect plants when they are applied, in solution, to a superficial abrasion of the plant leaf surface.

Most crop plants are in the process of modification by the insertion of genes, which controls resistance to specific herbicides, fungicides and insecticides. Other methods of protecting crops against viral and fungal pathogens through the application of genetic engineering techniques are also under development. For example, some 70% of the US cotton crop in 2000 is expected to be based on genetically engineered varieties.[22] Similar percentages for soya, maize and potato are also expected. As much of the damage to crops is dependent on weeds, fungi and caterpillars, the prevention of this devastation leads to higher yields and lower agricultural prices. Additionally, some crop plants are engineered to express a gene that codes for the production of a toxin derived from *Bacillus thuringiensis* (Bt toxin), which is lethal to insect pests.[23]

Not all the modifications relate to interspecies biological warfare. There are efforts expended on changing the carbohydrate composition of potatoes, increasing the methionine content of plant proteins, thus making them more nutritious, and the removal of the toxic lipids from rape plants. Investigations are also seeking ways to make plants more tolerant to growing under conditions of high salt concentrations in the water supply and, where droughts are common, it is desirable to have plants that are tolerant to low-water environments. Tomatoes have been engineered to have increased shelf lives and products derived from these plants have proved popular in some areas. Other parameters such as ripening times, colours and the nature of the flower structure may also be modified. Trees may be modified to express higher growth rates with the production of less lignin, increased habitat ranges and stress resistance as well as yielding woods of higher quality. The deliberate production of sterile hybrids can give plants that have hybrid vigour but lack seeds from which they can be repropagated. The control of the production of the progenitors of such plants provides a commercializable property.

Pharmaceuticals such as vaccines may also be made from genetically engineered plants.[24] Such systems may yield some one to two *kilograms* of viral protein material per acre planted per annum. Other biopharmaceuticals that are required on the kilogram scale rather than the micro- or milligram scales can be produced from genetically altered plants. Prime targets are the production of human serum albumin, which has a large-scale use in blood substitutes, the generation of human antibodies, some of which may be used therapeutically in the cure of toxic shock, and the blood clotting factors which can help patients suffering from haemophilia.

Ethical concerns in plant genetic engineering

The thought that the genetic composition of our food materials may have been deliberately altered has inspired many to examine the issues of the genetic engineering of plants thoroughly. In November 1994 a consensus conference was held in London to examine the concerns of a wide cross section of people on plant biotechnology.[25] This was an acute issue at this time as the genetically engineered 'flavour-saver' tomato had just received its distribution licence. The outcome of this conference was that the lay panel wanted genetically engineered food to be clearly labelled as such, with the ready availability of comprehensive information on the changes that had been engineered into each product. The food distributors at the time held that special labelling might stigmatize the product so that people would be reluctant to purchase it (as had been the case, uniquely in the UK, when γ-ray sterilized foods appeared on supermarket shelves). However, recent experience has shown that the labelling of tomato purée as originating from a genetically engineered tomato had increased sales (although contributory factors could have been a marginally lower price plus an improved – less burnt – flavour).

Present concerns have been centred on the newly engineered variants of common food plants. However, over the last century there has been a continual change in the genetics of these plants through a concerted mutation, crossing and selection process which has resulted in much higher-yielding types of crop plants. These plants account for our ability to keep up with an expanding world population. So it is illogical to object to newly genetically engineered plants because they have been so modified. Rather we have to look for other reasons for the basis of the strength of the rejectionists' views.[26]

Once, it was the spectre of the Four Horsemen of the Apocalypse (plague, famine, civil war and death) which haunted the imaginations of a cowed populace. Now, the prospects of a decrease in the amount of biodiversity are regarded as alarming. Additionally, the threat that the pollen from a plant, genetically engineered to tolerate a particular herbicide, will fertilize a weedy relative of that crop plant and over-grow the agricultural zone is a cause of anxiety. Before considering the ethical aspects of these phenomena, it is useful to determine the extent to which their manifestation exposes us to harm.

Biodiversity, or the number of species per unit area, is a parameter whose value has varied throughout biological time. Over the last 600 million years the number of species on this planet (as judged by the fossil record) has fluctuated considerably. There have been about five occasions when some 20% to 90% of all then present species became extinct.[27] The last such was the event sixty-five million years ago which included the demise of the dinosaurs and led to the emergence of the mammals. We also have to consider that new species arose to take the ecological niches vacated by the species that passed on. So the worldwide ecosystem is conversant with wild changes in the number of species. As new plant variants come on stream, they tend to dominate the agricultural practice of the day and, as mono-cultures, they are uniformly susceptible to particular pests or viruses. However, they tend to be backed up by other variants which, although not as productive, are less susceptible to these attacks. Whether it causes more benefit than harm to proceed in this way is still an open question. It is clear that increases in agricultural effi-ciency, stemming from the monoculture approach, is of value. But this is achieved at the expense of opportunities for improvement which could have resulted from an unknown variant which was not provided with a chance to express its capabilities to the full. At this time the balance of benefit is with the monoculturists, but it is well that we bear in mind the inherent weaknesses of this approach and prepare ourselves to respond rapidly and overcome the problems resulting from wipeouts.

A second aspect of biodiversity is based on a decrease in the number of species of plants in those parts of the tropical rain forests that have been denuded of trees to make way for other forms of agri-culture. The loss of these plants is thought to result in a decrease in the possibilities for the discovery of medicinals: a serious contention, as some 80% to 90% of the current pharmaceutical armamentarium is derived from plant-based products. Nevertheless, there has been a recent revolution in the strategies of the pharmaceutical companies. They have come to focus on the three-dimensional molecular structures of existing biomolecules as the source of information for 'rational' drug design. From this data they synthesize and examine millions of alternative molecular structures for their biological effects (the combinatorial approach to drug discovery). Yet the screening of native organisms for natural products still occupies a considerable proportion of research budgets, and while this has opened new areas, such as the algae and fungi, the need to examine native and exotic plants continues. The exploitation of the flora of other, often developing, countries has to be effected through appropriate agreements with those countries so that benefit, possibly in the form of a royalty, may accrue to the country of origin of the source material.

That the pollen from a transgenic crop can travel several kilometres and fertilize related plants should not surprise.[28] But whether such fertilized plants will become pests is a less likely event. An even less likely scenario is that the gene for herbicide resistance becomes incorporated into the genome of an unrelated plant which is a natural weed; this would provoke a need to respond with a newly engineered crop plant resistant to another herbicide. The danger from chemically resistant transgenic plants is twofold. On the one hand, it is possible that the weed which is targeted by the herbicide, to which the transgenic plant has been made resistant, will mutate and no longer succumb to the chemical. This means that the plant to be protected will have to be re-engineered to be resistant to another herbicide that will kill the weeds which have become resistant to the first herbicide. Multiple cycles of this nature may be anticipated. Whether combinations of resistant genes coupled with mixtures of herbicides will be a longer-lasting answer has not been determined, but there is little doubt that this way of improving crop yields will be explored in all its aspects. What applies to the plants which have been genetically engineered with exogenous herbicide genes is also applicable to plants engineered with insect-, fungus- or virus-resistant genes. In each of these cases variants of the pests will emerge for which a different transgene will have to be introduced into the plant.

The other danger is that companies supplying the herbicide and the genetically resistant plant will so exploit their monopoly position as to render the new technology unavailable to any other than the already rich. Of course, their patent monopoly rights will only last some sixteen to twenty years, after which any supplier may mimic and market the inventions. Yet the problems inherent in making a herbicide (special chemical synthesis) and transgenic plant (resistance gene and transfection process) preclude an easy entry into the field, even in an effort to copy what has already proven successful. This barrier may be overcome by well-funded governmental research institutions.

Were developed nations to become so competent that they were able to produce all the food and plant materials they wanted from indigenous plants and their genetically engineered variants, then there could be knock-on negative effects to the developing world that once supplied this market. Efforts have to be directed towards some form of compensation for this market loss.

The addition of selected animal genes for expression in food plants may also present problems, especially when the origin of the genes is from animals which, for example, Jews and Muslims are forbidden to eat, such as porcines. Others, who are vegetarians, might object to the introduction of any animal gene into a plant that is used as a food for humans. While the previous conditions may indeed be effected, it is most unlikely that the exact gene which originated in an animal would be inserted into a plant in an unmodified form. A shorter gene, with expression-control promoters or with some of the redundant third bases changed to enhance expression, is often used. Again, one could hardly object to genes that are common to all living organisms being transferred. As the reason for the rejection of food animals is based on the nature of the whole animal and/or the processes which are undertaken to render it suitable for eating, a gene taken from such an animal does not evoke either of these situations and therefore may be considered in a different light. Nevertheless, any exploitation of an animal, including the extraction of its genetic material, might be considered unacceptable. In this case a chemically synthesized gene could be constructed which would never have experienced the animal environment. These may be technical fixes to obviate an ethical dilemma, but they do put the magnitude of the ethical questions raised into perspective so that reasonable people might come to acceptable and pragmatic conclusions about their actions *vis à vis* plants genetically engineered with animal genes.

As the agent which effects the genetic engineering of the plant may be a form of DNA which can have an independent existence, in the form of a virus or bacterium, it is held that such agents may leave the plant and transform other species. Were they, for example, to provide an antibiotic-resistance gene (a gene which is normally contained in these vectors because it enables the modified organism to be selected for further use) to a pathogenic bacterium found in nature, then humans might be put at risk of contracting disease. The gene coding for kanamycin resistance is often used for this purpose because the antibiotic kanamycin is not used to cure humans of bacterial disease as it is too toxic. So it is not a matter of concern if bacteria become kanamycin-resistant as a result of obtaining this gene from a genetically engineered plant as the antibiotic used to kill such bacteria would inevitably be other than kanamycin.

A recent (May 1998) ruling of the European Parliament has endorsed the Patent Directive of the Council of Ministers, which establishes two crucial provisions. The first is that discoveries of the sequence of bases of the genes of a living organism are not in themselves patentable. Inventions which incorporate the base sequence of genes that are identical to those found in living organisms may be patentable providing an industrial application has been specified. This latter definition has been adopted by the US patent office in the year 2000. This means that the genes of existing living organisms cannot become the property of a patentee. Thus foods, plants and animals cannot be monopolized merely because somebody has managed to sequence the bases of one or more genes of those entities. Indeed, varieties of plants may be protected as intellectual property if there has been an inventive step in their construction, but this does not tie up the use of the parent plants whose genomes might have been used in the novel construct. A genetically engineered plant may be rightfully considered an invention. It had not previously occurred in nature and could be regarded as a novel addition to the biosphere.

Those who are disquieted by modern developments based on science and engineering will not derive comfort from the new engineering capabilities of making genetically engineered plants. So although these applications may not achieve universal acceptability, it would be difficult to so construe traditional ethical teachings, to reject these developments. Nevertheless, as we cannot foretell the future, it is well that we adopt a cautious, pragmatic approach to the latest organisms. We have to be in control at all times, should anything which is both harmful and unforeseen occur, we need to be able to limit the damage and prevent further injury.

Non-human animal modifications

Many of the issues generated by our ability to deliberately genetically modify plants transfer to the animal situation. Unnaturalness, usurpation of the function of a deity and the prospects of the emergence of an uncontrollable monster elicit negative responses which, when orchestrated effectively, can delay progress. The protests of the 'Green' movement in Germany has set back that country's efforts to obtain technical and financial benefit from biotechnological developments some ten to twenty years. Current efforts have led to a surge in the number of biotechnology companies in that country. However, a number of genetically engineered animals have been constructed and their presence has stimulated research to discover the most appropriate ethics.

Animal constructs

The wish list for the modification of animals is not dissimilar to that of plants. Some of the characteristics which are considered desirable in a food or draught animal are faster growth rates, increased weights at slaughter, improved efficiencies of feed utilization and resistance to temperature extremes and pathogenic micro-organisms or helminths, plus decreased aggressive tendencies coupled with an ability to control the reproductive cycle. Some cattle or pigs are altered to provide low-fat steaks or bacon. Other uses, such as the production of pharmaceuticals or body organs for xenotransplantation into humans, are also under intensive investigation. This in turn has led to the emergence of methods for the cloning of animals, first from embryo cells and latterly from adult nuclei which have been derived from cells of known functionality.[29] The modification of rodents and other animals, often primates such as the rhesus monkey, which was engineered to be susceptible to the human immunodeficiency virus so that they might serve as models for human diseases, has achieved commercial fame. An application such as the Harvard 'oncomouse' (a rodent which has been genetically engineered to be highly susceptible to human cancer-inducers) has achieved a degree of notoriety. The genetic apparatus of certain insect pests has been modified so that all the males are rendered sterile. These, when admitted to the field, compete for mates with fertile males, and where they are successful, they break the breeding cycle and lead to the decimation of the pest.

It is of interest and importance that considerable efforts have been directed towards the genetic modification of fish, particularly those that are 'farmed'. Here the ability to efficiently utilize supplied feed is crucial, as the profit margins are narrow from the highly competitive situation that pertains. Such animals are also exposed to fish vaccines, which is another area for the deployment of genetically engineered microbes. Nevertheless, some such fish have rates of growth of up to ten times the natural rate and reach proportionate sizes. The occasional escape of such animals from the confines of the 'farm' can constitute a problem.

Towards a new suite of relationships between humans and animals

Although 'man was given dominion over the animals'[30] it was not in the interest of humans to exploit them to the extent that they ceased to exist. Rather, for those animals which did not pose a threat to human existence, a caring and respectful relationship has been developed over the last 13,000 years. During this period, animals have become domesticated and provide support to human communities in the form of a food resource, as a warning system, as a method for testing the toxicity of potential foods or environments, in a draught capacity and as pets or companions. The use of animals in competitive situations so that humans might wager resources on the outcome of the trial is also of ancient origin[31] (horse racing was an Olympic sport from 700 BCE).

Special attention has been given to the ethical issues involved in the genetic engineering of pigs so that their tissues may be compatible with the immune system of humans.[32] Thus a failing human heart, kidney, liver, lung and so on may be replaced with the equivalent organ produced in a pig. As the use of pig heart valves for the replacement of their ineffective human analogues has been commonplace for some time, it is difficult to sustain an ethical argument which denies the use of pig parts for human benefit, even though this would mean the demise of the pig. The deliberate modification of the pig so that it may be even more useful in this regard can be considered a step along a slippery slope towards the commodification of all animals and, possibly, eventually, humans.

But we have controls that prevent the progression of a trend leading to a situation which we would regard as unacceptable. In making determinations as to where to stop, we have regard to any unnecessary stress or discomfort foisted on the animal. We also have to consider the possible safety hazards which could result from the transplantation of pig tissue harbouring endogenous retroviruses that could become replicatively active were they transferred into the environment of a human cell. These cells may possess genes that complemented those of the pig retrovirus so that from two defective viruses a single viable virus might emerge and cause disease. The release of such engineered pigs into the wider environment would not constitute a hazard in that damage, caused by the engineered modification, would be virtually inconceivable. But when genetically engineered salmon escape from the pens of the fish farms they can have a substantial effect on local wild fish stocks. However, as in most predator–prey relationships an oscillating condition prevails, this then becomes the new natural state.

Similar provisions, that seek to prevent non-essential pain, stress and discomfort, apply to other farm animals which may engineered to produce pharmaceuticals such as the α_1-anti-trypsin, haemoglobin, albumin and others. The attempted production of human growth hormone in pigs led to the development of animals which were both larger and clearly stressed in that their bones were too weak to support their weight. These experiments were discontinued. Efforts to efficiently produce pharmaceuticals in engineered animals has led to the development of cloning techniques, so that it is now possible rapidly to expand a single productive animal into a commercially useful herd.[33] The ethical implications of this work lies more in the area of the use of the cloning tool in human replication than in the animal area where breeding programmes involving *in vitro* fertilization and the use of artificial insemination have been performed for many years. In these latter situations, it is the economic conditions that direct the techniques that are used.

It is also in the economic implications of the use of genetically engineered animals that there is a need for greater care in the implementation of such programmes. For example, the modification of a cow to produce its own endogenous bovine somatotrophin (BST) (as opposed to the repetitive injection of this material which has itself been derived from a genetically engineered bacterium) would increase milk yields considerably. Two issues result from this prospect. One is economic, in that it would take many fewer cows to deliver the same yield of milk. This would compress and condense the industry so that there would be fewer milk producers with the consequent displacement of many traditional farmers from their work. It is, therefore, essential to consider schemes for the redeployment of these otherwise redundant individuals in parallel with the implementation of the high-efficiency cattle. The other is that it is likely that the milk and urine from the changed animals would contain larger concentrations of BST. This could have effects on the people who drink milk and water, so extensive testing of the hormone levels of local water supplies and milk products would be essential.

Transgenic fish also pose economic problems. The intensive farming of these animals requires the massive use of other non-commercial fish caught at sea. For example, the production of salmon in a fish farm takes five times their own weight of raw fish to bring the farmed fish to maturity. Through the intense demand for the salmon, the local natural stock of fish has been seriously depleted resulting in the installation of a quota system. This, in turn, has led to a decrease in the numbers of fishermen. The success of the genetically engineered salmon, as a desirable product with a high commercial value, has led to unemployment and deprivation in the local community. Perhaps there is a clear heuristic in this situation, in that some of the commercial success of the salmon fishery should be channelled into retraining with the establishment of new industries for those whose livelihoods have been affected. As a general principle this might take the form of using some of the benefits of the new gene technologies to reduce any material disbenefits which are a direct result of their application.

If there is less criticism of the ways in which the new engineering tools are applied to the animal kingdom, it may be because, as far as food is concerned, it is always possible to adopt a vegetarian ethic. The benefits which accrue from the efficient production of pharmaceuticals is not contested, while the attempts to develop food animals which are more in keeping with a fat-free, low-cholesterol and low-salt diet is again generally lauded. As the way we behave to animals may reflect the way we would behave to humans, we have generally been mindful of inflicting the minimum of pain and discomfort at any stage of the animal-rearing process. These attitudes carry over to our behaviour *vis à vis* the genetically modified varieties of animal.

The situation with humans

Humans are a special case. As we proceed along the time line of evolution, we come to humans as a recent development, and as a departure which has definable and unique properties. Some might say that such features extend to an ability to reason, laugh, use words and language for communication or live in societies and possess, in addition to our material being, something which is spiritual and outside the cause-and-effect system. Others would hold that a human is completely defined by the materials that constitute its being. This latter view precludes a spiritual dimension or the existence of a 'soul'. It is clear, however, that humans are only reproductively fertile when mating with other humans: this assigns us to our own species. We may also be different from all other living entities in that we alone have been able to master fire and use it for our benefit. This single capability has provided us with metals, energy, transportation systems,

electronic communications and many more of the panoply of materials and capabilities we enjoy. Although we, like the rest of the animal
kingdom, have dabbled with selective breeding to enhance the survivability of the species, humans have latterly acquired abilities
deliberately to achieve particular changes to the essence of their
nature. It is the ethical implications of this new-found power which is
the cause of much contemporary concern and is the subject matter of
this section.

The power tools of human change

Hierarchies are established by a process of competition using force
(physical and/or intellectual power) and/or display. The acquisition of
money or, more ostentatiously, jewels, cars, yachts, race horses and so
on, provides additional opportunities to make a hierarchical statement. It is common that, in human communities, mating is based on
hierarchical equivalence. This is a form of eugenics which is one of the
blunt tools which may be used in an attempt to improve the quality of
the species. As radio and television leads to the profusion of manners
and behaviours which become the fashion of the society the need for,
and power of, the previously strict hierarchical structure becomes
more difficult to maintain. Other and less acceptable eugenic techniques involve the restricted mating (or sterilization) of those who are
deemed socially subnormal.[34] The extension of these practices into
genocide, where whole communities are expunged, is an activity that
is condemned by all national and international agencies at this time.
Nevertheless, we have to recognize that genocide has been used both
historically and in the contemporary world by a dominating group
that seeks to achieve advantage. However, the clear message of the
Holocaust (1939–45) is that neither eugenics nor genocide can be
regarded as acceptable tools for the engineering of future human
societies.

Euthanasia (gentle or easy death) is a practice which is growing in
certain countries. Laws forbidding suicide have largely been revoked
in Western societies. Physician-assisted suicide is a contemporary
concern, for there are now many with strong voices in society who
would wish to end their lives with dignity and without experiencing a
protracted period of pain, discomfort and degradation. The practice
of infanticide, however, remains outlawed. But this does not mean
that it is not practised in some parts of the world. Reasons for infanticide range from a surfeit of children, or a preference for male as
opposed to female offspring, or vice versa. Sometimes efforts to

resuscitate a newborn which expresses incurable and debilitating disease are set aside.

A panoply of tools, which can be used to control fertility, has been developed recently. A listing of such tools would include

- *in vitro* fertilization
- the possibility of gamete selection for the choice of the sex of a child
- the examination of the genes of an embryo to determine whether it may have a gene which predisposes it to disease
- the ability to raise a child who had a birth weight of about half a kilogram or more
- legislation enabling abortion in many countries and states (but by no means all)
- the contraceptive pill and the condom
- current work leading to the development of a contraceptive vaccine which can be administered by mouth
- cloned humans
- ova made from combining the nucleus from one ovum with the anucleate cytoplasm of a second ovum.

These tools enable human populations to control their reproductive destiny with greater efficacy than has been possible before. But they afford other opportunities, such as a need for surrogate mothers, the prospects of selling fertilized embryos of known potential and the development of a system which can bring fertilized embryos to full-term babies in a totally artificial environment. This last activity is presently outlawed in many countries, but this does not mean that it is impractical or that such laws will remain on statute books indefinitely. In the developing world we are watching a decrease in the number of children born to fertile women while in the developed world women are having fewer children (as careers bite into the time available to raise children); older women are also bearing children. This means that the population projections of the 1960s[35] will be biased towards the high side and an impending catastrophe of over-population could well be averted. Recognizing that for humans to attempt to colonize other star systems would require voyages of thousands of years or more, it may be possible to avail ourselves of some of the above tools and populate the exploratory vehicles with fertilized embryos. These, kept at the temperature of space (2.3° Kelvin), might be expected to survive indefinitely, particularly if sufficiently well shielded from X-rays and other penetrating radiations. The revival of these embryos, their growth (in artificial wombs) into humans and their education would have to be effected by robots. The terraforming of planets and their subsequent colonization is a matter which is likely to occupy our minds in the near to middle-term future.

Knowledge of the sequence of bases in each of the approximately 30,000 to 140,000 genes of the human genome, coupled with new-found and developing capabilities to add, remove, modify or copy these genes *in situ*, means that humans can modify some of those aspects of their destiny which are genetically determined. It also means that we can know about ourselves in such a way that we can better appreciate our relationships with the other living beings of the biosphere and the story which describes our origins and subsequent development. Other consequences of our ability to read our genes is that we may be able to predict with high degrees of certainty our propensity to genetically determined diseases, our sexuality, our parentage, the human groups to whom we are most related (ethnicity) and the potential we might have to excel or disappoint in a wide variety of activities, sports or recreations.

There is a general agreement that the correction of genes whose expression leads to disease states is worthy. However, present laws require that such modifications should apply only to the somatic tissues of the individual with the defective genes and not to the gametes of that individual.[36] As we discover the genes, whose expression is partly or mainly responsible for such human characteristics as intelligence, height, athletic ability, musical ability, skin colour and muscularity, the use of genetic engineering to enhance these abilities or appearances of people becomes a matter of choice.[37]

Another tool, which is presently just over the horizon, is the prospect of an ability to clone human beings from the cells of mature individuals. It would not surprise people working in the field of *in vitro* fertilization and embryo development that it might be possible to use human embryonic cells to obtain a clone of the original ferti-lized ovum. The use of cells from mature animals, excised and grown in laboratory-scale cell cultures, may also be used in animal cloning experiments with a small but reasonable chance of success (*circa* 1 to 10%). What we are learning is that when the nucleus of a cell which has divided some fifty times is inserted into the cytoplasm of an anucleated ovum, the clock of the inserted nucleus is reset to time zero. The practical and ethical implications of this situation have yet to be explored fully. But these abilities, taken in conjunction with the genetic engineering tools we have and those which are still under development, will create a radical departure from the kind of evolutionary situation which has taken four billion years to go from the origin of life to humans.

While we may yet take full advantage of a pragmatic trial-and-error approach to the determination of the direction in which advantage might lie, the efficiency with which we might engage in this activity could be orders of magnitude greater than that of evolution by *natural* selection and variation. In this latter case, the grist of variation for use in the selection mill would have been generated by a series of seemingly random events as would the selection procedures. The substitution of haphazard events by changes which have been engineered and designed would accelerate the evolutionary processes many fold. So, having outlined many of the new ways in which humans may be engineered and shown that there are serious ethical issues which arise, it is appropriate that we examine how we may resolve a selection of the conundrums engendered by the alternative ways in which we might behave.

New tools, new ethics

Breaking with tradition is difficult. Even if our past ways of behaving result in outcomes with which we are less than pleased, we have a horror of the untried and a suspicion of the unknown. The code of Hammurabi (*c.*1700 BCE), the Bible and the teachings of those philosophers who ventured into the realm of ethics, from Aristotle onwards, have provided a rich resource from which people have chosen their guidelines for behaviour. But these authors could not have conceived of the power that has come into the hands of humans in the last century or so. It therefore becomes the duty of those who are prepared to take up the baton to examine the prospective uses of these new tools and to design a suite of ethics which will enable us to use them always with the intention of maximizing benefits and minimizing harms.

Whatever we do, we have to express care. This requires us to acknowledge that we are members of a community and that, while benefiting from the facilities that only a community can provide, we have to have a mind to the welfare of our fellow citizens. This means that we have to be open and above board and that we share our failures as well as our successes. It means that we have to be honest and disclose all we know in as unbiased a manner as possible, and that when we have conflicts of interest, we should say so, up front. We are also required to disclose the level of confidence we have in our assertions and the basis of that confidence. We cannot continue to proceed in a manner which is based on secrecy, on the maintenance of a state of conflict with adversaries, on duplicity and dissembling. The distrust which this engenders saps the basic strength of our communality. It creates mountains of paperwork, to assure taxpayers that they are getting value for their communal contributions and that people in commerce are adhering to the laws and ordinances that regulate the conduct of business. It spawns regulatory agencies and standards bureaux whose unwillingness to take risks on behalf of the community results in endless delays and costs reckoned in the hundreds of millions of dollars (US). Some might express their care by the adoption of an attitude of prudence. Inherent in this concept are the features of foresight, wisdom, sagacity and sound practical and political judgement. Others would want to stress the need to make practical progress by adopting a pragmatic approach to ethics.

At the turn of this century there was considerable philosophical activity in the USA which focused on the term 'pragmatism'. This was derived from the Greek πραγμα (*pragma*), meaning 'thing', 'matter', 'business', as opposed to πραχτιχζ (*practicos*), which means 'practical', 'empirical' or 'quack'. The then negative connotations of the practical were sufficient to give more prominence to the similarly firm foundation of a reality based on 'things'. (Where in this case 'things' means businesses or matters involving deeds.) Indeed the pragmatists C.S. Pierce and W. James were driven to come to some sense of what 'truth', as opposed to appearances, is. They concluded that notions of truth are to be approached from the standpoint of whether it made any practical difference, or was of any positive value, to hold to one or other version of what may be held to be true. In many ways it would seem that they hijacked the connotations of πραχτιχζ and associated them with the word pragmatism. However, they were probably misguided in so ardently seeking to come to a definition of truth and would not have been quite so keen were they to have been aware of later developments in sensory perception and/or of quantum mechanical considerations.

Knowledge of the truth is unattainable. Socrates (470–399 BCE) realized this, as have most philosophers since. All our concepts of reality are derived from the data from our sense organs. If these are delivered in digital form, the numbers have been massaged by whatever electronics have been used in the process of number generation. Sense data are necessarily unique to the person, are never 100% perfect and are limited by our sensitivity to wavelengths, frequencies and molecular stimuli (for smell and taste); we even have a limited range of sensitivities to pressure and temperature. So the reality we sense is at best both partial and distorted to some, if only minor, degree (see also my discussion on the nature of science in the first chapter). Further, we cannot know everything, as there is a necessary 'injury' to the system when it is under observation (Heisenberg's uncertainty principle). Moreover, quantum theorists have used the concept of an unknown random event to posit the existence of multiple superposable universes. To give substance to this contention they quote the thought experiment which is called the case of Schrödinger's cat (E. Schrödinger 1887–1961). This requires us to imagine a box in which there is placed a living cat and a device which responds to an external random event by killing the cat. As the killing event is random we cannot predict it or know when it happens. So to our present knowledge the cat in the box may be alive or dead; or both alive and dead; hence the coexistence of superposable universes; a concept I find untenable. So our concepts of the objective world are necessarily flawed and subjective. This does not render them of less value to us, we merely have to be on guard lest we become so suffused with hubris as to believe with 100% certainty that our concepts are factual, truthful and that we can prove that observed phenomena are linked by particular causal relationships.

A further aspect of pragmatism involves the experimental or empirical method of trial and error to arrive at a view of reality or, more importantly, a sense of direction in which one might proceed to achieve a result which is of utility or value to society. This method requires that one learns from what has been done by generating theories, generalizations or rules. These rationalizations may help design the next and more effective experiment. The empirical does not exclude the rational; indeed, rationality is an essential part of empiricism. This approach may be termed 'rational empiricism' or 'refined empiricism' to distinguish it from the blunt trial-and-error type of approach which may be designated 'basic empiricism'. But to chase the 'rational' without a firm foundation in observation and experimentation begins a journey into Cloud-cuckoo-land, where anything that can be logically derived from its premises goes. Sometimes this is heuristic; most times it is wasteful.

Perhaps it is because we have been led into chasing the 'purely rational' for too long that we have become embedded in a mire of conjectured or theoretical risk and disaster, which has been applied to the area of genetic modification of living organisms. By adopting this new approach, we may well take advantage of the groundwork which has already been done by the pragmatists. This requires that we engage a cautious, careful, open and empirical approach to the process of discovering how to obtain most effectively the benefits from the new tools which have recently become available to us.

Notes

1 *The Khoran and Tales from the Thousand and One Nights* (1968 [*c.*850 CE]), London: Penguin Books.
2 Asmodeus (Ashmedai) (1916) *The Jewish Encyclopedia*, vol. 2, New York: Funk and Wagnalls Company, pp. 217–20.
3 D.J. Kelves (1986) *In The Name of Eugenics*, Berkeley and Los Angeles: University of California Press, p. 426; P. Weingart (1989) *German Eugenics between Science and Politics*, Osiris, 2nd series, vol. 5, pp. 260–82; A.D. Smith and M. Zaremba (1997) 'Outcasts from Nordic super-race', *The Observer*, 24 August, p. 6.
4 L.M. Silver (1998) *Remaking Eden*, London: Weidenfeld and Nicolson, p. 317.
5 J. Dewey (1938) 'Experience and education', in M.J. Adler (ed.) *Great Books of the Western World*, London: Encyclopaedia Britannica Inc., vol. 55, pp. 99–134.
6 Hippocrates (1923) *The Oath*; translated by W.H.S. Jones, The Loeb Classical Library, vol. 1, London: William Heinemann, pp. 289–301.
7 T.L. Beauchamp and J.F. Childress (1994) *Principles of Biomedical Ethics*, Oxford: Oxford University Press, p. 546.
8 H.G. Mittenburger (ed.) (1980) *Safety Aspects of Baculoviruses as Biological Insecticides*, Bonn: Bundministerium für Forschung and Technologie.
9 J.S. Cory, M.L. Hirst, T. Williams, R.S. Halls, G. Goulson, B.M. Green, T.M. Carty, R.D. Possee, P.J. Cayley and D.H.L. Bishop (1994) 'Field trial of a genetically improved baculovirus insecticide', *Nature*, vol. 370, pp. 138–40.
10 M. Williamson (1996) *Biological Invasions*, London: Chapman and Hall, p. 244.
11 HRH the Prince of Wales (1998) 'Seeds of disaster', *The Daily Telegraph*, 8 June, p. 16.
12 UNICEF (1996) *The State of the World's Children*, Oxford: Oxford University Press, p. 99.
13 R.E. Spier (1989) 'Ethical problem?: get a technical fix', *Vaccine*, vol. 7, pp. 381–2.
14 R.E. Spier (1998) 'Ethical aspects of vaccines and vaccination', *Vaccine*, vol. 16, pp. 1788–94.
15 G.H. Wilson (1967) *The Hazards of Immunisation*, London: The Athlone Press, p. 52.
16 Editorial (1998) 'Birth control for alley cats', *Nature Biotech*, vol. 16, p. 315.
17 E. Geissler (ed.) (1986) *Biological and Toxin Weapons Today*, Sipri: Oxford University Press, pp. 7 ff.
18 UNICEF, *The State of the World's Children*.
19 N. Rufford (1998) 'The West's secret weapon to win the opium war', *The Sunday Times*, 28 June, section 1, p. 13.

157

20 I. Brodie (1998) 'US to guard public from germ attack', *The Times*, 27 May, p. 17.
21 Nuffield Council on Bioethics (1999) *Genetically Modified Crops: The Ethical and Social Issues*, London: Nuffield Council on Bioethics, p. 164.
22 D. Robertson (1998) 'Monsanto bypasses Mycogen with Bt synthetic genes', *Nature Biotech*, vol. 16, p. 230.
23 W.H. McGaughey, F. Gould and W. Gelernter (1998) 'Bt resistance management', *Nature Biotech*, vol. 16, pp. 144–6.
24 K. Dalsgaard, A. Uttenthal, T.D. Jones, F. Xu, A. Merryweather, W.D.O. Hamilton, J.P.M. Langeveld, R.S. Boshuizen, S. Kamstrup, G.P. Lomonossoff, C. Porta, C. Vela, J.I. Casal, R.H. Meloen and P.B. Rogers (1997) 'Plant-derived vaccine protects target animals against a viral disease', *Nature Biotech*, vol. 15, pp. 248–52. See also T. Arakawa, D.K.X. Chong and W.H.R. Langridge (1998) 'Efficacy of a food plant-based oral cholera toxin B subunit vaccine', *Nature Biotech*, vol. 16, pp. 292–7.
25 L.P.M. Lloyd-Evans (1995) *Science and Engineering Ethics*, vol. 1, pp. 93–6.
26 E. Perrenboom (1998) 'German Greens attenuate their genetic resistance', *Nature Biotech*, vol. 16, p. 130.
27 R.A. Kerr (1994) 'Who profits from ecological disaster?' *Science*, vol. 266, pp. 28–30.
28 A.M. Timmons, Y.M. Charters, J.W. Crawford, D. Burn, S.E. Scott, S.J. Dubbels, N.J. Wilson, A. Robertson, E.T. O'Brien, G.R. Squire and M.J. Wilkinson (1996) 'Risks from transgenic crops', *Nature*, vol. 380, p. 487.
29 I. Wilmut, A.E. Schnieke, J. McWhir, A.J. Kind and K.H.S. Campbell (1997) 'Viable offspring derived from fetal and adult mammalian cells', *Nature*, vol. 385, pp. 810–13.
30 Genesis 1: 26, 28.
31 *Encyclopaedia Britannica* (1998) CD ROM version.
32 Nuffield Council on Bioethics (1996) *Animal-to-Human Transplant: The Ethics of Xenotransplantation*, London: Nuffield Council on p. 146.
33 J.B. Cibelli, S.L. Stice, P.J. Golueke, J.J. Kane, J. Jerry, C. Blackwell, F.A. Ponce de Léon and J.M. Robl (1998) 'Cloned transgenic calves produced from nonquiescent foetal fibroblasts', *Science*, vol. 280, pp. 1256–8.
34 Ibid., n. 3.
35 D.H. Meadows, D.L. Meadows, J. Randers and W.W. Behrens III (1972) *The Limits to Growth*, New York: Signet, p. 207.
36 J.L. Fox (1998) 'Germline gene therapy contemplated', *Nature Biotech*, vol. 16, p. 407.
37 Ibid., n. 4.

8

COMPUTERS AND SOCIETY

Simon Rogerson

Introduction

Advances in computer technology, coupled with the growing convergence of computing, telecommunications and mass media, present many opportunities and dangers to individuals, organizations and society as a whole. Computers can be shaped to do any activity that can be described in terms of inputs, transforming processes and outputs. It is the nearest thing to a universal tool (Moor 1985). Consequently, society and its organizations are becoming more dependent upon computer technology. There is an increasingly wider access to, and wider application of, this powerful resource. Those responsible for the development and application of computer technology are faced with decisions of increasing complexity which are accompanied by many ethical dilemmas. Moor (1985) and Maner (1996) explain that computer technology is a special and unique technology, hence the associated ethical issues warrant special attention. Indeed, Tucker (1991) points out that there is a need to understand the basic cultural, social, legal and ethical issues inherent in the discipline of computing. Furthermore, Gotterbarn (1992) suggests that professionals must be aware of their professional responsibilities, have available methods for resolving non-technical ethics questions and develop proactive skills to reduce the likelihood of ethical problems occurring.

The nature of computer ethics

The field of computer ethics is evolving and has been defined in different ways. Walter Maner, who coined the term 'computer ethics' in the mid-1970s, defines computer ethics as representing a new field of applied professional ethics dealing with problems aggravated, transformed or created by computer technology. Deborah Johnson (1985) defines computer ethics as being the study of the way in which computers present new versions of standard moral problems and dilemmas, causing existing standard moral norms to be used in new and novel ways in an attempt to resolve these issues. James Moor (1985) defines computer ethics as the analysis of the nature and social impact of computer technology and the corresponding formulation and justification of policies for the ethical use of such technology. He suggests that it addresses policy vacuums and conceptual muddles brought about by the advancing technology. Finally, Terrell Ward Bynum (1997a) suggests that the overall goal of computer ethics is to integrate computing technology and human values in such a way that the technology advances and protects human values, rather than doing damage to them.

The mid-1990s has heralded the beginning of second generation computer ethics. The time has come to build upon and elaborate the conceptual foundation while, in parallel, developing the frameworks within which practical action can occur, thus reducing the probability of unforeseen effects of computer technology application. It is a multi-disciplinary generation drawing on philosophy, sociology, psychology, computer science, information systems, law and others.

Privacy

Privacy is a fundamental right of individuals and is an essential condition for the exercise of self-determination. The ability to control personal information is an important factor in sustaining privacy. Organizations are increasingly computerizing the processing of personal information. This may be without the consent or knowledge of the individuals concerned. There has been a growth in databases holding personal and other sensitive information in multiple formats of text, pictures and sound. The scale and type of data collected and the scale and speed of data exchange have changed with the advent of computers. The potential to breach people's privacy at less cost and to greater advantage continues to increase.

However, sometimes individuals have to give up some of their personal privacy in order to achieve some overall social benefit. For example, a social services department might hold sensitive information about individuals that provides an accurate profile of individual tendencies, convictions and so on. The sharing of this data with, for example, the local education authority in cases of child sex offenders living in the area might be considered morally justified even though it might breach individual privacy.

Computer privacy is a new twist on an old ethical problem and involves issues which have not been previously raised or cannot be predicted. For example, advances in genetic data have led to some interesting ethical questions as it can accurately define genetic relatives and thus establish hereditary traits and diseases. Individuals have certain rights to how and where that information is distributed but in order to exercise those rights they will undoubtedly learn of their genetic profiles – and that is the new twist. Knowledge of one's genetic profile will undoubtedly affect the individual's self-perception, self-esteem and lifestyle. Thus privacy in this situation must also include an individual's right not to know.

Balancing the rights and interests of different parties in a free society is difficult. The acceptable balance will be specific to the context of a particular relationship and will be dependent upon trust between concerned parties and subscription to the principle of informed consent. This balance might incur the problem of protecting individual privacy while satisfying government and business needs. Such problems are indicative of a society that is becoming increasingly technologically dependent.

Industry and commerce

Within industry and commerce privacy continues to be an important issue and one which regularly presents tensions between competing obligations. There are two important types of privacy: consumer privacy and employee privacy (Spinello 1995). At one level privacy is about corporate ethos and how individual rights are valued. This leads to the level of consideration of what protection should be in place. This in turn leads to a lower level, which is concerned with the tools that might be used to manage privacy such as encryption, codes of practice and role definitions for staff.

Consumer privacy covers the information compiled by such data collectors as marketing firms, insurance companies and retailers, the use of credit information collected by credit agencies; and the rights of the consumers to control information about themselves and their commercial transactions. Indeed, the extensive sharing of personal data is an erosion of privacy that reduces the capacity of individuals to retain control of factors which may affect their lives. Organizations involved in such activities have a responsibility to ensure privacy rights are upheld. Consumer privacy focuses on the commercial relationship. Expanding this concept to client privacy includes consideration of non-commercial relationships where privacy is equally important. For example, medical, penal and welfare relationships have, without doubt, serious privacy relationships. According to Spinello the issues that need to be addressed regarding the transfer of consumer data (and client data) include

- the potential for data to be sold to unscrupulous vendors
- problems with ensuring the trustworthiness and level of care of data collectors
- the potential for combining data in new and novel ways to create detailed composite profiles of individuals or categories of people
- the difficulty of correcting inaccurate information once it has been distributed across many different files.

Employee privacy deals primarily with the growing reliance on electronic monitoring and other mechanisms to analyse work habits and measure employee performance and productivity. These practices can affect an employee's right to control or limit access to personal information provided to an employer, the right to choose what he or she does outside the workplace, the right to privacy of thought and the right to autonomy and freedom of expression. In the modern workplace there are increasing opportunities to monitor activity. It is important to ensure the use of monitoring facilities does not violate the privacy rights of employees. Some of the potential problem areas are

- network-management programs on personal computers that allow user files and directories to be monitored and to track what is being typed on individual computer screens
- network management systems that enable interception and scrutiny of communications among different offices and between remote locations
- email systems that generate archives of messages that can be inspected by anyone with the authority or technical ability to do so
- broad-based electronic monitoring programs that track worker productivity and work habits
- closed-circuit television surveillance systems that are computer controlled, have extensive archiving facilities and digital matching facilities.

Privacy legislation

Privacy legislation is not universal and is influenced by political, economic and cultural factors. Where it exists in some countries it can be ineffective. This is because the legislative time frame is always much slower that the technological. Furthermore, given that communities are becoming increasingly free of geographical and temporal constraints, the viability of privacy legislation is questionable. Resolution of privacy problems is thus heavily reliant upon organizations fulfilling their obligations as a supplier, as a client, as an end user of the technology and as a community member, as well as upon their being committed to self-regulation.

In the UK the Data Protection Act 1998 (DPA98) came into force on 1 March 2000. It sets rules for processing personal information and applies to some paper records as well as those held on computers. DPA98 is enforced by the Office of the Information Commissioner, which is also responsible for freedom of information. DPA98 provides a model for legislation and its principles provide a foundation for a framework that can be used to address the issue of privacy, develop a reasonable privacy policy and ensure that computer technology usage is sensitive to privacy concerns. The following extracts from a publication of the Office of the Information Commissioner (2000) provides some detail for this framework.

The rules of good information handling –
the principles

Anyone processing personal data must comply with the eight enforceable principles of good practice. They say that data must be:

- fairly and lawfully processed
- processed for limited purposes and not in any manner incompatible with those purposes
- adequate, relevant and not excessive
- accurate
- not kept for longer than is necessary
- processed in line with the data subject's rights
- secure
- not transferred to countries without adequate protection.

Personal data cover both facts and opinions about the individual. They also include information regarding the intentions of the data controller towards the individual.

Processing personal data

Processing may only be carried out where one of the following conditions has been met:

- the individual has given his or her consent to the processing
- the processing is necessary for the performance of a contract with the individual
- the processing is required under a legal obligation
- the processing is necessary to protect the vital interests of the individual
- the processing is necessary to carry out public functions
- the processing is necessary in order to pursue the legitimate interests of the data controller or third parties (unless it could prejudice the interests of the individual).

Processing sensitive data

Sensitive data include: racial or ethnic origin; political opinions; religious or other beliefs; trade union membership; health; sex life; criminal proceedings or convictions. Sensitive data can only be processed under strict conditions, which include:

- having the explicit consent of the individual
- being required by law to process the data for employment purposes
- needing to process the information in order to protect the vital interests of the data subject or another
- dealing with the administration of justice or legal proceedings.

The virtual society

The development of an expanding set of international information networks, known as the Internet, has been one of the most influential applications of computers and telecommunications. This phenomenon has led to an enormous growth in people being connected to the Internet. In 1991 there were eight million, growing to twenty million in 1995. By December 2000 this had risen to nearly 400 million people and it is estimated that this will grow to 775 million by 2003. It has evolved from a closed world of specialists and experts to a common and commercial universe open to the general public. The networks of the virtual society offer exceptional possibilities for exchanging information and acquiring knowledge, and provide new opportunities for growth and job creation. However, at the same time, they conceal risks to human rights and alter the infrastructure of traditional public and private operations. Johnson (1997) explains that the potential benefit of the Internet is being devalued by antisocial behaviour, including unauthorized access, theft of electronic property, launching of viruses, racism and harassment. These have raised new ethical, cultural, economic and legal questions which have led many to consider the feasibility and desirability of regulation in this area. Similarly, it is questionable whether counter-measures will be very effective either. The absence of effective formal legal or technological controls presents grave dangers to the virtual society.

The international aspect of the Internet, the transient nature of the content and the rapid evolution of the techniques and strategies raise specific difficulties for the application of penal and commercial law. It is extremely difficult to determine which laws apply, who is responsible and what proof is required in the event of a transgression. It is probably impossible to create international law that can provide legal guarantees for this global community. This would require agreement on universal rights and wrongs which may well be possible for obvious cases such as the dissemination of child pornography but is very difficult for debatable issues such as individual privacy and intellectual property.

The virtual home

The home will be the physical location of the virtual society. Many of the organizations with which people interact have used computer technology to provide new forms of interaction that can take place from the home. Working, studying, shopping and banking can all now be done from the home. According to Venkatesh (1996), in the 1980s employment, children's games and word-processing were already accessible from home and the 1990s has seen a significant expansion of computer technology application in the home. This includes child and adult education, family communication and correspondence, news coverage, travel bookings, medical services, home banking, retail purchasing and household management. It is clear that this application will continue to expand and will create a critical mass that will sustain the virtual society.

Virtual behaviour

Johnson (1997) suggests that there are three general ethical principles that promote acceptable behaviour in the virtual society:

- know the rules of the online forums being used and adhere to them
- respect the privacy and property rights of others and if in doubt assume both are expected
- do not deceive, defame or harass others.

The outcome of not subscribing to such principles is likely to result in chaos overwhelming democratic dialogue, absolute freedom overwhelming responsibility and accountability, and emotions triumphing over reason (Badaracco and Useem 1997). For organizations operating in the virtual society these principles can be expanded into a number of explicit actions:

- Establish an electronic mail policy that forbids forgery of electronic mail messages, tampering with the email of other users, sending harassing, obscene or other threatening email and sending unsolicited junk mail and chain letters.
- Clarify the responsibilities of those involved in providing information. The publisher is the producer of the online information and is, in the main, responsible for that information. The producer therefore must be identifiable at all times. It is arguable that people can only be held responsible for things they can control. Access providers take this line, refuting responsibility for the wrongdoings of users, because their contribution as access providers is purely technical.
- Develop international cooperation that will encourage the creation of common descriptions for Internet services, encourage transparency (which would benefit users) and respect for trademarks, and will increase the possibility of global access to the Internet on demand.
- Encourage the development of legitimate electronic commerce that upholds consumer protection through the use of standard contracts and technical mechanisms. Many issues need to be

166

taken into account, including the validity of the electronic signa-ture, the solvency of the purchaser, the legitimacy of the vendor, the security of the transaction and the payment of appropriate sales taxes.

- Establish a body for handling customer complaints and review-ing Internet activity of the organization. This body would be in contact with public and private international groups that are competent in Internet affairs.
- Train employees in ethical Internet practice and promote Internet awareness within the wider community.
- Promote a greater equality of access to the Internet through multilingual and multicultural support. This counters the current situation where the Internet is an Anglo-Saxon network with 80% of servers being North American and 90% of exchanges taking place in English.

Such actions provide a means for self-regulation that would combat the regulatory flux surrounding the Internet and might lead to effec-tive policies regarding transparency, responsibility and respect for appropriate legal frameworks.

The nature of work

With the advent of computers there has been a shift from tradition-ally stable organizational structures towards more flexible working arrangements. New computer-enabled working practices are creating more dynamic structures that are highly flexible and capable of responding to environmental uncertainty. For example, with the advances in telecommunications and information systems many jobs can be redefined as telework, which involves working remotely via a computer link. There are right and wrong ways to organize telework but, if handled properly, industry can gain through reduced operating costs; society can gain through reduced levels of road traffic and strengthened local communities; workers can gain through not having to pay the financial and physical prices of commuting; workers' families can gain by not having to move to different towns frequently; disabled people can gain new access to work; and parents can combine work and childcare in new, more flexible ways. The potential problems must not be ignored. For example, teleworking might result in the breakup of social groups in the workplace and the disenfranchisement of those without the resources to participate, both of which could lead to increased stress for individual workers.

Teleworking scope

The impact of computer-enabled work will continue to grow. Work that is capable of being transformed into computer-enabled work must have a low manual labour content, be undertaken by individuals rather than teams, require minimal supervision, be easily measurable and not depend upon expensive or large equipment. The range of workers that can be transformed into teleworkers is large and includes professional and management specialists such as financial analysts, accountants, public relations staff, graphic designers, translators and general managers; information technology specialists such as software programmers and systems engineers; support workers such as bookkeepers, proofreaders, draughtsmen, researchers, data-entry staff, telesales staff and word-processor operators.

There are yet further applications of telework possible with recent technological developments. Professions that are now thought of as being 'hands-on' can increasingly be conducted 'down the line'. For example, surgeons have conducted operations by remotely controlling robotic tools in a hospital hundreds of miles away. Equally, banking, once thought to involve large numbers of staff sitting in local branches, is increasingly being conducted by telephone rather than by face-to-face contact.

Ethical dilemmas

With imagination, huge numbers of jobs could be transformed into telework. However, this change in work practice raises many ethical dilemmas and as computers evolve so the dilemmas change. The following list illustrates some of the dilemmas that can arise:

- The ability to employ people and sell goods and services globally through technological support may result in localized areas comprising people who have redundant or over-priced work skills and people who cannot afford the goods and services produced. Has an employer a responsibility to the local community to ensure such situations do not arise or are minimized?
- Is it right to exploit low labour costs in the economically poor areas of the world, ignoring the injustice of wage differentials and an employer's responsibility to the community in which its employees live?
- Given the access to a global workforce and an increased need for flexibility to respond to the dynamic needs of the marketplace

then the permanency of jobs and job content is likely to change. Is this acceptable to individuals and how might organizations support individuals in coping with this often stressful situation?

- Computer-enabled communication only supports some of the elements of human communication. The loss of non-verbal communication or body language and the creation of electronic personalities could have an impact on the way people interact. Will this have a detrimental effect on individuals and the way they work?

- The workplace provides an area for social interaction at many levels. Individuals cherish this interaction. Commuting provides psychological space that separates work from home which is important to some people. The move to teleworking radically changes this situation, potentially causing social isolation and disruption in home life. How can organizations safeguard individuals when adopting teleworking?

Information: the new lifeblood

Information is the new lifeblood of society and its organizations, and our dependence grows daily with the advance of computer technology and its global application. Information empowers those who have it, but it also disenfranchises those who do not. Wealth and power flow to the 'information-rich', those who create and use computing technologies successfully. They are primarily well-educated citizens of industrialized nations. The 'information-poor' – both in industrialized countries and in the developing world – are falling further and further behind.

Information is essential for organizations to make effective decisions. It is used to identify situations where decisions must be made. It can help search for and generate choices, and provide insight into the possible outcomes and effects of selecting a particular alternative. It is through information that results of decision-making are communicated to others. It is through information that decision-makers gain knowledge which can then be used in both current and decision-making. Information has thus grown to become one of the most valuable assets of an organization.

Information properties

There are several important properties of information that will influence the actions of information providers. Failure to consider these properties and ensure integrity of provision is wrong as such inaction could lead to organizational loss and individual stress. These properties are summarized as follows:

- Information must be presented in a concise and clear form. The addition of unimportant issues may distract the recipient's focus of attention on the salient aspects. The language used to convey the information may also hinder the recipient's comprehension of the important issues.
- Information must be communicated at the right time. There is no point in conveying issues relating to a decision a day later than when the decision was made, if the message was solely meant to aid the decision-making process. Too much information at the same time can also be detrimental, resulting in information overload.
- Information must be relevant to the recipient. An irrelevant message is of no value and is simply unwanted data.
- Information must be accurate and complete. Information that is inaccurate or incomplete can be worse than no information at all, as erroneous decisions may be made on the basis of that information.

Responsibility for information provision

The provision of the majority of information is likely to use computer-based information systems. The integrity of information relies upon the development and operation of these systems. For example, effective and appropriate data validation and verification must be used during input, processing and output. With the advent of data-matching systems, care must be taken not to use statistical models that draw dubious conclusions. Responsibility for these activities is a complex issue. In cases of large information systems no single individual can fully understand or be held responsible for the whole system. It often turns out that the organization and several individuals within the organization have a shared responsibility.

It is important to understand the nature of responsibility. A person has a duty by virtue of his or her role within the organization and is responsible for undertaking or failing to undertake something which causes something else to happen. Blame is attributed when this outcome is wrong or harmful and might lead to legal liability. Issues of specific responsibility often include several of these concepts. For example, a computer programmer knowingly reduced the testing procedure for a program in order to meet a deadline by not using the test data that was supplied for rare cases. This resulted in a major failure in operation several months after implementation. In this situation the programmer was to blame because the failure to complete the specified testing had caused the program to malfunction and the programmer had a duty to undertake adequate testing as part of his or her professional responsibilities. In this circumstance the programmer may be found legally liable.

Organizations should develop conventions and expectations that assign responsibilities for activities in which computers play a role in information provision. Individuals must be aware of their responsibilities regarding the authenticity, fidelity and accuracy of data and information. They should be encouraged to accept these as part of their responsibilities to society.

Computer misuse

As computers become more widely used, the risk of misuse increases and the impacts of such acts are likely to be greater. For example, in the UK there was a threefold increase in the number of computer misuse incidents reported in 1993 compared with 1990, with virus infection, fraud and illicit software accounting for 40% of the total incidents. Computer misuse covers a wide spectrum of activity summarized as follows (Audit Commission 1994):

- fraud through unauthorized data input or alteration of data input, destruction, suppression or misappropriation of output from a computer process, alteration of computerized data and alteration or misuse of programs but excluding virus infections
- theft of data and software
- use of illicit – unlicensed and pirated – software
- using computer facilities for unauthorized private personal work
- invasion of privacy through unauthorized disclosure of personal data and breaches of associated legislation, and disclosure of proprietary information
- hacking – deliberately gaining unauthorized access to computer systems, usually through the use of telecommunication facilities
- sabotage – interfering with computer processes by causing deliberate damage to the processing cycle or to the equipment
- computer virus infections – distributing programs with the intention of corrupting a computer process.

Spinello (1995) argues that organizations and individuals are ethically obliged to protect the systems and information entrusted to their care and must strive to prevent or minimize the impact of computer misuse incidents. He suggests that those stakeholders at greatest risk from a computer misuse incident might be party to decisions made concerning security arrangements. He argues that computer misuse offences should not be treated lightly, even if the detrimental outcome is negligible, because, at the very least, valuable resources will have been squandered and property rights violated. Spinello also points out that a balance has to be struck regarding stringent security measures and respect for civil liberties. There is a dual responsibility regarding computer misuse. Organizations have a duty to minimize the temptation of perpetrating computer misuse while individuals have a responsibility to resist such temptations.

Intellectual property

Intellectual property rights (IPR) related to software raise complex and contentious issues. Society has long recognized that taking or using property without permission is wrong. This extends not only to physical property but also to ideas. IPR is difficult to assign and protect, and requires careful deliberation. It is generally accepted that software is a kind of intellectual property and that to copy it or use it without the owner's permission is unethical and often illegal. There are, however, those who argue that software ownership should not be allowed and that software should be freely available for copying (Stallman 1992).

Copyright and patents

In the UK, the law recognizes that computer software deserves protection and the principal instrument of protection is copyright. Under current legislation a computer program is classified as a 'literary work' and can be copyrighted if it is an entity that 'exhibits originality, qualification and ownership'. Copyright ownership relates to several aspects of software. One can own the 'source code' of a computer program, the 'object code' of a program and the 'look and feel' of the computer program's interface (Bynum 1997a).

A further aspect that can be owned is the 'algorithm' which is the sequence of commands that the source and object code represents. The ownership of the algorithm patent is highly contentious as it enables the owner to deny use of the mathematical formulae that are part of the algorithm. The contention is that this effectively removes parts of mathematics from the public domain, places unjust 'patent-search' burdens on program developers and results in the stifling of competition and in decreasing software variety (Bynum 1997a). In the UK, patent legislation explicitly excludes the granting of a patent for a computer program. However, an invention that is more than just a program may be patented so long as it satisfies the other require-ments of patent law, namely it shows it is novel, an inventive step forward and capable of being applied in industry. Thus computer-related inventions such as program-controlled machines can be patented.

Ownership

Ownership might not be clear. Johnson (1994) argues that a con-sequentialist framework is best for analysing software IPR because it puts the focus on deciding ownership in terms of affecting continued creativity and development of software. Software may be developed by a number of people, each making a contribution. Individuals might have difficulty determining which elements belong to them and to what degree they can claim ownership. Individuals may be employ-ees or contractors. The development of software on behalf of a client raises fundamental IPR issues. It is important that agreement con-cerning the ownership of IPR is reached at the outset before any development commences.

If an organization or group of individuals invests time, money and effort in creating a piece of software it should be entitled to own the result by virtue of this effort and be given the opportunity to reap an economic reward. For the sake of fairness and equity and to reward initiative and application, one should have the right to retain control over intellectual property and to sell or license the product. However, the extent of these rights is debatable. Parker, Swope and Baker (1990) explain that there is a responsibility to distribute software that is fit for the purpose and so the owner does not have the right to dis-tribute software that is known to be defective and that has not been thoroughly tested. Software embodies ideas and knowledge that can often benefit society as a whole. To have unrestricted rights may curtail technological evolution and diffusion, which might disadvan-tage society. Some reasonable limit must be placed on the IPR so an equitable balance is struck. For example, current copyright legislation in the USA protects the expression of an idea and not the idea itself.

This constraint appears to achieve a balance between the right to private property and the common good.

While there is reasonable agreement in countries of the West that individuals or groups of individuals have intellectual property rights, interpretations in other countries and situations are sometimes different. For example, IPR safeguards in countries of the Far East are minimal, mainly due to a different philosophy that tends to treat intellectual property as communal or social property. In the poorer developing countries the view often taken is that the right to livelihood takes precedence over other claims on which IPR are based. It is only when prosperity increases that there is shift from a social well-being interpretation of IPR to one with more emphasis on the individual.

IPR is a complex and contentious issue in the computing field. Where software contains ideas and knowledge that can benefit society as a whole, clashes can occur between the owner, who has the right to exploit the product commercially, and society, which has a general right to access it and benefit from it. An equitable balance must be found that takes into account these competing rights. From an ethical perspective there are two fundamental questions that summarize this debate and that need to be answered regarding software. Who owns the software? Who has the right to modify, distribute or use it?

Developing information systems

Developing computer-based information systems (IS) is frequently a complicated process involving many people from different functional areas. There are many operational decisions to be taken during this extended activity. As well as economic and technological considerations, which are usually covered, there are ethical and social issues that need to be taken into account – these are often overlooked.

It is best to undertake the complex development process of IS using a 'project team' approach. Effective project management is a vital ingredient in achieving a successful outcome. The objectives for the project need to be agreed at the outset. In deciding the objectives their implications need to be considered, in terms of the actual outputs:

*   What will happen to them and how will they be distributed?
*   How will they be kept secure if they are sensitive?
*   Who will use them?
*   Who will have access to them, for monitoring purposes?
*   Who will be affected by them?

The project team should be well briefed on these issues and have the opportunity to debate them fully to establish its own conclusions. It should consider all the implications, including ethical implications. It may need to call on resources from inside and outside the organization. To confine the discussions within close boundaries, in an attempt to save money and time, is misguided at best and catastrophic at worst. Broader issues will inevitably arise during the course of the project. If the team members are unprepared, they will lack direction and perform poorly. The sponsor of the project therefore needs the vision and the authority to ensure that the project team is supported and coached to consider everything, including the related ethical and social issues.

Within computing there are numerous activities and decisions to be made and many of these will have an ethical dimension. It is impractical to consider each minute issue in great detail and still hope to achieve the overall goal. The focus must be on the ethical hot spots because they are likely to influence the success of the particular information systems activity and promote ethical sensitivity in a broader context. The scope of consideration is an ethical hot spot and is influenced by the identification and involvement of stakeholders, both of which are often difficult to achieve (Rogerson 1997). There is empirical evidence to suggest that the perception of what should be considered in IS projects is very narrow, whether it concerns the possible scope and level of use of the system or the range of people who could or should be involved. Indeed, with the exception of hardware and software suppliers, all stakeholders involved are within the organizations and in close proximity to the projects (Farbey, Land and Targett 1993). Such restricted stakeholder involvement reduces the likelihood that all relevant ethical issues are properly considered.

Appropriate people from the whole range of stakeholder groups should be consulted. Participation by owners and employees is obvious but it may be desirable for other groups to take part in particular situations. For example, if a manufacturing company wishes to improve links with suppliers and customers, then it would make sense to involve representatives from both groups. Similarly, if an organization wished to form a strategic alliance with a competitor in an attempt to increase market share through synergy, then participation by that competitor would be essential. The drive for efficiency gains through applying IT by a large local employer could mean a reduction in the workforce or employing a different workforce group. In such circumstances the involvement of unions and relevant community groups is probably desirable.

The widespread use of, and dependence upon, IS within organizations and society affects the lives of most individuals. The project management process must consider, from the start, the views and concerns of all affected parties, showing the principles of due care, fairness and social cost. Concerns over, for example, deskilling of jobs, redundancy and the breakup of social groupings can be then aired at the earliest opportunity. Fears can be allayed and project goals adjusted if necessary. Another ethical hot spot is to do with informing the client (Rogerson 1997). No one likes unpleasant surprises, so early warning of a problem and an indication of its scale are important. The key is to provide factual information in non-emotive words so the client and project manager can discuss any necessary changes in a calm and professional manner. The adoption of the principles of honesty, objectivity, due care and fairness helps to ensure a good working relationship with the client. Failure to adopt such approaches might harm an organization's reputation and market credibility, cause problems to the morale of internal staff and damage relationships with business partners.

There are numerous methods for developing IS. Many deal inadequately with the ethical dimensions of the development process, tending to stress instead the formal and technical aspects. During the process of development, managers and the project team must consider the consequences that implementing the system has for people, society and the organization, because these affect the attitudes of the users and the success of the system. These broader issues are summarized as (Wood-Harper *et al.* 1996):

- Whose basic values will influence the study of the situation and the development of the IS and are these acceptable to all stakeholders?
- How will ethical considerations be included?
- Which methodology should be used?
- What approach should be used if there are conflicts of interest?

IS developers should adopt the principles of objectivity, due care, fairness and consideration of social cost and benefit, and in particular they should

- include the social design of computerized systems and work settings in the overall systems development project
- build systems that are attractive to those whose work is most affected by them

- undertake the development of IS in parallel with any necessary reorganization of work resulting from changes in responsibilities, relationships and rewards.

Responsibility of computer professionals

In discharging their professional duties computer professionals are likely to enter into relationships with employers, clients, the profession and society. There may be one or more of these relationships for any given activity. Quite often there will be tensions existing between all of these relationships and particularly between employer–employee and social relationships. The responsibilities of the computer professional are thus onerous. These should be accepted and the resultant duties undertaken taking into account the obligations as a supplier, as a client, as an end user and as a member of society (Collins *et al.* 1994).

There are three skills that a computer professional should possess in order that professional duties might be undertaken in an ethically sensitive manner:

- the ability to identify correctly the likelihood of ethical dilemmas in given situations
- the ability to identify the causes of these dilemmas and suggest appropriate sensitive actions to resolve them, together with an indication of the probable outcomes of each alternative action
- the ability to select a feasible action plan from these alternatives.

Professional codes can be useful in helping computer professionals discharge their duties ethically because a code provides a framework within which to work and indicates acceptable work practices. Codes should address three levels of ethical obligation owed by computer professionals in their working relationships. The first level is a set of ethical values shared by virtue of the professional's humanity. The second level demands a higher order of care for those who might be affected by the professional's work. Finally, the third level comprises several obligations which derive directly from factors unique to the computer profession (Gotterbarn, Miller and Rogerson 1997). In short, professional codes can inspire, guide, educate and provide support for positive action.

Conclusion

The social impact of computer technology is growing at an increasing rate. Computers are changing where and how we work, learn, shop, eat, vote, receive medical care, spend free time, make war and establish social relationships. The computer revolution, therefore, is not merely technological and financial, it is fundamentally social and ethical. It is clear, therefore, that activity related to the development and use of information systems and the underpinning computer technology must include explicit action which addresses the ethical issues surrounding the development and use of such systems. The rise of computer ethics over the past two decades has brought much-needed ethical and social perspectives. However, more and more of the world is becoming 'wired'. We are entering a generation marked by globalization and ubiquitous computing. The stakes are much higher, and consequently considerations and applications of computer ethics must be broader, more profound and, above all, effective in helping to realize a democratic and empowering technology rather than an enslaving or debilitating one.

References

Audit Commission (1994) *Opportunity Makes a Thief*, London: HMSO.

Badaracco, J.L. and Useem, J.V. (1997) 'The Internet, Intel and the vigilante stakeholder', *Business Ethics: A European Review*, vol. 6, no. 1, January, pp. 18–29.

Bynum T.W. (1997a) 'Global information ethics and the information revolution', in T.W. Bynum and J.H. Moor (eds) *The Digital Phoenix: How Computers are Changing Philosophy*, Oxford: Blackwell.

Bynum, T.W. (1997b) *Information Ethics: An Introduction*, Oxford: Blackwell.

Collins, W.R., Miller, K.W., Spielman, B.J. and Wherry, P. (1994) 'How good is good enough?', *Communications of the ACM*, vol. 37, January, pp. 81–91.

Farbey, B., Land, F. and Targett, D. (1993) *How to Assess Your IT Investment*, Oxford: Butterworth Heinemann.

Gotterbarn, D. (1992) 'The use and abuse of computer ethics', in T.W. Bynum, W. Maner and J.L. Fodor (eds) *Teaching Computer Ethics*, Research Center on Computing and Society, Southern Connecticut State University, pp. 73–83.

Gotterbarn, D., Miller, K. and Rogerson, S. (1997) *Software Engineering Code of Ethics*, SIGCAS newsletter, July.

Information Commissioner (2000) *The Data Protection Act: A Brief Guide for Data Controllers*, The Office of the Information Commissioner, Wilmslow, accessed at wood.ccta.gov.uk/dpr/dpdoc.nsf 1 February 2001.

Johnson, D.G. (1985) *Computer Ethics*, first edition, Upper Saddle River, NJ: Prentice-Hall.

Johnson, D.G. (1994) *Computer Ethics*, second edition, Upper Saddle River, NJ: Prentice-Hall.

Johnson, D.G. (1997) *Ethics Online, Communications of the ACM*, vol. 40, no. 1, January, pp. 60–5.

Maner, W. (1996) 'Unique problems in information technology', *Science and Engineering Ethics*, vol. 2, no. 2, pp. 137–54.

Moor, J.H. (1985) 'What is computer ethics?', in T.W. Bynum (ed.) *Computers and Ethics*, Oxford: Blackwell.

Parker, D.B., Swope, S. and Baker, B.N. (eds) (1990) *Ethical Conflicts in Information and Computer Science, Technology and Business*, Wellesley, MA: QED Information Sciences.

Rogerson, S. (1997) 'Software project management ethics', in C. Myers, T. Hall and D. Pitt (eds) *The Responsible Software Engineer*, Berlin: Springer-Verlag, pp. 100–6.

Spinello, R.A. (1995) *Ethical Aspects of Information Technology*, New York: Prentice-Hall.

Stallman, R. (1992) 'Why software should be free', in T.W. Bynum, W. Maner and J.L. Fodor (eds) *Software Ownership and Intellectual Property Rights*, Research Center on Computing and Society, Southern Connecticut State University, pp. 35–52.

Tucker, A. (ed.) (1991) *Computing Curricula 1991: Report of the ACM/IEEE-CS Joint Curriculum Task Force*, New York: ACM Press.

Venkatesh, A. (1996) 'Computers and other interactive technologies for the home', *Communications of the ACM*, vol. 39, no. 12, December, pp. 47–54.

Wood-Harper, A.T., Corder, S., Wood, J.R.G. and Watson, H. (1996) 'How we profess: the ethical systems analyst', *Communications of the ACM*, vol. 39, no. 3, March, pp. 69–77.

9

ETHICAL ISSUES ENGENDERED BY ENGINEERING WITH ATOMIC NUCLEI

Raymond E. Spier

Foundations

A historical perspective

Fire, derived from the energy locked up in molecules, was transformed from a destructive and devouring element to a friend of humankind over a period of what may have been several thousand years, some half a million years ago. We are the only animal species to have achieved this mastery over one of nature's primeval attributes. Over the last 100 years we have been experimenting with the beneficial liberation of the energy that holds the particles of atomic nuclei together. At some stage in the future we may well take advantage of the energy that is stored in the form of the sub-atomic material particles themselves. As with all new developments, humans are required to re-examine their behaviour and answer the basic ethical questions posed by the need to achieve benefit and prevent harm from the unfolding opportunities. This process is particularly apt when confronted with the prospects of energy derived from the breaking down of atomic nuclei (nuclear fission) as the magnitude of the resulting effects is on a scale which presents unprecedented challenges to our control capabilities. But this is not different from the situation when we tamed the power of fire. It is just that, in nuclear engineering, we are at the beginning of a process which requires further expenditure of time and effort to achieve an equivalent level of control as we have in molecular engineering and incendiaries.

To put the atomic situation in perspective, it is useful to recognize that Röntgen discovered X-rays made from cathode rays in 1895, which was followed by Becquerel's (1852–1908) discovery, in the next year, that phosphorescent materials, one of which was a uranium-containing crystal, could blacken shielded photographic plates in the absence of light. By 1903 Marie Curie (1867–1934, the first winner of two Nobel prizes) and her husband Pierre, with the help of chemist A. Debiern, had isolated two further radioactive materials from pitch-blende: polonium and radium, where the latter was prepared as a metal. When Becquerel carried a small vial containing this radium in a vest pocket in 1901 he noticed that his skin adjacent to the pocket was 'burned', thus becoming the first person to perceive the biological effects of radioactivity. Such people were the pioneers; the amounts of radioactivity they were exposed to were enormous by modern standards. For example, one gram of radium generates 37×10^9 emissions per second (this is defined as one curie of radioactivity; where the emissions are a combination of α-particles or helium nuclei (consisting of two protons and two neutrons), β-rays or electrons, γ-rays and neutrons). Whereas the normal background radiation, made up from cosmic radiation and the radioactivity of naturally occurring materials, such as granitic rocks and the gas radon, to which we are all exposed on a continual basis, is some 20 to 30 detectable emissions per second.

Radiation and people

All living organisms containing nucleic acids (ribo- and deoxy-ribonucleic acids or RNA and DNA respectively) as their genetic materials are subject to changes in those materials. The mere act of replicating the DNA of cellular organisms in the standard reproductive processes of mitosis and meiosis (for egg and sperm formation) can lead to imperfections in the copied DNA *vis à vis* the original. In addition to these endogenous sources of genetic variation, the food we eat, drugs, smoking and the sunlight to which we expose ourselves have also been implicated in changes to our genes. These changes (mutations) are for the most part benign and many of them may even be corrected by the biochemical machinery of the cells, but some mutations are in genes whose products lead to the uncontrolled reproduction of those cells, resulting in a cancer. As we age the number of accumulated gene changes increases our propensity to develop a malignant cancer, to the extent that some 50% of UK female deaths and over 30% of male deaths in the age range 35 to 64 are attributed to cancer.[1] Over 99% of such individuals would not have been exposed to concentrated sources of radioactivity as a result of their work or leisure activities. Nevertheless, exposure to so-called 'ionizing' radiations does damage nucleic acid and does lead, among other effects, to cancer.

Units of radiation and their relationships

There are two ways of defining radiation. The first is dependent on the effect of the radiation on a physicochemical detection system while the second determines its effects on human bodies (the biological effect). As components of the first system we have the curie, defined as 37×10^9 detectable emissions per second. Correspondingly we have the becquerel, which is defined as one detectable emission per second. When it comes to the definitions which involve biological effects, it is important to distinguish between the different types of radiation because the neutron and α-particle radiations have about one-twentieth the effect of the equivalent energy of β- and γ-radiation. Thus the absorbed dose of radiation is called the rad; the röntgen equivalent man is the rem.

- One rad is an absorbed dose of radiation when 100 ergs are absorbed by 1 gram of tissue, or 10^{-2} joules/kg of tissue.
- One röntgen is a measure of exposure (not absorption) to high voltage X-rays or γ-rays which produce one electrostatic unit of charge (one detectable emission or one becquerel or one disintegration per second) per 0.001293 gm of air (1 cc) at NTP.
- One rem is roughly the same as one rad when the radiation is of the β- and γ-radiation type.
- One rem is roughly the same as 20 rad when the radiation is of the neutron and α-particle type.
- One gray is equivalent to 100 rad.
- One sievert is equivalent to 100 rem.
- So, for X- and γ-radiation, one sievert is the same as one gray.
- For β- and γ-radiation, one sievert is the same as about 20 gray (this depends on the particular nucleide or species of atom).

For example, the whole body exposure of a human to 400 rem will kill 50% of adult humans and 100 rem of concentrated X-rays will burn or damage the skin. It is recognized that 0.1 rem/day is a safe dose for people working in the nuclear industry, while background radiation exposes ordinary people to 0.1 rem per year. Alternatively, when the background radiation is expressed in grays it is approximately 0.001

grays per year or 1 milligray per year or 1 millisievert per year. In America, those members of the population who do not deal with radioactive materials during their routine daily business are exposed to 0.91 millisieverts (mSv) per year from cosmic or terrestrial and food sources. In addition they experience some 0.04 mSv per year from the fallout from nuclear explosions and 0.002 mSv per year from the generation of nuclear power. This is augmented, were they to have obtained a medical or dental X-ray, by 0.4 to 10 mSv.[2] The press regards an exposure of 0.2 to 0.3 gray as a low-level exposure. If the exposure occurred in one burst, there would be more damage than if the same total exposure were applied over an extended period. The effects of radiation doses in the two to fifty gray area are severely damaging and can cause death.[3]

Finding meaning in statistics

While the exposure figures quoted above provide a basis to judge the consequences of further increases or decreases in the background radiation, it is again important to put such considerations into a wider perspective of costs versus gains. For example, within the home we are prone to accidents from falling off ladders, scalding, cuts and scratches from broken glass and burns from heaters and open gas flames. Some 5000 people in the UK die from such accidents each year and three million need medical attention.[4] These figures are larger than deaths and injuries from road accidents (3500 and 330,000 respectively). Annual deaths in the UK from cancer, by comparison, are 156,500.[5] While every increase in the intensity of the background radiation is likely to have an effect in increasing the number of cancers, it is unlikely that the numerical effects of such increases will be seen in the cancer statistics. That is not to say that such increases in mortality should be ignored. On the contrary, we have a duty to do all we can to decrease such damage. However, a cursory perusal of the statistics would indicate that additional effort in the areas of the pre- vention of smoking-associated lung cancer and diet-associated cardiovascular disease will have pay-offs many orders of magnitude greater than that obtainable by decreasing background radiation. Notwithstanding such considerations, we are yet left with the ques- tion of whether we would wish to have any benefits from the exploitation of the controlled release of energy stored up in atomic nuclei when we realize that the cost may be in terms of human lives, however few that might be.

To assess the possible benefits of, and hence examine the ethical issues raised by, the release of nuclear energy we need to examine the various fields in which the properties of radioactive atoms and their fission products are used. It would seem that there are four main areas in which such properties are realized: scientific investigations on the way molecules interact and the genetic code, medical applications in terms of diagnosis and therapies, nuclear power applied to the production of electricity and the propulsion units of ships and nuclear power as a component of a country's military armamentarium.

Adding to knowledge

This section examines the use of radioactive materials in a laboratory environment. The amount of activity used in radioactive tracers, when measured in a scintillation counter, can be of the order of several tens to hundreds of thousands of disintegrations per minute per experimental vial. The commonly used isotopes are tritium (hydrogen-3), carbon-14, sulphur-35, phosphorous-32, iodine-131. These are all β-particle emitters except for the iodine (used less commonly) which emits γ-rays. The path length of the β-particle is of the order of millimetres and the particle does not penetrate through the glass walls of containing vessels and test tubes. This is to be compared with the three million γ-rays and 250,000 β-particles emanating from natural sources which pass through an individual per minute.[6] It is not likely that exposure to the radioisotopes used in laboratory experiments will lead to radiation-damaged individuals even if such materials were to be mishandled, spilled or ingested (in small quantities).

It is generally assumed that additions to the knowledge base are attributable to following a practice known as the scientific method.[7] While this may be the case, it is not the whole story as it is often necessary to effect some engineering process to acquire the equipment or materials necessary to effect that method. The engineering of materials which contain radioactive atoms, so enabling their detection, has been a major source of knowledge in the area of biochemistry as well as in other areas of chemistry and physics. The production of elements which do not occur naturally in quantities sufficient for their detection has become a target activity for nuclear physicists. The transuranic elements, of which we have the examples seaborgium (106), bohrium (107), hassium (108), meitnerium (109), unnnnilium (110), unununium (111) and ununbium (112) have been produced as a result of such work.[8]

It is of interest, from an ethical viewpoint, as to whether the production of something which is undetectable in nature (as some of these elements, such as 110, exist for fractions of a microsecond) is not contrary to some principle which forbids acts which result in unnatural ends. A second ethical issue might be that, through our improved understanding of the nature of the forces which bind atomic nuclei together, we might achieve weapons of even greater destructive capacity than those already in existence. Or might we not inadvertently produce an element whose decay products (the materials which remain after an atom has expressed its radioactivity; these may in their turn be radioactive) could cause a self-perpetuating nuclear reaction leading to destruction and radioactive contamination on an unprecedented scale? In acquiring this knowledge, humans become more adept at devising reductionist explanations for the origin of matter and for the origin and nature of the universe. This in turn may lead to challenges to the conventional sources of such information in the ancient scriptures. While this, of itself, may not be of major import, the implications of the weakening of the basis from which moral systems have ensued can be a cause for concern. As there is then a moral void, this needs to be filled with theories of behaviour that can command sufficient respect and following to provide the guidelines for contemporary citizens.

These, and other, arguments will occur many times when different aspects of atomic engineering activity are surveyed. As there are many approaches to ethics,[9] it will be useful for the reader to appreciate this author's perspective. In reading the lessons regarding the way living organisms behave and taking into account all the living organisms present on Earth today, as well as those that existed during the evolution of these present-day organisms over the last four thousand million years, it is clear that survival is a dominant motive for behaviour. Therefore the maximization of that parameter is a potent guideline for human behaviour today. This assumes that humans are a species of animal and are not imbued with any additional spiritual (outside the cause-and-effect system) properties. However, survival is a complex term in the modern world of humans. It is clear that humans function in groups of various sizes – some more permanent than others, some of greater cohesion than others. The unique time and circumstances of any one situation determine the loyalties of an individual to other individuals. Such loyalties are also dependent on the age of an individual and his or her wealth. Clearly the very young and the very poor can but look after their own survival. As people become older and richer they can perceive that their survival is tied into community activities and objectives leading, in times of special threat, to greater national and international groupings. Today, threatened with a projected asteroid collision in 2028 (as *The Times* 13 March 1998 has it, it is now calculated to miss Earth by 600,000 miles) as one of our greatest dangers, we are forced to recognize the commonality of the world's life forms where the survival of all individuals is best served by our conjoint activities.

Learning of our nature and the way we work

Radioactive, and therefore detectable, isotopes of the elements can be used as tracers. This is achieved by measuring the effects of such radioactivity as a response in a Geiger counter, or by counting scintillations caused by the effect of radiation on sensitive chemicals, or in the blackening of a photographic emulsion. The first such uses of the radioactive isotope of phosphorus, P-32, for the unravelling of human physiology were by Hevesy in 1934. This was augmented by work on photosynthesis in 1941 when Ruben, using the O-18 isotope of oxygen, showed that the oxygen, which was produced by chlorophyll-containing plants when exposed to light, was derived from water. Later, Calvin, using a radioactive isotope of carbon, C-14, revealed the way carbon dioxide in the air was converted to glucose in the plant. Tracers such as those used in the above experiments have also found use in agriculture in tracing what happens to the water supplied via irrigation systems, to the nitrogen atoms supplied in fertilizers and to the pesticides used to control insects and in tracing the distribution of geothermal sources.

These experiments and applications were conducted in an intellectual environment that did not connect the nature of the knowledge generated to ethical issues. The latter was for consideration by politicians and others, not the scientists themselves. Recently this has changed. In 1977 the team of Maxam and Gilbert and a second team of Sanger, Nicklen and Coulson discovered the different ways we might read the sequence of the bases which make up the genes. A culmination of these discoveries, both of which used radioactive nucleotides (although the Sanger method can use a colorimetric marker also), is that we can approach the problem of determining the sequence of the bases in all the genes in the human genome, some 3×10^9 bases, by the year 2003. While this ability is not, of itself, riddled with ethical problems, the implications of the possession of such knowledge is.

Reading the roughly 100,000 genes of humans is to acquire knowledge of the nature of our potential for being. (As things stand in 2001, it would seem that from studies of many sets of identical twins, some of whom were brought up in different homes and others in the same home, that some 50% or so of the characteristics of personality, intelligence and activity are genetically determined while the remainder is dependent on environmental factors.) Our genetic endowment, coupled with its interaction with its environment, determines the actual outcome of what makes us the way we are. As knowledge advances we are learning to recognize the genes which code for the proteins whose nature predisposes us to particular disease or capability states. Whether a child is susceptible to cystic fibrosis or Huntington's chorea can be determined by an examination of the sequence of the bases in particular genes. Susceptibility to certain cancers (such as breast cancer) can also be determined by a similar examination of other genes. This knowledge has implications for the way we behave. For example, we might consider the option of determining *in utero* the genetic make-up of a foetus whose family history might predispose us to think that there was a likelihood of inheritance of the gene for Huntington's chorea. Were this to be found, there would then be an option to consider a termination of the pregnancy. There are clearly some people who would find such an option ethically repellent, while others would accept it as a valuable alternative. Progress in this area will clearly lead to more such decision options.

A corollary to these issues is that knowledge of our genetic make-up is of considerable value to life-insurance companies, mortgage lenders, employers and the police. Such organizations might use information about our defective genes to deny us insurance (or to charge especially high premiums), to dispute the magnitude of a mortgage, to prevent our employment and to provide the police with information that might implicate us in actions with which we were not connected. Marriage decisions might also be based on an examination of the complementarity of particular genetically defined characteristics (as is already the case with the Tay-Sachs syndrome for some Jewish groups). This would have profound implications for those who did not possess such matching genes and might dispose such individuals to the bachelor condition. Collateral issues are raised in determining who might have access to this information and whether it can be added to other databases to determine whether we might be more or less susceptible to the wiles of a particular sales campaign.

Following the 1984 discovery of Jeffries, that by using a radioactively labelled probe it is possible to characterize the genetic material of an individual human (or other DNA-containing living or dead organism) one may obtain a genetic 'fingerprint' of that individual. Such identifiers are almost exclusively unique to individuals. Thus family relationships can be ascertained with a high degree of reliability, which is particularly of value in cases of disputed paternity. Moreover, as the sample required for testing is minuscule (a hair, a fingerprint smear, a spot of blood and so on) the forensic use of this technique in bringing criminals to justice is legion, notwithstanding the possibility of mistakes. But it could go beyond that. Consider a universal database of the genetic fingerprints of each living human being used to keep track of the activities and whereabouts of everybody. Civil liberties might be held to be at risk. On the other hand it would be the deliberate wrongdoers who are likely to suffer the most. This balance between the powers of the state and those of the individual becomes crucial when the use of these radioactive probes is brought out of the refined atmosphere of the laboratory and dropped into the hands of the civil authorities.

But progress will not let us stop at this point. As we know more about our genes (see also chapter 7 in this volume) we could conceive of options to genetically re-engineer humans with enhanced capabilities in defined areas such as intelligence, height, speed, voice quality and so on. This brings us up against a further suite of ethical issues. Do we have the right to re-engineer humans according to our own precepts (or, 'do we have the right to play God')? Would this not be an unnatural event? And could this not lead to disasters which are exemplified in Mary Shelley's 1818 story of the creation of a monstrous being by the fictional Victor Frankenstein? Answers to such questions are difficult, but were we to consider the ability to introduce a particular gene or characteristic into a human at will to be a 'tool' then we can apply the ethical guidelines we use for tools to the ability to genetically engineer humans. This enables us to recognize that a tool may be used for benefit (a hammer knocking in nails) or harm (a hammer used as a weapon for murder). We do not specifically regulate the use of the hammer for beneficial ends by the implementation of laws, rules, guidelines and education. Rather, we define the kinds of behaviour we require of humans in that we do not permit them to kill others, irrespective of the instrument they might consider using. We explore the potential uses of new tools whose properties we have not yet determined with care. Again, our experience in taming fire, so that its beneficial uses are enabled, is a heuristic for the use of a new tool. Our approach has been, and will of necessity still be, one of cautious experimentation so that the applications can be surveyed and assayed for their propensity to deliver harm or benefit. This pragmatic and controlled experimental programme can be used to determine how a new tool might be used for benefit and its application for harm prevented.

Applications in the health care industry

Radioisotopes find uses in the three main areas of health care activity. In prophylaxis they are often used in the early stages of vaccine development when the nature of the genetic material of the pathogen or putative immunogen is determined and before the final vaccine material is prepared. For immunoassay and immunoelectrophoresis, radioactive iodine has proved to be of considerable use in areas where the amount of material to be detected is low or where the quality of the reactants results in responses which are difficult to detect. X-rays have many diagnostic uses as do radioactive tracers in whole-body and organ examinations. The use of radioactivity to cure sick patients dates back to the days when the biological effects of radioactivity had just been discovered. In addition to these uses on human subjects, health care benefits also accrue when insect pests can be controlled by the γ-ray sterilization of laboratory-produced male insects, whose non-fertile mating activities decrease the level of germ-carrying insects. Further, γ-rays are used for the microbial decontamination of foodstuffs as well as the examination of the quality of welds in oil pipelines.

Diagnostic applications

Radioisotopes are commonly used in analytical techniques involving antibodies and antigens as the primary reacting species. Such radioimmunoassays are widely used, as they are sensitive and enable the detection of minuscule quantities of materials in, say, blood samples. They are commonly used to test for toxic materials in foods and for the presence of narcotics or psychoactive drugs in suspected drug abusers. The level of exposure of researchers and laboratory technicians to radioactive emissions is not considered a hazard when 'good laboratory practices' are implemented. Also, as the information generated adds to knowledge about the way biological systems operate, or helps in the diagnosis of disease, it is not normally the subject of ethical review. However, information, like most other tools, can be used for benefit or harm. It is up to both the generators of such information and civilly minded individuals to be mindful of such occurrences and to be vigilant in their circumspection of this data.

While radioactive materials are used in brain scans based on the detection of positrons (positron-emission tomography), most diagnostic techniques make use of X-rays or γ-rays. Such procedures result in exposures to radiation of between 10 and 250 mSv per procedure; some 10 to 250 times the annual background exposure level of about 1mSv per year. Of course, people who agree to such exposure levels should have provided an informed consent before examination. Furthermore, individuals do not normally expose themselves to such radiation levels casually; they have an expectation that the cause of their disease state might be discovered.

Doctors and diagnostic technical staff members who frequent these examination areas are well aware of the risks presented by exposure to the radiations they use and are carefully monitored for the amount of radiation they are exposed to on a weekly basis. Scientists who use X-ray microscopes may be particularly at risk, as the ways in which the radiation beams are controlled and directed need constant attention to achieve pictures of the highest resolution. This was of especial concern with the older-style instruments. The same exposure standards, which apply to workers in the nuclear industry, would apply to such individuals. As there is not any occupation that is totally devoid of risk of personal injury or damage, the risks taken by members of the medical profession are regarded as acceptable. However, as the patients are subjected to the highest exposure levels it is important to devise new and less damaging means of effecting diagnoses.

Therapeutic applications of radiation

Cancers are the primary target of radiotherapeutic treatments. The dose levels are often the maximum the patient will tolerate without an exacerbation of the disease state. In general every effort is made to focus the radiation on the affected part and, to this end, use is made of directional beams of radiation or the insertion of radioactive materials within the tumour. Whole-body radiation of 10 sieverts (10,000 times annual background exposure) will cause the cessation of the development of bone marrow. But while a whole-body dose of less than 6 gray given at one time is almost certainly fatal, several tens of grays given over a long period of time to small tissue volumes can be tolerated. Clearly such exposures are damaging in their own right. However, when faced with probable death from inaction, or the ineffectiveness of drug treatments, the balance of benefits often falls on the side of the application of radiation, so applied as to concentrate its lethal effects on the diseased organ.

The radioactive materials used in these treatments do not disappear. Iodine-131 has a half-life of about eight days; Cobalt-60's half-life is ten months to five years depending on the isomer. These materials find their way into the environment via the sewers. The dilution effects engendered by this process render them harmless.

Most ethical systems would hold the preservation of life as a basic premise. And medical ethics' four requirements, to preserve a patient's autonomy, to be beneficent, not to be maleficent and to be just, can be achieved using established informed consent practices. The use of radioactive materials to achieve extensions of the lives of cancerous patients is therefore not a disputed procedure even though, in many cases, it is not particularly effective. It is, of course, paradoxical that radiochemicals can both cause and cure certain cancers; we are left with the requirement to maximize benefit by selecting those conditions that will serve us most in the furtherance of our ethical guidelines.

Nuclear power applications

At this time, some 35% of the European Union's electricity supply is generated by the controlled fission of uranium-based nuclear reactors; in France this figure is 76%.[10] There are also over 700 nuclear-powered naval vessels (including some 40% of the US Navy) sailing the seas.[11] These figures stem from the relative cost and effectiveness of nuclear energy in particular applications. This is based on the fact that weight for weight the energy, which can be liberated from uranium, is 2.5×10^6 times that which can be obtained from coal. So although the raw uranium costs some 500 times more than coal and even though only 0.5 to 0.8% of that material is 'burned' in the nuclear reactor, the 'levelized lifetime cost' per kWh of electricity (which includes all the costs of decommissioning, processing, storage of waste materials and so on) while providing a 5% return on investment, can be determined. For these conditions, it has been shown that the ratio of coal generation to nuclear generation costs varies between 0.95 and 1.79.[12]

There are nuclear reactors based on the use of enriched uranium, where some 30% of the fuel is used up. Also, as the fission of uranium results in the production of plutonium it is possible to extract that material and use it as a source of fuel. In this way it is possible to obtain more fuel from a 'spent' uranium reactor than was put into the reactor in the first instance. These fast-breeder reactors have not proved themselves to be economic at this time, but could become so

191

in the future. But readers will note the close and inevitable connection between the nuclear power industry and the military munitions effort. As plutonium is a key component of nuclear bombs, the production of this material in power reactors gives these installations a semi-military status. Hence many of the conditions which pertain to the maintenance of military secrecy have been applied to those establishments dealing with the generation of electricity from nuclear fuels. This closed information policy has led to a serious level of distrust between the public, government and the operators of nuclear installations.

For ship-based nuclear propulsion systems, the arguments which favour the nuclear option versus that of oil are that the reactors are compact and weigh much less than the combination of fuel oil plus engine, that they do not require an air intake and do not generate gaseous emissions (they do have wastes and need refuelling every few years), that they do not discharge oleaginous pollutants while voiding ballast and servicing engines, that when operating at maximum speeds they do not burn disproportionate amounts of fuel and that the propulsions systems are more reliable. It is stated that 2500 reactor years at sea have not resulted in any significant nuclear accident. Nevertheless, we do not yet have a civil nuclear-based shipping industry, with the possible exception of Russian icebreakers. We also have to watch with care the consequences of the running down of sections of the Russian naval fleet. Some of these nuclear reactor-containing ships are decomposing at their anchorages. Monitoring the levels of radioactivity in the Northern seas is a high priority.

Further applications of nuclear technology are under investigation in the use of low level heat resources produced as a by-product while generating electricity for domestic and industrial heating applications. This would be particularly applicable where there are dense concentrations of domestic housing. Another, and perhaps more appropriate, use of nuclear power is in the generation of water fit for irrigation from sea water by the process of reverse osmosis. This requires the application of numerous large pumping units and can be sited at a desert location alongside a coastal region. Additionally, there are numerous opportunities for the use of nuclear power in 'off-Earth' activities as in the provision of electricity for satellites, the propulsion of rockets or the establishment of colonies of humans on the moon, Mars or the Jovian moon Europa.

Ethical issues pertaining to nuclear power

Few would deny the contention that some clear benefits may be derived from the appropriate and carefully controlled generation and application of nuclear power. Such a situation would take account of the plutonium produced, the storage, for many thousands of years, of the radioactive waste generated and the risks of a damaging accident occurring at a nuclear power plant. In the formative phases of the nuclear industry there have been many accidents with little loss of life (three people died at the SL-1 reactor accident in Idaho in 1961) or contamination of areas outside the plant site, which have been described in detail.[13] This statement would cover the events at Three Mile Island where, on 27 March 1979, a reactor became uncontrollable (largely as a result of incorrectly connecting an instrument air line and a plant air line, leading to instrument failure) and was only prevented from exploding by voiding radioactive hydrogen gas into the air and radioactive cooling water into the Susquehanna river (website: www.wowpage.com/tmi/). It would not cover the incident at Chernobyl, in the Ukraine, on 26 April 1986. Here a reactor exploded, liberating a cloud of radioactive materials, which was deposited as radioactive caesium and strontium as far afield as Scotland. Of the 237 people who suffered from acute radiation syndrome, some thirty-eight people died from radiation exposure. 15,000 people lost their ability to work following disease and of the 12,000 children who received large doses of radiation to the thyroid gland, 800 developed thyroid cancer (website: www.iaea.or.at/worldatom/). The doses of radiation received by the children varied from about one to nine grays. A further consequence of this event was the dehabitated and uncultivated land that extended for many tens of kilometres from the site of the reactor failure.

To place the accident record of the nuclear industry into perspective it is well to recognize the continuing loss of life in other industries connected with providing our societies with energy. For example, between 1974 and 1978, for each million miners digging coal in the UK, some 210 died each year as a result of accidents. Or, between 1967 and 1976, for each million offshore oil and gas workers in the North Sea, some 1650 died from accidents.[14] In the construction industries during the same time frame, of one million workers employed, 150 died from work-related accidents; these figures would pertain to the construction of nuclear power stations as well as gas, coal or oil-fired installations.

That people die from work-related accidents is not a justifiable cause for ethical complacency. We do not live in a risk-free world even though we deplore every instance when we think somebody's death has been caused by preventable circumstances. There is the prospect for personal damage from the food we eat, the air we breathe and the information we obtain. All such sources of sustenance are not proscribed because of their possible harmful effects. Rather we take a view that our behaviour (ethics) should be such that we minimize the harm and maximize the benefit. We do not deliberately eat food that smells or looks 'off'; we stay out of confined spaces where smoking is permitted or where people with infectious diseases are housed; we learn to critically evaluate the information we deploy when providing goods or services to our fellow citizens.

The magnitude of such risks can be discovered by personal experience or by reference to an extended literature on risk assessment. But the risks associated with the nuclear power industry cannot be readily determined. By direct, indirect or surreptitious means we have learned of leakages of radioactivity, accidents in atomic reactors, the real costs of decommissioning and the health effects of the radiations to workers and the people in areas surrounding nuclear power plants. Public servants, elected representatives, industrial spokespersons and military officials who offer information on matters related to the nuclear industry are renowned for their unwillingness to provide a full and accurate account of their bailiwicks. Indeed, these communications have been more characterized by obfuscation, misinformation and dissimulation.[15] In mitigation, it may well be that some of the information requested could be used to determine the ability of a country to make certain strategic weapon systems, which, if known publicly, would enable potential enemies to design and implement counter-systems. Or, it could be argued that adverse publicity in connection with leaks and so on would bring the plants (manufacturing or power generating) that are producing materials vital for a deterrent nuclear force into opprobrium. It is also necessary to add that, while the authorities have been unwilling to divulge details about the workings or malfunctionings of atomic reactors prior to the 1990s, in the latter years of that decade there has been a sea-change in attitude, in that more information is becoming available and the information is more timely. The Internet may have been a cause of this improved openness. Or it may be that it has been decided that, in the absence of a Cold War, we can be more open about what we used to believe it was valuable to hold secret. Nevertheless, it is vital for citizens to have access to all available information, which would enable them to make determinations for themselves as to the risks involved in the generation of power through nuclear reactors. Were they to think that some vital, or even less than vital, information was being withheld, then their suspicions would be aroused and their distrust of the system in all its aspects provoked.

Were we to test the nuclear power operations which generate electricity against a variety of ethical standpoints we would find that it would be perverse to consider this method of generation of electrical power unethical or wrong for all times and circumstances. Do the ends justify the means (consequentialism)? To produce power efficiently is desirable; to produce it with a minimum damage to the environment is also of great value. Clearly, nuclear power gains from the absence of the so-called greenhouse gas generation and from the absence of the oxides of sulphur in the off-gasses. There are, however, the possibilities of reactor accidents and environmental contaminations as in the Chernobyl incident. In addition, the waste materials need to be stored in a way which does not contaminate the environment and which can be held in a harmless situation for thousands of years or indefinitely. Many would hold that this is an impossible task and that a consequence of this would be to desist from all work which seeks to obtain benefit from atomic nuclei. Others would rise to the challenge and devise new techniques to achieve the desired end. Such a development may be attained if the ideas of Fergus Gibb are given support. He would deposit large amounts of highly radioactive materials at the bottom of boreholes penetrating some four kilometres below ground. The heat from the radioactivity would melt the local rock and cause a fusion between the radioactive materials and the surrounding and containing stony materials. When the radioactivity had declined the fused melt would cool and solidify. As groundwaters do not circulate to such depths it is thought that it would be unlikely for any radioactivity to leach into the waters circulating about the planet's surface.[16]

The accident record is likely to improve as we learn to control the nuclear reactions in the atomic pile and to engineer the supporting equipment to a standard where failure has minimal effects and where the back-up systems are as reliable as the front-end equipment. Also, we can expect that the processing of the wastes of these reactors will improve to the point where some of the material will be recycled for more energy generation while the intensely radioactive material that has to be stored will be concentrated and stabilized to meet the criteria for indefinite containment.

Would one wish to have a nuclear generating installation sited next to one's back yard? (Golden-mean ethics; do unto others as you would have them do to you; this ethic has echoes in other ethical systems such as those of deontology or duty, contractarian ethics or the Kantian 'categorical imperative'.) For a variety of reasons it would be unsuitable to site a nuclear reactor system in the middle of a town. There is a need for an extensive site of low cost near an ample supply of water (for cooling systems) and as power stations are hardly held in aesthetic esteem, it is well that they are situated in areas where people are not ordinarily resident. In which case, from necessity, we do not need to respond to the original question as others will be as unaffected by the siting of the station as one would be oneself. However, we do have a duty to deal fairly with those members of our society who, through their own wishes, are closest to a source of danger. Adequate and immediate systems of compensation should be available as well as all the relevant information, so that they might assess the risks of their activities as accurately as possible.[17]

None of the absolutist or divinely based ethical systems has had to contend with the prospects of nuclear power generation (the Judeo-Christian Bible and the Koran are silent on this, as are Hindu and Buddhist scriptures). However, it is possible to obtain some guidance via the efforts of those who interpret the fixed scriptures, the hermeneutics. We are therefore left with relativist ethical systems which would seek to determine a cost–benefit relationship from which a decision as to whether or not to proceed is made. In the above discussion it would appear that there are prospects that the generation of electricity from nuclear power should have a role in our efforts to improve our lot. It would be left to the determination of people local to the site of a nuclear power plant as to whether the balance of advantage is favourable to them. If not, they have the right to protest and work to prevent its construction. If so, they have the benefits from having a cheap and clean local energy supply which, if it can be arranged, might even provide them with home heating from the low grade waste heat source which needs cooling before discharge into local waterways.

Nuclear power and the military

Throughout recorded history societies have sought to acquire and deploy destructive powers of greater and greater magnitude. The latest product of this cycle is dependent on the release of the energy stored in the nuclei of atoms. Atomic (nuclear) bombs delivered by conventional aircraft, rockets, depth charges, land mines or guns are, whether we approve or not, a part of the most advanced military armamentaria.

Following their first use, at Hiroshima and Nagasaki in 1945, they have never been used as agents of destruction. Nevertheless, such weapons have to be fabricated, tested and stored if they are to have any uses. At each such stage there are serious ethical questions to be examined.

Fabrication issues

Many of the technical problems involved in fabricating nuclear weapons are common to the use of nuclear materials in the power generation industry and have been examined in the previous section. People are exposed to radiation damage in the recovery of the uranium ores and in the processing of these raw materials to materials enriched into those isotopes of uranium whose concentration can trigger a nuclear explosion, such as the uranium-235 and plutonium-239 which is derived from uranium processed in a nuclear reactor. Some ten kilograms of plutonium can be formed into a single bomb and a 1000 Mwe power station can produce about 100 kg of plutonium per annum. Adding isotopes of hydrogen (deuterium, H-2 or tritium, H-3) to a plutonium or uranium nuclear bomb increases the explosive power considerably so that modern nuclear bombs have the destructive power of hundreds of millions of tons of TNT.

The most salient of the ethical issues to be associated with the fabrication of nuclear bombs revolves about the need for secrecy with regard to information about power reactors, which produce plutonium at the same time as they generate electricity for the grid. Once a culture of non-disclosure of information has been established in an industrial plant it tends to become pervasive and all-encompassing; it is safer (for jobs and careers) to err on the side of confidentiality rather than disclosure when asked about the workings of the plant. So when elected representatives in the UK parliament ask for information, from which it is possible to calculate the net amount of plutonium available (for the production of weapons), the minister in charge of the power industry does not divulge the sought-after figures. Similar blocks to information have been experienced by journalists in the USA who wanted data about the workings of the Hanford (near Richland in Washington State) and Rocky Flats (outside Denver, Colorado) weapon fabrication plants. However, in recent times the operational history and current activities of both of these facilities is finding its way into the media.[18]

While in the previous section these issues have been raised in connection with nuclear power generation, it is useful to examine the questions involved in the secrecy of the state of the national weaponry in relation to the need-to-know demands of journalists and citizens. Obviously, the state of one's weaponry (types, numbers, sizes, state of readiness, deployment) is crucial information for a declared or undeclared enemy. It enables counter-measures to be taken and pre-emptive actions to incapacitate a war-winning weapon planned. Historically, such information was guarded zealously, but the geostrategic situation has changed radically since the advent of nuclear weapons. Now, there is a strong case for disclosing the details of one's armoury so that potential aggressors are deterred from attacking. A stalemate is established such that neither side can possibly see that they will emerge from a 'hot' conflict with any advantage. For not only will death and destruction have occurred on both sides to extents which can hardly be imagined, but the aftermath of a nuclear exchange will be to contaminate the land, sea and air to degrees which will preclude civilized living.

As there is a need to disclose the extent of one's nuclear arsenal and the means whereby it can be delivered (to date reliable means to protect against rocket-borne nuclear weapons have not been developed), it is both practicable and desirable to provide the information to as wide a constituency as possible. Collaterally, details of the way the safety aspects of the weapons production process are implemented and monitored can become public knowledge. People are well aware that all industrial activities pose risks of damage to people and the environment. What they need from the nuclear weapons industry is comprehensive information which will enable them to assess the relative costs of a weapons programme in comparison to the equivalent costs of a fishing industry (most dangerous in terms of deaths of personnel) or construction industry. Given such openness it is possible to satisfy ethical questions as to how to behave in the future.

Weapons testing

The testing of nuclear weapons poses problems which other weapon test systems do not raise. Three areas of difference may be considered: the effect of a nuclear explosion *per se*, the radioactive fallout consequent to the explosion and implications of the demonstration of the feasibility of such a weapon. The magnitude of the explosion creates shock waves, which can be detected on the other side of the planet; they may trigger earthquakes or volcanic eruptions. Fallout from testing nuclear bombs has provided an additional 0.04 mS per year to the natural background radiation of 0.91 mS per year (a 4.3% increase). The realization that this increase in background radiation was harmful led, in 1963, to a Nuclear Test Ban Treaty which switched atmospheric tests to underground tests (at least for the USA and the then USSR). However, the crucial consideration, in the testing of nuclear weapons, is that at the end of a 'successful' test period the world has to live with the demonstrated feasibility of effective nuclear weapons.

Until the Test Ban Treaty there had been deep unrest at the pollution of the atmosphere with radioactive contaminants derived from atmospheric tests of bombs. Relocating the tests to underground vaults decreased the intensity of this protest but did raise other questions about seepage of the contained radioactivity into groundwaters for eventual recycling or the penetration of the cavities produced by overbearing seawaters. Other efforts, such as the Non-Proliferation of Nuclear Weapons (1968), the Strategic Arms Limitation Talks of 1972 and 1979, Intermediate-Range Nuclear Forces (1987) and the Strategic Arms Reduction Talks of 1991, have resulted in considerable decreases in both the testing and the number of deployed nuclear weapons.

At the time of writing (2000) there are few concerns about the testing of nuclear weapons save for the rejuvenation of areas of the world (the Bikini Atoll, for example) where the blight of radioactive contamination had destroyed the fauna and flora of the area. Such sites are recovering slowly but not to the extent that humans may live there freely. So, from an ethical standpoint, the damage has been done; the people who benefited from the tests were not the people who were disadvantaged by having been removed from the test sites, nor were they the people who were exposed to the highest levels of radioactive contamination. Those who gained have a duty to compensate those who suffered. They also have to undertake to examine the ethical implications of their actions before they engage in activities that may have regrettable consequences in the future.

Weapons storage

A weapon store is a target; its location and holdings should be a closely guarded secret. It is also a place from which weapons, or weapons-grade explosive materials, may be stolen. In societies where there is little trust between the governors and the governed, secrets present ethical problems. Are people being exploited unknowingly? Is the risk of damage fairly distributed about the society? Do the 'enemy' know more than the citizens? Who needs to know what?

Some of the distrust is allayed when selected members of the public are brought into the circle of the people who know and are trusted with all the data under a secrecy agreement. The responsibility of the people's representatives would be to ascertain that the governmental organization was operating in a just manner. Were this not to be the case, then it could be that they would perceive that they have a higher responsibility and break the secrecy agreement in the interest of the greater good of the society. In the UK selected members of the press are given information under a 'D-notice' designation, which means that it is for their information only and not for publication. This enables these journalists to write, in a manner which skirts about the issues which are held secret, in a way which would not contradict those secrets were they in the public domain.

Since the dissolution of the USSR in 1991, the prospect of the acquisition of weapons-grade nuclear materials by unauthorized parties has been an ever-present threat. Clear and well-founded controls on such material are a necessity. Although it is unlikely that any terrorist group will purloin sufficient material to make more than one or two explosive devices, the delivery of such weapons by vehicular transport into the heart of our societies is not impossible. The vigilance of all citizens is required to prevent such occurrences; just as we all have to be on our guard for unclaimed packages at airports or town centres.

In the development of the new weapons technology it would have been difficult to foresee all the inherent problems; even were most of them anticipated, it would have been hard to forego a weapons program. Once such a program had begun, the result would be virtual invincibility, particularly when this program was inspired by the state of war which then existed between the Allies and Axis powers. Over fifty years later, when the genie is out of the bottle, we have to design ethical systems to enable us to live with the conditions we find in this post-Second World War world. In particular, and in view of the issues connected with the sometime need for secrecy, we have to engage in a review of the relationship of the individual to the state. The inherent difficulty of this task stems from the transitory nature of any particular state of society. We have to formulate relationships which are to pertain under dynamic conditions. The size, cohesiveness and location of the groups with which an individual might be associated will change with time and circumstances. But it should not be beyond our capabilities to design systems of priorities which will cover most foreseeable situations. From this relationship the issues of secrecy and security may be reviewed; whatever the outcome of such a review it is essential that the nuclear weapons we have yet to destroy do not cause us more danger than is necessitated by their currently required presence.

Weapons use

As a result of conventional bombing, the cities of Berlin, Dresden[19] and Tokyo each lost about 100,000 of their civilian populations while London lost some 30,000 in air raids. The atomic bombing of Hiroshima and Nagasaki was the first and only operational use of nuclear weapons, causing civilian losses of 60,000 and 10,000 respectively. In all these cases there were many more wounded and homeless, but the atomic bomb blasts rendered the areas radioactive; a situation from which these towns have since recovered. In 1945, before the bombing, the population of Hiroshima was 342,000; in 1988 it had risen to over 2,800,000. Whether the Americans needed to drop the atomic bombs on the Japanese cities is a hotly contested issue and was so when the decision to proceed was made. Although on the one hand it may have led directly to the nuclear arms race, it may also have had the effect of demonstrating the awesome destructive power of such weaponry and therefore made the race into a stalemate. With hindsight a thorough examination of the ethics might conclude that the bombing was unjustified; the war was won; it was just a matter of time before the Japanese surrendered. But in the heat of battle, as memories of costly victories and even costlier defeats coupled with reports of the maltreatment of prisoners and captive civilians, it would be churlish to deplore the decision that was made.

Other ethical issues raised by the availability of nuclear bombs hundreds of times more powerful than those of the Second World War pivot about two key issues. The first involves the position of citizens who do not wear military uniforms, the second pertains to the issue of deterrence, based on the possible killing of millions of people if not most of humanity.

Citizens as hostages

When we consider the ways in which a war might be waged we are reminded of the provisions of St Thomas Aquinas (1225–1274), who began to define allowable military practice (*jus in bello*).[20] He did not comment on the position of those who do not wear military uniform. However, the Geneva Convention (IV) of 1949 recognizes the special position of civilian persons and those connected with hospitals and the Red Cross. It is well recognized that 'unintentional' collateral damage involving human mortalities might result from an act of war. Such events are regarded as regrettable but inevitable; they do not generally evoke moral opprobrium. Wanton killing of civilians, however, is regarded by many ethicists as wrong.[21] Those civilians who do not wear military uniform are designated non-combatants or innocents (Latin *nocens*, 'harm'). But is this designation safe?

During a war which requires the deployment of all the available resources of the society to achieve the objectives of the conflict it is difficult to envisage individuals who are not engaged in supporting the war effort. During the Second World War all non-essential metal objects (particularly those of aluminium) were collected from all households in the UK. All people were enlisted in the blackout efforts to deny German bombers targets; and all people were on their guard against loose conversation, which could inform an enemy spy. The Battle of Britain was as much won in the aircraft factories as on the runways of Biggin Hill or the dogfights over Kent. Those factories were supported by exertions in agriculture, food distribution, education, construction and a myriad of other activities directed to the war effort. These people wanted to win the war; they did not want to be a subject people. Their intentions included the killing of adversaries which they did through the agency of the uniformed military, yet those men and women in civilian clothes who cracked coded enemy messages at Bletchley (Station X) may be considered to have caused the loss of more enemy lives than batteries of long-range guns. If we exclude the pacifists, we can be confident in our opinion that when the society as a whole is under threat, all the people become engaged in the conflict with a view to securing their survival. Thus the issue of non-combatants arises when only a subset of the society is at war, as for instance, in 'peace-keeping' operations, or when an attempt is made to influence the political structure of a country by interfering in a civil conflict. In which case it may be concluded that, were two societies engaged in a total war (mutual survival at stake), then all the members of those societies are technically 'front line troops'. The ethical position that such people are different and therefore immune from the exigencies of war cannot command respect.

Deterrence

Is it ethical to create an armoury with such destructive power that an aggressor would be virtually committing suicide in an assault? When the defender is equally well armed would it not be tantamount to mutual suicide to engage in a conflict? Whether ethical or not, for many of the last fifty years the world has been in this kind of situation. The acronym MAD, for 'mutually assured destruction', is not inappropriate. As stated here, it would seem that a stand-off situation is entirely satisfactory; except for the cost of producing and maintaining the weaponry. But there are dangers from destabilizing causes. A new technical discovery could enable one side to imagine that it had such an advantage that it might, via a first strike, gain an outright winning advantage. A third party (terrorist group or nation state) might, by causing massive, yet token, destruction to one of the protagonists, instigate an all-out exchange. A maverick element in one of the two protagonists might trigger a war, notwithstanding the many turnkey operations under the control of the most senior leaders being required to unleash a nuclear weapon. In the face of the existence of such destructive power we have to contend with a novel ethical situation.

One approach to such behaviour, which is likely to gain acceptance among most ethicists, is to reduce (eventually to vanishing point) the nuclear arsenals. To some extent that lesson has already been learned, and the gradual, supervised destruction of a sizeable component of the nuclear arsenal is presently in hand. But that will still leave a residuum of nuclear weaponry whose destructive power is yet capable of provoking the onset of a 'nuclear winter' with the loss of much of the Earth's biosphere. It is therefore essential to continue this process of nuclear weapons reduction to levels below which it is impossible to assuredly destroy an enemy.

Of course, it is possible to envisage *de novo* a situation before such destructive arsenals had been built up, and ask the question of whether it is ethical to proceed with the generation of such a force that mutually assured destruction is the necessary outcome. Looking back at the history of our present situation, it would seem that we should not have embarked on this massive accumulation of nuclear weaponry. This conclusion would be reached virtually irrespective of the ethical system used. One might also ask, at the time when the first atom bomb was under construction, or even before, when the possibility of its construction was theoretically postulated, was it possible to foresee the developments that have occurred? And, if it was so envisaged, would it not have been prudent to have made the ethical decision to desist from the experimentation which showed that the bomb was not only a theoretical construct but also a practicable reality? To judge this issue in context, we must remember that a situation of all-out world war was ongoing at that time, and that America had lost the major portion of its Pacific fleet at Pearl Harbor on 7 December 1941. (In 1939 a group of European physicists migrated to America and advised President Roosevelt that it was possible to make a nuclear weapon. The president created a team to investigate the possibilities in May 1941. Enrico Fermi demonstrated the first self-sustaining nuclear chain reaction by the end of that year at the same time as the Pearl Harbor disaster.) It would have required a superhuman character to resist the development of what could be a war-winning device by pointing out the future implications of a build-up of nuclear weapons which could threaten the existence of life itself.

Aquinas was probably correct in asserting that the rulings of the ten Judaic Commandments may be set aside when loss of life is at stake (due to disease or attack by enemies). In considering the issue of deterrence based on the massive accumulation of nuclear weapons, we have to ask whether this can be a sufficiently stable situation to enable the emergence of a new world order, based on nation-state cooperation for the maintenance of peace. We cannot but recognize areas for potential conflagrations: Iraq, Libya, Yugoslavia, Indonesia, Rwanda, Israel, Kashmir, Ireland and so on. Yet we may be able to view these situations as analogous to other non-nuclear wars which have occurred under an unused nuclear umbrella. To a utilitarian, the achievement of peace is a worthy goal; an individual who relies on personal feelings to generate ethical guidelines may have serious misgivings with regard to the deterrence situation (Bertrand Russell, for example); someone who bases actions on the golden rule would think that a stand-off is a tenable option, while a prudent prag-matist would recognize the present situation for what it was worth and cautiously proceed to make it more secure. Although the many ethical approaches to this problem do not provide a consistent outcome, we are faced with the practical need to determine how to proceed. This author would take the view that we have to move with care and caution to a situation where the threat of biosphere annihi-lation has been replaced by the establishment of systems, organizations and codes of conduct that enable the peaceful develop-ment of all nation states. It may well be that international police forces have to have weapons of destruction; but these should be pro-portionate to the needs and in any case should never be based on nuclear weapons.

Conclusions

We are living in a world where the properties of radioactive atoms can be used for benefit or harm. A portion of the knowledge we have acquired can unleash such destructive forces that the whole of the biosphere is threatened with annihilation. This must be prevented at all costs. If we are to control the powers of the atom and promote their beneficial applications we have to adopt policies which enable all citizens to be aware of the situation in those industrial plants which are the transforming agents of nuclear energy to electricity or motive power. There will be a need for non-executive directors drawn from the public to sit on the boards of such organizations. The present national and international agencies may need additional support so that they may be more effective in their benign purposes. So, from the existence of weapons whose destructive effects cannot be confined to a specific locale, the need for nation states to choose non-violent means in matters of settling inter-state disputes becomes not just facultative but obligatory. In time we may be able to implement the internationally constituted equivalent of police forces, but until we do, we have to emphasize what Aquinas held to be the chief of the cardinal virtues: prudence.

Notes

1 *Social Trends 27*, 1997 edition, a publication of the UK Government Statistical Service, London: The Stationery Office.
2 *Encyclopaedia Britannica*, CD98, multimedia edition.
3 R. Berkow (ed.) (1992) *Merck Manual of Diagnosis and Therapy*, sixteenth edition, Rahway, NJ: Merck Research Laboratories, pp. 2516–19.
4 *The Health of the Nation* (1991) Cm 1523, London: HMSO, p. 73.
5 *Social Trends*, p. 133.
6 *Encyclopaedia Britannica*.
7 R.E. Spier (1995) 'Science, engineering and ethics: running definitions', *Science and Engineering Ethics*, vol. 1, pp. 5–10.
8 R. Stone (1997) 'Transuranic elements names finally final', *Science*, vol. 277, p. 1601.
9 Ruth Chadwick (ed.) (1997) *The Encyclopaedia of Applied Ethics*, London: Academic Press; Peter Singer (ed.) (1991) *A Companion to Ethics*, Oxford: Blackwell Publishers.
10 *Social Trends 27*, p. 196.
11 R.M. Adams (1995) *Nuclear Power for Commercial Ships*, website: www.openweb.com/AAE/ship_paperhtm.
12 *Nuclear Power Economics and Technology: An Overview* (1992) Paris: Nuclear Energy Agency, OECD, p. 43.
13 W. Patterson (1997) *Nuclear Power*, Harmondsworth: Penguin Books.
14 'Risk assessment' (1983), report of a Royal Society Study Group, The Royal Society, London, p. 89.
15 J. Valenti, L. Ackland and K.D. Steele (1998) 'Nuclear waste, secrecy and the mass media', *Science and Engineering Ethics*, vol. 4, pp. 181–90.

16 R. Edwards (1999) 'Dead and buried', *New Scientist*, vol. 163, no. 2204, p. 21.
17 K. Shrader-Frechette (1997) 'Nuclear power', in *Encyclopaedia of Applied Ethics*, ed. Ruth Chadwick, London: Academic Press.
18 J. Valenti, L. Ackland and K.D. Steele (1998) 'Nuclear waste, secrecy and the mass media', *Science and Engineering Ethics*, vol. 4, pp. 181–90.
19 'F-for Freddie', *The Observer* colour supplement, 23 December 1973.
20 Thomas Aquinas (c.1274) *The Summa Theologica* Part II of the second part QQ40.
21 See articles on 'War and nuclear war', in Ruth Chadwick (ed.) (1997) *Encyclopaedia of Applied Ethics*, London: Academic Press.

10

SCIENCE AND THE MILITARY

Michael Atiyah

Warfare

From the very earliest times man has used his intelligence to produce weapons with which to kill both his animal prey and his human enemies. In Darwinian terms this has been the basis of his evolutionary advantage and the intelligence of *Homo sapiens* can be seen as the final outcome of this process. Survival of the fittest has proved an effective if harsh mechanism.

Moving from the individual to larger social units, such as nations or civilizations, it has been argued that evolution still operates at the organizational level and that war between nations eliminates the weak and degenerate. This view would no doubt have been held by the Romans and much more recently and explicitly by the Nazis.

In contrast, the great religions of the world have evolved an ethical outlook in which behaviour to fellow human beings is much more considerate. It is true that militant religion has also been a driving force behind many of the most ferocious wars in human history and, at the present day, religious fanaticism in various guises is a conspicuous source of violence. Despite this, religious thought in its highest form aspires to non-violence, as in the Christian precept of turning the other cheek or in the long-established Quaker tradition of pacifism.

Ethics is not the exclusive province of religion; secular philosophers, ancient and modern, have expounded at great length on the topic. Even social Darwinists allow that altruism and love of one's neighbours serve an evolutionary purpose. There is much common ground between these various schools of thought, even if they start from quite different axioms.

In practice much depends on how extensive one's 'neighbourhood' is. In former times the world, measured by contemporary means of transport and communication, seemed a very large place, populated by many disparate groups. The 'Huns' who overran Eastern Europe under Attila, the 'Red Indians' who suffered Christopher Columbus and his successors or the African tribes encountered by nineteenth-century explorers seemed alien races. Even more recently Australians lived in fear of the 'Yellow Peril'.

Today, at the beginning of the twenty-first century, modern technology has effectively shrunk and unified the world, producing what economists have termed the 'global village'. In theory our interdependence should make conflict both undesirable and unnecessary. We are all 'neighbours' and though we may not positively love each other we shall have to learn to live peacefully together.

If technology has unified the world economically it has also, in parallel, produced weapons which could effectively destroy our entire civilization. Whatever one's views about wars in the past, as perhaps an inevitable part of human historical development, global war in the future could effectively terminate our history.

This philosophical preamble about the role of war in human history was meant to set the stage for a consideration of the ethical problems faced by scientists and engineers in this whole area. (I will occasionally distinguish between scientists and engineers but in general I shall lump them together and use 'scientists' for both.) Swords, bows and arrows and gunpowder were created by our predecessors. In this century we have moved on to machine guns, tanks, bombers and guided missiles. Finally there are the ultimate weapons of mass destruction, chemical, biological and nuclear. If engineering predominated in earlier times, scientists can take their full share of dubious credit for the latest inventions.

To what extent are scientists and engineers to blame for the horrific weapons which they have helped to produce? It is sometimes claimed that scientists simply search for an understanding of nature and it is others (politicians, generals and possibly engineers) who misuse their discoveries. An alternative defence is that scientists are forced to work for military purposes and that they have little choice except to obey, particularly in wartime.

Unfortunately these claims are not borne out by the historical facts. For example, the famous German chemist Fritz Haber worked enthusiastically to help produce poison gas during the First World War. It is also well known that Frisch and Peierls wrote to the British authorities in 1940 pointing out the potential basis for an atomic bomb, and that Szilard and Einstein had written on similar lines to President Roosevelt.

While Haber's actions now evoke little sympathy, the initiators of the atomic bomb project were motivated by the well-founded fear of a potential German bomb. Certainly German physicists were aware of the possibilities. It has been claimed by some historians that Heisenberg did not want the German project to succeed and steered it in unproductive directions. If true, this would have been an excellent example of high scientific ethics. Given Heisenberg's tremendous standing as a physicist it is even possible that he might have been successful. As it was, the German effort was technologically inadequate and could not compete with the Manhattan Project. Moreover, the famous 'Farm Hall' conversations (now published[1]) hardly substantiate the claims made on Heisenberg's behalf, though he does say (after hearing about Hiroshima) that he was glad the Germans failed.

In addition to major weapons, such as nuclear or chemical, there are also many minor ones which scientists and engineers have been responsible for developing. While all weapons designed to kill people are objectionable, some are worse than others. Napalm, which burns victims alive, was used in Vietnam and vivid pictures of screaming children on fire remain in our collective memories. Anti-personnel mines, which are difficult to detect and mutilate innocent civilians long after the official conflict is over, are currently attracting much opprobrium.

The list could be made much longer. We have devised, developed, produced and used a whole range of gruesome weapons. We can try to excuse our conduct and put the blame on others or on circumstances beyond our control. Certainly, in time of war it is very hard for any citizen, scientist or otherwise, not to assist in the 'defence of his country'. Heroes and martyrs do exist but they are rare.

Since recrimination over the past is not particularly fruitful we can ask about the ethical responsibilities of scientists in the present and future. What can we do to prevent the use of the formidable weapons that the world now has at its disposal? What can be done to prevent the science of the future being directed to producing new weapons yet undreamed of? Although all citizens have responsibilities in these matters, scientists have a special role for a variety of reasons which it is worth spelling out in detail.

- Since science provided the essential basis for modern weapons, scientists collectively have a special responsibility to prevent their use.

- Scientists have the knowledge and authority to explain to the public at large the enormous destructive power of modern weapons.
- When agreements to monitor, reduce or dismantle arsenals are being developed and implemented, scientists have the technical expertise to advise and assist.
- Scientists are in the best position to forecast possible military applications of new scientific discoveries.
- Scientists worldwide form a natural fraternity that transcends national boundaries and can be used to advocate rational policies.

At the present time international conventions have been agreed that ban chemical and biological weapons and scientists have been actively involved in the detailed specification of these conventions. Although progress is being made with nuclear weapons they remain the biggest threat to the future of mankind, so I shall devote some time to discussing the present position.

Nuclear weapons

At the height of the Cold War between the United States and the Soviet Union, some 70,000 nuclear weapons were stockpiled. This awesome arsenal was more than enough to eliminate all human life from the face of the earth. In terms of conventional explosive power, it was the equivalent of two tons of TNT for each inhabitant of the earth. This insane position had been reached by a combination of mutual fear and distrust. One has unfortunately to recognize that a number of leading scientists on both sides (such as Edward Teller in the USA) were encouraging this arms race by constantly developing more advanced technology. Very elaborate strategies were evolved to spell out in what circumstances and at what level nuclear weapons would be used. It all hinged on the theory of mutual deterrence, threatening near annihilation to the enemy in retaliation to a first strike. Both the plausibility and the ethics of this policy are highly suspect. What good would it be to the United States, devastated by a Soviet nuclear assault, if the president were to press his button in retaliation? Revenge on this scale is hardly credible and a moral burden too awesome to contemplate. Yet the peace and stability of the world were supposed to rest on this shaky foundation. Essentially a game of poker was being played with incredibly high stakes.

Fortunately the dangerous absurdity of this arms race eventually dawned on those in power, or perhaps one should say they were persuaded to change course by the combined efforts of military men, policy advisers and scientists acting through bodies such as the Pugwash movement.

The advent of Gorbachov, followed by the collapse of the Soviet Union, accentuated the process and in a few years' time the stockpile of nuclear weapons will have been reduced by a factor of five. This is a great step forward but there is no room for complacency. If the world is to be saved from the terrible threat of nuclear disaster the process must continue while the political climate is favourable. A world without any nuclear weapons is now a realistic goal that is supported by many knowledgeable authorities (see for example the report of the Canberra Commission).[2] Scientists worldwide should be pressing for this goal to be universally adopted.

If we eventually reach this goal then a major continuing problem will be to prevent the re-emergence of nuclear weapons in contravention of international agreements. It is at that stage that the worldwide fraternity of scientists should really come into play. The safety of the world will depend on scientists abiding by the international rules and reporting any of their colleagues who flout them. A similar situation already exists for chemical and biological weapons, where international inspections and controls have to be supplemented by the 'whistleblowing' vigilance of individual scientists.

This policing role of scientists in underpinning international agreements should be widely welcomed on ethical grounds. It is also realistic and practicable. By contrast a general blanket appeal to all scientists not to work on military research is highly laudable but hardly realistic. Without the backing of a specific international agreement, an abstract appeal would lack the legal and social force necessary to ensure widespread compliance.

I have concentrated so far on the nuclear issue because of its overriding importance and the possibility of further progress in the near future.

Unfortunately the possibility of lethal weapons exploiting scientific discoveries will clearly not end with those currently available. Already lasers are being considered for various military purposes. Their use to blind the enemy was at one stage being seriously discussed and they figured prominently in the 'Star Wars' programme. It is hard to forecast future possibilities, but human ingenuity, combined with human malevolence, is unfortunately capable of producing many unpleasant surprises. Is it possible to forestall such developments?

Perhaps in the wake of agreements on the major current threats of chemical, biological and nuclear weapons an attempt should be made to draft an international convention that would prohibit novel military uses of science. If it proves too difficult to agree on anything so vague perhaps one could agree on an umbrella convention, supported by a standing scientific committee which would, as science progresses, identify possible prohibitions. This might be workable since the scientific community can probably identify possible hazardous applications of new science a decade or so before they become technically feasible. In this way the stable door can be shut before the horse has bolted.

The arms trade

While preventing global war with weapons of mass destruction is the top priority, and hopefully within reach, local wars conducted by more conventional methods are everywhere in evidence: Bosnia, Africa, the Middle East. While the underlying causes of these conflicts are rooted in past history, the widespread availability of modern weapons, including the humble rifle, fans the flames and accentuates the carnage. Without the vast arms industry of the Western world these minor wars would not be as lethal as they are. How can we justify the huge arms trade that fuels these tragedies?

Perhaps we should begin by openly recognizing the nature and scale of the problem. The bulk of the arms exports are provided by a small number of major powers (USA, UK, France, Russia, China) competing among themselves. Their reasons are both economic and political. In the first place the domestic market for their arms industries are deemed inadequate to cover the costs of their large military programmes. As with other industries, economics requires a large export market. Put another way, a cut in exports would lead to unemployment at home and a squeeze on the defence budget. This is highlighted whenever, for example, there is a major order in the UK for military aircraft from Saudi Arabia. Very large sums of money are involved and thousands of jobs depend on the order going ahead. International competition is fierce and there are no holds barred in this lucrative trade.

Although the economic motive is usually the driving force, there are also political considerations, and these were prominent in the days of the Cold War. The major powers were keen to maintain their political influence in various parts of the world, primarily in the Third World among the newly independent states.

Supplying them with weapons was one of the best ways of ensuring their dependence. If you have acquired a large force of tanks it does not pay to quarrel with your source of spare parts. When the political motives dominated, military equipment was often supplied free, or on advantageous terms, as 'aid'. In economic terms this can also be compared with the use of 'loss-leaders' by supermarkets. A few free gifts attach your clients more closely.

A third and sometimes incidental purpose of the arms trade was to try out new weapons in active service. Military men know that there is no substitute for actual combat conditions against an appropriate enemy to test out the new technology. A few minor wars, conducted vicariously through client states, would provide an excellent demonstration of the latest weapons and have the inestimable advantage of only involving casualties for foreigners.

While all these reasons are compellingly positive from the point of view of the arms exporter, they appear in a different light at the receiving end. Weapons acquired ostensibly for 'defence' are frequently unleashed on neighbouring states, in civil wars or on popular uprisings. Innocent civilians end up as the victims, and it is little consolation to know that they have been killed or maimed by some sophisticated new device, the invention of intelligent and skilled scientists and engineers from the more fortunate parts of the world.

The economic consequences are equally disastrous. Developing countries with innumerable problems of poverty, population growth and overexploitation of natural resources are desperately in need of genuine aid to help them solve their social and economic problems. The vast sums that are spent on armaments could much more profitably be spent on peaceful purposes. The security of the world would be genuinely enhanced in this way.

How do Western politicians justify their continuing support of the arms trade? One argument is always that the arms manufacturer and salesman just produces the goods; he is not responsible for their misuse. A similar debate on a more domestic scale has just been taking place in the UK on the availability of handguns. In the aftermath of the Dunblane massacre of schoolchildren, public opinion has in the end forced the government to impose quite severe restrictions on the personal possession of guns of various descriptions. As everyone recognizes, this alone may not prevent future tragedies in which crazed individuals slaughter unsuspecting members of the public; it will, however, make it more difficult for them to acquire the necessary weapons. A similar principle applies to the international arms trade. Reducing this will not by itself eliminate the tragedy of conflicts and wars, but it may make them less likely and less lethal.

Another argument put forward in defence of the arms trade is the standard free market response. We are simply reacting to a demand from the external customer. Leaving aside the enormous political pressure put on these customers by the governments which supply the arms, the argument also ignores the doubtful status of the customers. Many of the countries which are major purchasers of Western arms are led by dictators or cliques who are hardly motivated by the best interests of their citizens. Moreover, these leaders frequently owe their power and position to the support of foreign countries, and the acquisition of weapons is a key factor in this support. To put it more crudely, the major arms suppliers have set up client states to purchase their weapons.

Ironically, the ending of the Cold War and the consequent cut in the military budgets of the major powers has, if anything, had the opposite effect on the arms trade. The domestic market having been reduced, there is increasing pressure to look for exports. This applies in particular to the countries of the former Soviet Union, where the economic pressures are greatest.

Occasionally a client state turns on its patron, as happened with Iraq in the Gulf War. This brings home to the weapons exporters the dangerous game they are playing. Public opinion is aroused, as with the Dunblane massacre, and there is talk of a global attempt to reduce the arms trade. So far, however, such attempts have been brief and half-hearted.

As I have attempted to indicate, there are many aspects of the arms trade to which there are strong ethical objections, but there is one which particularly stands out. Many dictatorial regimes have ruthlessly suppressed minority movements, using the unpleasant tools they have imported. In Iraq, in East Timor, in pre-1993 South Africa and in various parts of Central and South America such events have taken place. Governments supplying arms to these regimes always claim that the weapons they are providing are for external defence only and are not designed for internal use. This sophistry deceives no one, least of all the recipients of the arms. The Chinese used tanks in Tiananmen Square and Saddam Hussein used poison gas against the Kurds. Although these particular weapons may have been home-grown, it indicates that ruthless regimes are capable of using almost all battlefield weapons against their own populations.

Attempts by human rights activists to get their governments to deny military equipment to countries with particularly bad records have rarely been successful. For a while, after the election of President Carter, the United States took the lead in this direction but real-politik eventually returned. Only in extreme cases, such as South

Africa under apartheid, or Iraq after the Gulf War, have arms sanctions been maintained for long.

Given the manifest evils of the arms trade, where does this leave the individual scientist or engineer working in the defence industry of one of the major powers? There may be no real ethical conflicts in working genuinely for the defence of one's own country, provided this is not a euphemism for nuclear weapons. But the same weapons, exported elsewhere, may be used in ways which cause serious qualms. An individual, particularly if he is working on the underlying basic sciences, rather than on specific weapons, has little direct say in the ultimate destination of the outcome of his efforts.

It is clear that no action will be taken to restrict arms exports without substantial efforts to arouse public opinion, both nationally and internationally. Scientists, particularly those with detailed knowledge of the defence industry, are in a good position to take part in public debate designed to influence governments. Of course, there may be difficulties in speaking out. In many countries, including the UK, commercial and military secrecy is used to silence potential experts or whistleblowers. The situation is better in the United States where freedom of information is more highly prized and protected. A first step therefore is to press for greater freedom for the individual to speak out, without fear of harassment by his employers or by the state. The Matrix Churchill case concerning the supply of British arms to Iraq and the subsequent Scott Inquiry shows the dangers that can arise when freedom of speech is muzzled.

Because of the competitive nature of the arms trade it seems unlikely that any country could effectively act alone. Only the United States could lead unilaterally and, given the right climate of public opinion, one should not exclude that possibility. Ideally, however, this should be an area for the United Nations, particularly in view of the negative effects that military expenditure has on economic and social development. At the international level, therefore, scientists should act collectively to press for suitable steps by their governments and by the UN.

Surveillance

So far I have concentrated on the military applications of science in the context of wars, major or minor. However, there are wider applications of science in the civil area, which are ostensibly justified by security needs, and the ethical implications of these need to be carefully considered.

The increasing sophistication of modem communications means that the ability for surveillance has greatly increased. In a technical sense we are much closer to George Orwell's scenario of 'Big Brother is watching you' than we were fifty years ago. Moreover, even in democratic states, with an independent judiciary and theoretical parliamentary control, the threat of internal terrorism is being used to justify widespread 'bugging' of suspect individuals and organizations.

No one doubts that every reasonable effort should be made to protect the public from those who are planning acts of violence, and intercepting information is clearly an essential part of this process. The danger is that pressure from the state for information, together with the increasing technological capability to monitor information more thoroughly, may end up with an unacceptable approximation to the Orwellian vision. Even in the commercial sphere, concern about information and its use has already led to the Data Protection Act. But the speed of change in information processing and communications may overtake the more cumbersome machinery of parliamentary bills and legal controls. The engineer may put into the hands of the authorities systems and devices which are far in advance of what had been foreseen by the guardians of our civil liberties. Here then is the danger and also the opportunity for scientists, aware of their ethical responsibilities, to alert the wider community to what might be about to happen. Again, the obsession with secrecy that prevails in UK government circles will make it difficult for scientists to speak up. It is well known that the most advanced work in communication systems tends to start, for obvious reasons, in the military domain. Inevitably the scientists who are best placed to provide advance warning will be those most directly prohibited from divulging information about their work.

The only real safeguard against the combined hazards of technological advance and state security lies in having an open democratic society where information is freely available and scientists can speak without undue constraints. As with the major problems of nuclear security, the role of the individual scientist as whistleblower is crucial. The laws of the land, augmented where necessary by international law, should provide protection to such whistleblowers and defend their right to act in the interests of democratic freedom.

Closely connected with surveillance is the use of torture to extract information. This barbaric practice, which many naively assume disappeared with the medieval rack, is unfortunately still widespread and is constantly documented by bodies such as Amnesty International.

Present-day techniques are more subtle than medieval ones and they vary widely in different parts of the world. Some are primarily psychological while others involve physical maltreatment, including something unavailable in medieval times – the electric shock. Few civilized countries openly admit to the use of torture and potential public outrage remains a powerful deterrent in such countries. Unfortunately, there are parts of the world where there are few restraints on the degree of torture used.

Torture can be inflicted with primitive tools but sophisticated devices may sometimes be employed. Since there is considerable opposition to various animal traps, which cause unnecessary suffering to the victims, it should go without saying that devices specifically designed for the torture of human beings should be universally banned, and no scientist or engineer should agree to participate in their development and production. This may become more important in the future when scientific advances might open up new techniques for torture, involving perhaps more direct ways of affecting the mind of the victim. The mere definition of what constitutes torture and what is an admissible procedure of interrogation is not easy to decide and might become even more complicated in the future. Scientists will have to be on the alert.

The military–industrial complex

Behind all the specific issues lies the much deeper problem associated in Eisenhower's words with 'the military–industrial complex'. As a general-turned-politician he was uniquely well placed to understand and identify the problem. A critique that would have been routine from Marxist sources was much more telling coming from the president of the leading capitalist country. What Eisenhower was identifying was the pervasive extent to which the needs of the military were spread through large and important parts of US industry. The aircraft, electronics and computer industries, the heart of a modern economy, were extensively linked with the Defense Department. The size of the defence budget, and the constant search for high-technology weapons, ensured that military R & D was intimately tied up with the major companies involved.

This continuation of government military expenditure and the associated civilian industry produces an extremely powerful force that is very difficult to oppose. Moreover, each side enhances the other in a symbiotic relationship. The scientist or engineer is thoroughly trapped in between. He may have grave doubts about the military involvement but his whole livelihood is at stake. A cut in the defence budget is almost certain to have an impact on him and his colleagues. It is hard to lobby for something which is going to threaten your job or your grant.

The ethical dilemma for the scientist is clear. There may be a direct conflict between his wish for a peaceful world and his economic self-interest. What is a personal dilemma for the individual is also a major problem for the whole of society and for the politicians who lead it.

In drawing attention to the growing power and influence of the military–industrial complex, Eisenhower was recognizing this dilemma. By bringing the matter into the open, and encouraging debate on this difficult problem, he took an important step. The cosy relation between the military and industrial sectors flourishes best when questions are not asked. A rational policy can only be evolved when there is open discussion and full information.

So again we see the need for an open society in which scientists can speak out and contribute to public debate. But they can only do this if the legal and political climate is right. Even in democratic countries we have a long way to go before we reach that stage.

Conclusion

The pervasive role of modern technology and its particular importance in the development of sophisticated weapons means that scientists cannot avoid facing the ethical implications. Some scientists are directly involved in military work but many more are linked much more indirectly. Collectively the scientific community, both nationally and internationally, shares a general responsibility to mankind to minimize the harm done by science and to maximize its benefits.

The task is not an easy one, and scientists alone cannot solve the problems. They have to persuade the public and the politicians, but they are in a privileged position – they have knowledge. It is their role to spread this knowledge, to interpret it and to deduce the consequences. All of this can only be done effectively in an open society where information can be freely exchanged without legal hindrance or economic pressure. Scientists have to press for these freedoms to be more widely available and they have to join forces across national boundaries to help achieve these objectives. Fortunately, new technology in communication is itself providing new opportunities for sharing information. It is widely believed that the collapse of communism in Eastern Europe was hastened by the inability of the regimes to close off all sources of information. Perhaps, on a global scale, a similar phenomenon will make our task easier.

Notes

1   'Operation Epsilon: the Farm Hall transcripts' (1993), introduced by Sir Charles Frank, Bristol: Institute of Physics.
2   Report of the Canberra Commission on the Elimination of Nuclear Weapons, August 1996.

11

ENGINEERING, ETHICS AND THE ENVIRONMENT

Susan B. Hodgson and Slobodan Perdan

Introduction

The environment is one of the most pivotal places in which to explore the interplay between engineering and ethics. The role of engineers in relation to other humans and their natural environment is undoubtedly of great significance. Engineers have played a central part in creating technology which enables humans to transform the environment in unprecedented ways, changing radically the nature and scale of the environmental impacts of their activities. With the technology now available humans can modify almost any part of the Earth, leaving virtually no parts of it free of their impact. Indeed, the impact of human activities on the environment is not a new phenomenon. Since the earliest societies some human activities, such as the use of fire, agriculture and management of grazing animals, have transformed the natural world, and have had significant effects on natural processes. However, it is only through the development of modern science-based technology with new sources of energy that human actions and activities have had critical and sometimes irreversible effects on the environment. Moreover, enormously enhanced technological efficiency, industrialization and reliance on fossil fuels have brought about a number of environmental problems which are potential threats not only to humans themselves but to other organisms in the biosphere, and even to preserving life on the Earth. In the light of these problems we are becoming increasingly aware that our advancing technological ability to control and use nature for its resources also carries increased responsibility for the results of our activities. As Christopher Stone (1988) has pointed out, 'there is today a widespread feeling that our technology, our capacity to alter the Earth and the relations thereon, *is outstripping our ethics, our ability to provide satis-factory answers to how that power ought to be exercised'*.

This moral predicament is a good point from which to explore the ethical implications of our intervention in the natural environment and the role of engineering in it. We will approach the issue by describing the ways in which the natural environment is conceptual-ized to illustrate that the idea of the environment constructed by the engineer and the scientist already has important ethical dimensions.

The approaches

A scientist draws boundaries around an experiment: a biologist sets out a quadrant to identify and carry out species-counts of flora or fauna or has a petri dish and uses an electron microscope in the lab. Likewise, for the engineer, there is equipment for assessing the environment; its sites and features are identified and measured in some physical form. For any 'pure' scientist in search of the scientific truth, in pursuit of greater knowledge, the environment is an empiri-cal playground for experiments, the means by which to pose and test hypotheses. Observations by necessity are recorded, systematically controlled and calculated.

This approach is not surprising since to understand the environ-ment requires recording, classifying and describing. For example, to understand an animal's anatomy, its physical structure, a sample in formaldehyde can suit that purpose; the animal need not be alive. This process of analysing, recording and classifying data is necessary to understand how a species works.

However, lost is the animism when the life of the animal is reduced to an assemblage of body parts so that the organs' functions can be understood. Beyond breathing, there is the vitality of an animal inhabiting a community and interacting with other species. An envi-ronmentalist sees these interconnections and feels a moral imperative to preserve the community and to conserve the species. There is an inextricable link in the oxygen molecules which permeate human skin and those which fill the air available to all species. The environment contains stores of carbon, the conduit not only for energy and mass but also for our food and inspiration. Water courses through human veins as it does through the Earth's rivers. Boundaries do not exist between the environmentalist and the environment as the environ-ment is infused with matter – energy as well as spirit.

A tree threatened by a road-building scheme stands for much more than one tree; it is part of a forest community, an ecosystem, representing a vivid history and the potential loss and destruction of countryside through systematic road-building. Within this conceptualization, the action of a tree-hugger is a natural response to such a threat. This type of response in such situations in which the environment is threatened may not necessarily follow a sequence of logical steps, with a clear causality. The magnitude of response reflects a synergy stemming from a complex web of feelings and perceptions.

In contrast, drawing the boundaries between the system and the environment is a prerequisite for any engineering study or project. The environment is then defined as 'the physical surroundings, the external conditions' of the system within which engineers are engaged through work or study. As their interest in the system is that of instrumental, technical control, the engineers approach the environment in the same manner. The environment is seen as a matter that can be rationally managed, i.e. predicted, manipulated and controlled. The approach follows the immanent logic of the empirical–analytic science, primarily concerned with producing knowledge which can enable the prediction and control of events. As a practical application of this science, engineering is embedded in this approach. Inherent in this analytic approach is a dualism, a delineation of physical objects as separate from the human subject as an active observer.

Some of the first principles an engineer and scientist learns are based on a systems-and-environment delineation. The first law of thermodynamics states simply that matter and energy can neither be created nor destroyed. Boundaries separate the environment from the system under study across which a mass balance must be maintained. This physical law requires that inputs to the system must equal outputs from the system. This is a precise number, obtainable as a finite measurement.

These two contrasting illustrations can be explained more fully by taking a historical perspective and placing engineering within its scientific tradition.

The historical tradition for the engineer's concept of the environment

Rooted in the sixteenth century and stemming from the 'scientific revolution' of the sixteenth and seventeenth centuries, the analytic and experimental approach to the environment emerged from the works of Copernicus, Kepler and Galileo, from Cartesian philosophy, from the scientific methodology of Francis Bacon and from the mathematical theory of Isaac Newton. A fundamental component of the modern scientific mode of enquiry is the observation of nature in general as a mechanical system composed of separate physical entities, which in turn can be reduced to their component parts and functional units. Characteristics and internal relations of these component parts are thought to completely determine all natural phenomena. The scientists are observers who approach nature analytically, i.e. by breaking it down into component parts. They study and control nature as it is, or might be, useful for their own ends.

This scientific approach to the environment in which knowledge proceeds by orderly and systematic experimentation was revolutionary in replacing the older natural philosophy which was based on *a priori* principles and the pre-eminence of the Bible. Unlike its predecessor, which contemplated natural processes *per se*, the modern scientific outlook advocated study of nature in order to *control and dominate* it, to *survive* in it. For the contemporary practice of engineering, this scientific paradigm has become the conceptual framework for understanding the environment and developing and applying technology with it. This prevailing conception of science has dominated reality since these times. Capra (1982) summarizes this paradigm in the following words:

> Matter was thought to be the basis of all existence, and the material world was seen as a multitude of separate objects assembled into a huge machine. Like human-made machines, the cosmic machine was thought to consist of elementary parts. Consequently, it was believed that complex phenomena could always be understood by reducing them to their basic building blocks and by looking for the mechanisms through which these interacted. This attitude, known as reductionism, has become so deeply ingrained in our culture that it has often been identified with the scientific method. The other sciences accepted the mechanistic and reductionist views of classical physics as the correct description of reality and modelled their own theories accordingly.

This implied that humans were (are) above nature, and that nature was (is) there for no other purpose but to serve humankind. The Baconian creed that 'scientific knowledge equals power over nature' was accompanied by the idea of humans as 'masters and possessors of nature' (Descartes). This modern paradigm has been responsible for impressive advances in technology, industry and scientific discovery, and has contributed enormously to the well-being and health of humankind. New technology and scientific advances have brought us wide-ranging benefits, such as the discovery of penicillin to improve health and the creation of computers and satellites for global communication, that enhance commerce and culture. Yet the ascendancy of this paradigm has also generated some adverse effects. The belief that nature exists *primarily* to be exploited, manipulated and dominated for human purposes has nourished certain impaired and potentially disastrous technological and industrial practices, and eventually resulted in ecologically unsustainable modes of living. Development of experimental–analytical science and science-based technology, accompanied by the creed that nature must be 'bound into service', *intensified* human interventions in the natural environment, which in turn have brought about a number of the environmental problems. The pollution of the land, the air and the water, resource depletion, the extinction of species and the destruction of the wilderness are some of the most dramatic examples of environmental degradation which have emerged as a result of unconstrained technological confidence in managing the environment.

The rise of the engineering profession is inextricably linked with the development of the modern scientific outlook, resulting in the accumulation of technologically effective knowledge and practice. Technological optimism that stemmed from the new scientific paradigm has played a significant part in shaping the manner by which the natural environment is approached by engineers. The engineers, such as those who have applied scientific knowledge in developing, designing and implementing technologies, joined the scientists in the belief that nature exists to be managed. They have accepted the concept of the natural environment as a resource, rather than as something to be contemplated or enjoyed. Today, that concept is a part of the definition of their profession as 'the professional art of applying science to the optimum conversion of the resources of nature to the uses of humankind' (*Encyclopaedia Britannica*, fifteenth edition). Additionally, fundamental principles of mathematics and physics have been made a ground for the professional training of engineers. It is not surprising then that a world view of classical science has imposed certain assumptions about human–environment relations on the engineers, and at least partially determined the environmental ethics of their profession.

That ethics, based on a philosophy which has divided matter from spirit, appears to be exclusively *utilitarian*. It is essentially an ethics of maximizing the use of natural resources, driven by commercial self-interest. It addresses environmental issues by urging us to think of the constituents of nature as actually or potentially valuable resources, and to articulate them entirely in terms of economic interests. This ethics represents the attitude that says, 'We ought to preserve the environment (i.e. what lies outside the boundary) not for its own sake but because of its value to us (i.e. what lies inside the boundary)' (Fox 1984). That attitude is grounded in the belief that human needs, wants and interests alone should be taken as the basis for a whole system of principles and norms governing our conduct in relation to the natural environment. To put it in the jargon of moral philosophy, this type of environmental ethics 'treats only humans as morally considerable' (Elliot 1994). It ascribes only instrumental value to the natural environment and its non-human inhabitants, i.e. in this ethical framework all elements of nature serve as a means to the satisfaction of human interests. Since moral duties and obligations to the natural world are justified in terms of duties and obligations towards fellow human beings, protection and promotion of the well-being of humans gives us a rationale for environmental protection as well.

The prevalent method of acting on a utilitarian philosophy most often takes the form of a cost–benefit analysis in which monetary value is ascribed to the benefits which accrue to humans balanced against the costs which fall on humans. For example, in the case of a forest, cost–benefit analysis would consider the value of merchantable timber, the amenity value of forest walks and perhaps some value for the forest acting as a global sink for CO_2. Costs would include the labour, machinery and so on used to manage the forest. However, the utilitarian cost–benefit approach finds it problematic to value the forest as a living community of many different species or to see intangible aspects of wildness and 'naturalness' in the forest.

Many environmentalists feel that biodiversity has intrinsic value, i.e. that it is valuable not just because of its instrumental value for human purposes but because it is itself of inherent worth. Yet there is also a great instrumental value in biodiversity in addition to its 'intrinsic value'. Biodiversity contributes to human welfare in a number of ways, including new medicines, new genetic strains for food and other products, recreational enjoyment, scientific knowledge derived from its analysis and so on. According to the biologist Edward Wilson (1992), the loss of species would mean that 'new sources of scientific information will be lost. Vast potential biological wealth will be destroyed. Still undeveloped medicines, crops, pharmaceuticals, timbers, fibers, pulp, petroleum substitutes, and other products and amenities will never come to light'.

Undoubtedly, reasons of human self-interest can be found for seeking to ensure the preservation of biodiversity. The question is, however, how exactly the relationship between human self-interest and genuine concern for the environment is to be understood. It is questionable, for instance, if the concern for the species-preservation grounded in the recognition of the instrumental value of biodiversity can warrant an appropriate concern for maintaining biodiversity. There is a limit to the environmental concern which self-interest dictates, and it is highly unlikely that convergence between concerns based on human self-interest and typical environmental concerns will be exact.

Justifying moral duties and obligations to the natural environment for utilitarian reasons has implications for behaviour with regard to the environment. This type of environmental ethics will protect the environment provided it is shown to be beneficial for humans. If such benefits cannot be shown, i.e. in the case where human interests are not advanced, the natural environment will not be protected. It is an open question if this ethics is more an ethics for the use of the environment than it is an environmental ethics. It is also debatable whether such ethics can provide morally sufficient protection for the natural environment.

However, the alternative way of looking at the environment, to which many environmentalists and alternative scientists subscribe, is accompanied by an alternative environmental ethics. This alternative perspective, grounded in a different philosophy, has emerged as a critique of the dominant scientific paradigm as environmental degradation has become increasingly visible.

The environmentalist as concept of the environment

This concept of the environment is based on a newer science, *ecology*, dating from the nineteenth and twentieth centuries, in which the *relationships* of animals and plants are paramount. In the pioneer works of Alexander von Humboldt, collecting plants and fossils is for finding out 'how nature's forces act upon one another, and in what matter the geographic environment exerts its forces on animals and plants' and, more importantly, for finding out about the '*harmony of nature*' (Worster 1977). In ecology, plants and animals in their habitats together form an interdependent community and food web which are the defining characteristics of the environment. The dynamic interactions of the biotic organisms and abiotic elements are the integral parts of an ecosystem, which is larger than the sum of the parts.

However, this concept encompasses more than a new approach to science through ecology. It arises from the writings of the transcendentalists, including Thoreau and Emerson, during the eighteenth and early nineteenth centuries. Their philosophy goes beyond the limits of the analytical empirical world of direct experience to the metaphysical world of intuition and spiritual contemplation in which complete meaning in the environment is essentially unknowable. This non-scientific concept is perhaps best captured in art – the land- and seascape paintings of Turner in which shape, colour and light are fused to express the omnipotence of the sea. The American landscape artist Thomas Cole painted a human on the canvas as infinitesimally small (if at all) in relation to the physical power of the environment as expressed in craggy mountains and raging waterfalls. These 'environmentalist' painters felt in awe of nature, painting humans as diminutive dots on the canvas, contemplating their own mortality. As Alexander Pope said, 'In everything respect the genius of the place.'

More recently, environmentalists have argued that the mechanistic, reductionist and atomistic approach to the environment has been responsible for producing instrumental attitudes to the non-human world. They claim that this view has served as a rationale for an anthropocentric ethic which consists of conquering, dominating or merely managing nature for human benefit. An example of an actual ecosystem which has suffered from the narrow technological engineering approach is the Florida Everglades. With the utilitarian aim of protecting sugar cane plantations and providing new land for future residential development, the swampy Everglades were channelled. The delicate water balance necessary for the interaction of aquatic species was disrupted and, as the velocity and amounts of water flow increased, alligator eggs washed away and ultimately drinking water was threatened with contamination from saline intrusion.

In order to overcome anthropocentric arrogance, the environmentalists suggest a transformation in science and world views that will replace the mechanistic world view of classical science with 'a better code for reading nature' (Skolimowski 1981). This alternative is an ecological and holistic conception of reality emerging from various forms of non-scientific reflection, contemplation and understanding, as well as from recent developments in science.

In addition to the Western transcendentalism as an inspiration for the new conception, the environmentalists often enlist Eastern spiritual traditions (such as Taoism and Zen Buddhism), or the archaic wisdom of tribal cultures, such as native American religions and shamanism. That recourse to the non-scientific understanding of the world partially results from a distrust in the whole process of Western rationalization and in the methodological rationality of Western science and technology. The environmentalists hope that a more respectful and symbiotic perspective on the environment that characterizes those non-scientific views can help in finding ways of overcoming the subject–object relation of modern epistemology, and thus inspire harmonious attitudes to nature.

Yet what appears more important is that environmentalists find that the methodological separation between humans as subjects, and nature considered as a mere object of value-neutral description and causal explanation, has already been undermined within science itself. Some recent scientific developments, such as quantum physics, Gaia hypothesis, chaos theory and a number of other recent scientific theories, seem to disclose the limits of the epistemological conception of the detached scientific observer standing above and apart from the object of study. Environmentalists claim, for instance, that one of the fundamental principles of quantum physics, namely Heisenberg's uncertainty principle, has shown that observers are not independent of their experiments but are inseparably connected with them. They assert that the new physics' exploration of the atomic and subatomic worlds has led to a new picture of the physical universe as an intrinsically dynamic and interconnected web of relations. Classical physics' description of the universe, based on the assumption that matter is divisible into parts, has allegedly been replaced by a conception based on the primacy of process. Furthermore, according to the environmentalists, *scientific ecology* has shown that natural systems, particularly biological systems and biological organisms, demand conceptual models that are essentially holistic. They cannot be conceptualized adequately within mechanistic and reductionist frameworks, nor be understood completely by analytic dissection into physical components. As René Dubos (1969) describes the ecological view:

> It is not sentimentality but hard biological science. Man [*sic*] and the Earth are two complementary components of an indivisible system. Each shapes the other in a wonderfully creative symbiotic and cybernetic complex. The theology of the Earth has a scientific basis in the simple fact that man emerged from the Earth and then acquired the ability to modify and shape it, thus determining the evolution of his own future social life through a continuous act of creation.

The Gaia hypothesis of James Lovelock (1979, 1989) has also been taken as an example of the emerging holistic and organic scientific paradigm, and of a break with classical mechanistic science. This theory asserts that the Earth can be considered as a system that operates and changes by feedback of information between its living elements (flora and fauna) and non-living components (climate and geology). From an environmentalist perspective, the important message in the Gaia hypothesis is that the constituents of the Earth, its living and non-living parts, are inextricably intertwined and all function together, influencing the development of the whole environment. Moreover, chaos theory has emphasized the inherent unpredictability of many natural phenomena. This unpredictability is becoming apparent with the cumulative and synergistic effects of some environmental impacts over space and time. Increasing awareness of the complexity of the natural systems humans are interacting with, and level of uncertainty related to establishing the link between causes and effects in this context, have changed the understanding of human impacts on the environment. This has undermined confidence in the belief of classical science in predicting and controlling the effects and side effects of human intervention in the environment.

All these insights indicate a different, more holistic and ecological approach to the environment. They include the ecological idea of the natural environment as an integrated, organic whole rather than as a mechanical system divided up into compact, separate objects. From this perspective humans are seen as an integral part of their environment, 'not above or outside of nature' but as 'a part of creation on-going' (Devall 1980). This perspective is particularly popular among the 'dark greens' ('deep ecologists') who, as one of their champions has put it, reject 'the man-in-environment image in favour of the relational, total-field image' (Naess 1973). It appears that this 'total-field' conception challenges not only the methodological approach that separates humans from their environment, but also the very notion of the world as composed of independently existing elements. The world is seen as a complex, 'organic' whole that consists of a network of dynamic relationships and processes rather than separate objects-with-properties.

The environmentalists believe that the more holistic and ecological approach would eliminate the negative effects of the dominant paradigm – its reductionism, mechanistic materialism, excessive individualism and atomism. They argue that the holistic perspective with its emphasis on processes, interrelationships, interdependence and synthesis would be a more appropriate mode of understanding human relations with the environment. The ethically relevant implication of the new paradigm would be an ethics of empathy, compassion, respect and reverence with regard to nature as a whole, or at least for all living beings, like plants and animals.

Unlike utilitarian ethics, this ethics is grounded in the belief that we ought to preserve the environment not only for the sake of humanity's survival or well-being, but for the sake of the ecosphere itself, or at least of all living beings. The idea that humans are the source or ground of all value is viewed as anthropocentric arrogance. Morally appropriate behaviour with regard to the environment is to maintain the integrity of the ecosphere, not to conquer it or make it more efficient. This ethics attempts to be non-anthropocentric by viewing humans as just one constituency among others in the biotic community. It urges us to recognize that we are not members of human communities only, but also members of the 'biotic community'. Following this ecological insight, we should recognize that animals, plants and the ecosystems that sustain them have intrinsic value quite apart from any use or instrumental value they might have for human beings. Hence this ethics implies 'respect for . . . fellow members (of the biotic community) and also respect for the community as such' (Leopold 1989). The principle that 'a thing is right when it tends to preserve the integrity, stability, and beauty of the biotic community and wrong when it tends otherwise' (Leopold 1989) is very often quoted by the environmentalists as paramount for an ecologically sound ethics. Unlike anthropocentric utilitarian ethics that tend to be exploitative, ecocentric ethics are oriented more to nature conservation, and to minimum resource-taking strategies.

Is this conception of the environment and the ethics that it implies likely to conflict with the engineer's conception? The answer is obviously, 'yes'. However, the resolution of the conflict should not be an arbitrary choice of one, with the total rejection of the other, as both conceptions of the environment have contributed to the well-being, fullness and enrichment of our lives over the past centuries. Can we reconcile or find a way to converge these approaches? Can we strike a balance between the analytic and reductionist approach, and between the integrative and holistic approaches? Both outlooks have made significant contributions so it would be unjustifiable to claim the superiority of one over the other. The concept of the environment that is inherent in the prevalent scientific paradigm (and unquestionably accepted in engineering) appears to be indispensable in gaining technologically relevant factual knowledge. This technologically relevant type of knowledge is also an essential precondition for ethically responsible behaviour to the environment. As O'Neill (1993, p. 147) has put it, 'Problems of ozone depletion, global warming, acidification of water supplies, knowledge of the decline of bio-diversity, of the state of different habitats, of the effects of agricultural practices on local habitats and so on, could not even be properly *stated* without a scientific vocabulary, let alone be debated'. Paradoxically, we simply have no chance of coping with environmental problems such as global warming or resource depletion if we do not succeed in putting the technological ingenuity and power into the service of overcoming those damages which the same technological power has unleashed and continues to inflict on the natural environment. Needless to say, the role of the engineer in this endeavour is essential.

However, to restrict our cognitive interest and human energy in the environment to the type of reductionist, context-independent, value-neutral knowledge that is represented by the science paradigm is dangerous and could prove ultimately self-destructive. Ecological views are also scientifically sound and their emphasis on interrelatedness and interdependence of all phenomena may prove to be the crux of understanding and solving our environmental problems, most of which were unanticipated in the optimism engendered by the ingenuity of novel technological inventions such as modern transport.

The all-encompassing environmentalist perspective can be complementary to the scientific paradigm because it tends to overcome the narrow, instrumentalist conception of the human–nature relationship. This is particularly important for our ethics to the natural environment, since our present ethical orientation appears to be at least partially determined by the subject–object dualism of classical science and its instrumental concept of nature. An engineer who has practised for thirty years recalled a particular job which illustrates the unconscious or ingrained practice of this type of subject/object dichotomy in carrying out technologically oriented work:

> I don't remember being bothered about it (the production of weapons at the Royal Ordnance Factory), because I think we were working on improving the production of 'chemicals' and their end use was a long way off. Though I still have a steel plate with a hole punched through it by the end result of our process.

Overcoming the treatment of the environment as an object of control, domination and exploitation is demanded by our environmental predicament. Hence a novel attitude of respect or even reverence for nature may be indispensable as a motivation for the changes in our ethics that are required.

Model of environmental consensus-building and decision-making

The consensus model of environmental decision-making is an appropriate way of finding modes of reconciliation. This model pre-supposes a wide environmental dialogue or discourse whereby different conceptions of the environment and conflicting environmental ethics can be communicated through the participation of different individuals and groups. When considering the environmental issues, the causes of pollution and environmental degradation and their relative contributions to a deteriorating quality of life, we are very often confronted with various competing views and values, each having their own inherent significance to a particular group of individuals, and none of whom are able to claim overall validity. In these situations we are simply forced to confess that there is no single perspective which provides a privileged set of principles and concepts in terms of what the relevant issues are and how they can be articulated.

Dialogue or discourse allows different individuals and groups or parties to have a voice and be heard. Through discourse the contribution of each party or individual can be acknowledged – for example, in the case of engineers, the fact that they have helped create the technology to produce what we need or want for housing, recreation, entertainment, transport and food. While the value of engineering to society needs to be adequately recognized, other groups' responses and varying interpretations of that value need to be recognized as well. In the case of the environment, the engineering provision of our wants and needs has indirectly caused wide-ranging environmental impacts including overuse of finite resources, pollution and toxic waste. In this regard, engineers need to be sensitive to the fuller implications of their technological provision of goods and services as they have brought about both positive and negative effects through their production and development. For example, technological advances such as air travel and global communications have revolutionized the speed with which business transactions are completed as well as provided immense opportunities for travel and leisure. However, these apparently benign technological advances have irrevocably altered our sense of connection with the natural environment and have influenced enormous development changes and upheavals both spatially and temporally across the world.

An active dialogue can draw various groups' attention to the wider implications of technological impacts on society, which would not be visible with a single frame of reference, whether the engineer's defined but perhaps too bounded systems view or the boundless but perhaps too undefined environmentalist's view. Thus the absolute affirmation of one group's perspective and its associated values cannot be unconditionally valid. On the other hand, a complete acceptance of unrestricted relativism of values and perspectives will not be entirely helpful. While some anchoring of perspective is useful to provide some solid ground around which an argument can take place, we cannot presuppose a set of rules and principles; such autocracy would run counter to the inherent democratic nature of a consultative process. In addition, it is important that the aim of the discourse, the environment for all, is not construed as an economic interplay of zero-sum gaming, that is, a trade-off between costs and benefits. The discourse is one in which information is shared, not traded, and consensual knowledge is increased, not undermined.

Other methods which stand in contrast to this form of consensus-building for addressing environmental differences are those of the legal system. However, differences in opinion are further divided by the adversarial structure of the courtroom and the rules of the law. For example, expert witnesses express their opinions as either for or against a particular decision outcome. Where environmental damage has occurred, the judicial procedure necessitates the collection of evidence to apportion blame and allocate separate responsibility for redressing damage. The prosecution attempts to build up a case while the defence strives to knock it down; their objectives are directly opposite. Within a legal system, it is difficult to find common ground and consider the sharing of responsibility or the sharing of the obligations towards the environment. In addition, many individuals and concerned groups feel that they are excluded from participation because of their lack of knowledge about the procedures and the difficulties of understanding legal intricacies and the costs involved. Concerned environmentalists are also dissatisfied with the legal system's requirements for proof. Those that feel that a legal forum, for example a planning inquiry, will not adequately address their concerns have rejected this type of decision-making. In the case of the Manchester Airport runway development, protest seemed to be the only viable alternative for some environmentalists. With forceful protest on one hand and protracted legal procedures on the other, consensus-building can be considered as the method having the greater potential.

Given the scientific methodology which underpins the engineering discipline and its conception of the environment, engineers are likely to base decisions on a number of criteria which reflect the scientific knowledge which they consider legitimate and worthy of consideration. However, this knowledge has not traditionally included the other values which interested individuals and parties will have. If we want to settle questions concerning the wider implications of environmental issues of, say, global communication and transport, through a rationally motivated agreement, then we must ask what is possibly equally good or acceptable for all. In order to envisage a resolution, or acceptable agreements about collective understanding as to the environment, we have to take into account and mediate, by means of argument and discourse, all different rationales and different conflicting claims or quasi-claims through an equitable balance among interests. Importantly, while we should bring together and take into account all available scientific knowledge, we should also consider non-scientific reflection and understanding.

In this model, all the relevant interests are represented, and those involved agree on similar objectives in order to find a shared framework or arrive at a general way of working out a path that is acceptable to all. These common elements for shared objectives undoubtedly exist in that, put simply, we all want a 'clean' environment; we all want a decent quality of life. Thus this finding of a common ground for environmental discourse represents a process whereby our understanding of and opinions about the environment are outwardly expressed and formulated as a wider group or societal vision rather than restricted to one party's thinking.

The forum needs to be a place where engineers, scientists, environmentalists and other interested groups can reflect on different perspectives and have an opportunity to hear and listen to what others think and do. A dialogue across a diverse group of individuals will help mediate the tension between the two distinct conceptualizations of the environment and help maintain a broad platform instead of camps of increasing specialization. In sharing a table or forum for discussion, individuals from different groups start to share the lens through which they decipher the bits and pieces to comprehend the natural world. This act of listening is crucial to ensuring a true dialogue takes place. For any environmental issue, engineers should discuss, debate and even challenge the scientific information at hand, but they should not denigrate or dismiss the non-scientific.

Engineers have been well trained to express their professional competence in acquiring knowledge and translating that knowledge into practical products which are significantly different from those which have gone before (Spier 1995). Engineers have responded well to the outward manifestation of society's needs, which can be measured and quantified in terms of increased growth and production. This growth usually takes the form of physical objects and constructs for society as quantified by market mechanisms and government mandates, whether capacity of roads and bridges, numbers of video recorders in households or amount of memory on computers.

The professional activities of building roads, sewer systems, telecommunications, microchips and manufacturing systems are at the heart of many practising engineers. However, the environmental impacts of these engineering applications fall outside the traditional systems boundary of the discipline. By way of an anecdotal example, this point can be illustrated by an environmental issue discussed within a group by engineers and other interested parties. In this case, the environmental topic was transport. In starting the discussion of transport, an engineer focused on the technology, the internal combustion engine of a motor vehicle, and the improvements that could be made to this engine. However, a non-engineer pointed out that the environmental problem of transport is more than a car engine. It is the cumulative impact of car journeys and resulting traffic congestion causing impacts on human health and ecosystems. Others could have focused on the psychological dependency of car ownership and related cultural aspects of the car and have felt that these socioeconomic effects of road engineering projects have spiralled out of our immediate grasp. They could have justified this by pointing to such symptoms as road rage and stress at work due to commuting.

Landscape destruction, noise, species loss, congestion, stress – what are increasingly apparent but still difficult to measure are these wider indicators of a more qualitative and less tangible nature which reflect our fuller human needs and a broader definition of the environment. Dealing with these types of need is new to the engineering profession and so too is the communication role through which these types of need can be understood. As can be seen, the increased knowledge and experience considered legitimate to environmental dialogue for decision-making is broadening to include less tangible values derived from the ecological and environmentalist model. Each of these views contributes to the debate and requires adequate attention and consideration. The round table is helpful in providing a fuller perspective as an engineering professional's concern with 'positive' knowledge can crowd out other types of knowledge which are traditionally learned from family, culture or church, where facts as well as feelings are expressed. To give one example, an engineer described a person worried about gas leaking from overhead cables. The engineer's sentiment was, how could he/she believe such a ridiculous thing? This reinforced his preconception of the public as ignorant. However, public opinion is not necessarily based on misinformed science but rather on other forms of non-scientific knowledge. The exposure of these concerns in a discussion where science and technology is the arbiter of all value results in the public input being undervalued if not ridiculed. However, non-scientific opinions are not necessarily of less value and legitimacy in achieving environmental consensus. In this case, it is important for the engineer to try to understand how this person may have arrived at such an opinion, albeit a misinformed one. It could be that the person is associating the risk of one utility, gas, with that of another, electricity, and all utilities, whether gas, electricity or water, pose some sort of risk.

In a consensual model, the dialogue should not always take the form of the scientific expert telling the public what is and is not. The subject is not always technology and science, but other issues as well. The well-trained engineer needs to resist the temptation of always taking the dominant role of dictating the terms of the debate to the public, as the uninformed party. Through a balanced dialogue, support and strength is built up through argument, not necessarily in specialist technical knowledge *per se*, but in consensual knowledge shared across the public group, including the engineer, scientists and environmentalists, as well as the so-called misinformed public.

The overall aim is to find mutual understanding and show respect for every person as an autonomous moral agent so that different levels and types of knowledge and intelligence are acknowledged. This type of mutual empathic understanding and linkage can be found in the environmentalist model. As this concept shows, the qualitative aspects hold as much importance as the quantitative and are needed to counterbalance the scientific tendency of engineers commonly expressed as 'if you can't measure it or test it, it doesn't count'. In practice, this may mean respecting and accepting different types of knowledge.

In a sense, the consensual model is asking engineers to consider views and information *other* than engineering and is asking environmentalists not to reject out of hand the elements of engineering which do contribute to our social welfare. While engineers working within their discipline have yielded immense improvements through technology and in many cases raised our standard of living, we are at the stage where these disciplinary and systems boundaries are proving to be constraints for our shared creativity in preserving and enhancing our lives on this planet. The consensual model of ethics is one of inclusion and enlargement in which the community of concern embraces other nations and other species. Caring is extended to others different from ourselves, in contrast to the scientific community in which the tendency is to focus on the specialism, to narrow the boundaries for membership, to exclude others in the exchange of information. This is justified in order to increase and enhance specialized knowledge, although the end result may be the preservation of an elitist knowledge for the minority.

The consensual consultative model is goal-oriented, so that parties around the table agree on common aims, rather than task-oriented. The task-oriented approach can lead to a more narrow view as with each step of the task, one may not see the full implications of one's individual actions. This approach calls for a breaking down of the disciplinary boundaries and communication divided in the consensual model and a recognition of the legitimacy of different types of knowledge, understanding and experience.

Other influences

It is important to point out that the two conceptual models highlighted here are not the only dominant models influencing the engineer's approach to the environment. Indeed, it may be argued that the engineer's interaction with the environment is more heavily influenced by today's dominant economic model of liberalism and commercial imperative. The engineer or scientist can hardly satisfy his or her own conceptual model of the scientific method, with its requirements for scientific proof, when the economic model is pressing the engineer to get on with only the knowledge necessary to get the job done. The economic model continues to overshadow the engineering profession and restrict the engineer's outlook to the short term and thus limit the engineer's potential for realizing the fuller conceptual model of the environment advocated here.

To some extent engineers developing their careers in a commercially driven world will feel constrained by the perpetual profit-seeking behaviour and a macho business culture. While working within this corporate structure will appear to pose severe limitations on open dialogue and information-transparency for engineers, some signs of a shift in corporate behaviour are slowly appearing. Decisions do not always stop at the boardroom door. As the Advisory Committee on Business and the Environment recently pronounced in a consultative paper, corporations (and likewise corporate engineers) will need to move away from the 'decide-announce-defend position' and instead adopt one of genuine dialogue (ACBE 1996).

This model of consensus-building has achieved greater recognition in the government sector. One of the most internationally recognized and successful examples is the Montreal Protocol on Substances that Deplete the Ozone Layer adopted in 1987. By 1990, fifty-eight governments and the European Community, representing 99% of estimated world production of CFCs, had signed the treaty to phase out the production and consumption of CFCs. Establishing a scientific consensus was the necessary precursor to political agreement. Early on, the international scientific community shared and exchanged monitoring data and once the gravity of ozone-depletion problem was acknowledged scientifically, regardless of national boundaries, governments had a broad basis on which to build the negotiations for a political agreement (Benedick 1991). More recently, a large number of governments from both developed and developing countries formally endorsed a consultative process for the environment at the UNCED (commonly called the Rio conference) in 1992. Referred to as Agenda 21, this type of consensus-building embraces the process whereby different organizations undertake a consultative process with different populations to reach a consensus on a sustainable environment for the future. On a community level, the *Local Agenda 21 process* is one in which individuals are brought together through discussion-oriented round tables to define environmental issues and construct their concept of the local environment for the community. The idea is based on finding what is common ground through an interactive process of discussion and sharing of information, knowledge and experience. Through discourse, rapport and listening, a common dialogue evolves in the community and slowly some level of mutual understanding emerges.

This will mean that from time to time the corporate engineer will need to stand back from commercial pressure and ever-increasing technological specialization and development so that the wider context of this decision-making on the environment will be apparent. In this regard, codes of practice may have a role to play in providing guidelines for conduct but are limited in the extent to which they can provide a general framework. For the most part, norms are formulated for understanding acceptable behaviour through conscious and thoughtful communication and interaction with other groups. Overly detailed and prescriptive rules are not helpful as an engineer, encumbered by procedure, may lose sight of a code's overall purpose. Moreover, with the pace of change of new technologies or new applications, codes cannot address every possible outcome of a decision or anticipate the kind of decision that will have to be made. For example, CFCs were hailed as a chemical triumph in providing a safe, reliable form of refrigeration in contrast to the explosive properties of the ammonia which they replaced. No one could foresee their negative effects as in our systems view, in our everyday experience, they proved so stable but outside these boundaries of control they caused damage beyond our reach. With the proliferation of technological products, modern society has spun into an increasingly complex web of possible environmental risks based on scientific information which is difficult to manage and understand in its entirety.

Conclusion

The complexity and uncertainty of our contemporary life on this planet calls for an ethical conceptualization of the environment which draws on the engineering model as well as the environmentalist model, one which can be achieved only through active discourse and debate of all our views and viewpoints. Only by carrying out an open dialogue throughout the discussion of engineering activities can we constitute an appropriate ethical basis needed for delivering the norms and principles for protecting and enhancing the environment. This, of course, cannot be put into practice easily. But, as Brennan (1992) put it:

> If many different sets of values are in play when environmental issues are being discussed, the role of the policy-maker becomes more complicated. But life is complicated, and we will not make progress in tackling the grave difficulties we face unless we learn to avoid shallow thinking and simple solutions.

Here a consensus model of environmental decision-making comes into play.

This will mean enlarging the conceptual boundaries of the engineer for understanding the environment and from time to time reining in the all-encompassing conceptions of the environmentalist for understanding technology. Only through shared understanding and mutual respect of alternative views will we be able to confront and deal with the environmental problems that face us all.

Selected references

Advisory Committee on Business and the Environment (1996) 'Integrating the environment into business decisions: the consensus approach', draft report.

Benedick, R.E. (1991) *Ozone Diplomacy*, Cambridge, MA: Harvard University Press.

Brennan, A. (1992) 'Moral pluralism and the environment', *Environmental Values*, vol. 1, no. 1, pp. 15–33.

Capra, F. (1982) *The Turning Point: Science, Society and the Rising Culture*, London: Wildwood House.

Devall, B. (1980) 'The deep ecology movement', *Natural Resources Journal*, vol. 20, pp. 299–322.

Dubos, Dr René (1969) 'A theology of the Earth', lecture, 2 October 1969, Smithsonian Institution.

Elliot, R. (1994) 'Environmental ethics', in P. Singer (ed.) *A Companion to Ethics*, Oxford: Blackwell.

Elliot, R. (ed.) (1995) *Environmental Ethics*, New York: Oxford University Press.

Fox, W. (1984) 'Deep ecology: a new philosophy of our time?', *The Ecologist*, vol. 14, nos 5–6.

Leopold, A. (1989) *A Sand County Almanac*, Oxford: Oxford University Press.

Lovelock, J.E. (1979) *Gaia: A New Look at Life on Earth*, Oxford: Oxford University Press.

Lovelock, J.E. (1989) *Gaia: The Ages of Gaia: A Biography of Our Living Earth*, Oxford: Oxford University Press.

MacKaye, B. (1928) *The New Exploration: A Philosophy of Regional Planning*, New York: Harcourt Brace.

Martin, M. and Schinzinger, R. (1989) *Ethics in Engineering*, second edition, New York: McGraw-Hill.

Merchant, C. (1992) *Radical Ecology: The Search for a Liveable World*, London and New York: Routledge.

Naess, A. (1973) 'The shallow and the deep, long-range ecology movement: a summary', *Inquiry*, vol. 16, no. 1, pp. 95–100.

O'Neill, J. (1993) *Ecology, Policy and Politics*, London: Routledge.

Plender, John (1997) *A Stake in the Future: The Stakeholding Solution*, London: Nicholas Brealey Publishing.

Sagoff, M. (1989) *The Economy of the Earth*, Cambridge: Cambridge University Press.

Schama, S. (1995) *Landscape and Memory*, New York: Alfred Knopf.

Skolimowski, H. (1981) *Eco-philosophy: Designing New Tactics for Living*, London: Marion Boyars.

Spier, Raymond E. (1995) 'Science, engineering and ethics: running definitions', editorial, *Science and Technology Ethics*, vol. 1, pp. 5–10.

Stone, C.D. (1988) *Earth and Other Ethics: The Case for Moral Pluralism*, New York: Harper and Row.

Wilson, E.O. (ed.) (1992) *The Diversity of Life*, London: Penguin.
Worster, D. (1977) *Nature's Economy: A History of Ecological Ideas*, Cambridge: Cambridge University Press.

INDEX